Elite Cohesion in Mediatized Politics

ECPR Press

ECPR Press is an imprint of the European Consortium for Political Research. It publishes original research from leading political scientists and the best among early career researchers in the discipline. Its scope extends to all fields of political science, international relations and political thought, without restriction in either approach or regional focus. It is also open to interdisciplinary work with a predominant political dimension.

ECPR Press Editors

Editors

Ian O'Flynn is Senior Lecturer in Political Theory at Newcastle University, UK.

Laura Sudulich is Senior Lecturer in Politics and International Relations at the University of Kent, UK. She is also affiliated to Cevipol (Centre d'Étude de la vie Politique) at the Université libre de Bruxelles, Belgium.

Associate Editors

Andrew Glencross is Senior Lecturer in the Department of Politics and International Relations at Aston University, UK.

Liam Weeks is Lecturer in the Department of Government and Politics, University College Cork, Ireland, and Honorary Senior Research Fellow, Department of Politics and International Relations, Macquarie University, Australia.

Elite Cohesion in Mediatized Politics

European Perspectives

Eva Mayerhöffer

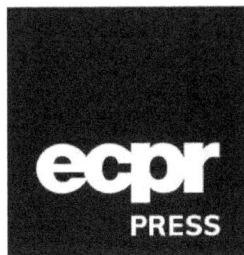

ecpr PRESS

Published by the European Consortium for Political Research, Harbour House, 6–8
Hythe Quay, Colchester, CO2 8JF, United Kingdom

This work is a revised version of a dissertation submitted to the Freie Universität Berlin
(D188)

British Library Cataloguing in Publication Data

A catalogue record for this book is available from the British Library

ISBN: HB 978-1-78552-284-0

Library of Congress Cataloging-in-Publication Data Is Available

978-1-78552-284-0 (cloth)

978-1-5381-5682-7 (pbk)

ecpr.eu/shop

Contents

Figures and Tables

FIGURES

TABLES

Chapter 1

Introduction

REDISCOVERING ELITES

In one way or another, society has always been divided into two basic groups: the elite and the general population. Having fallen somewhat out of view, this fact has once again become a subject of intense concern and debate. Extreme concentration of wealth, technocratic politics of necessity and not least a surge of populist parties and movements across the Western hemisphere have made elites one of the most pertinent issues in public and academic debate. This book takes a particular approach to this issue. For one, it deals with a relatively new type of elite that has remained somewhat below the radar, even though it plays an increasingly crucial part in a society permeated by informational flows and media technology: the *political communication elite*. Secondly, the book moves beyond the questions of who (are the members of elite) and how much (money, fame or decision-making power do they have) to the question of *elite cohesion*.

First, a few words on the political communication elite. The political communication elite draws together members of the political elite and the media elite in the creation and dissemination of political messages and news presented to the public. As such, the political communication elite is composed of two groups that could hardly be more different in terms of traditional elite status: whereas high-ranking politicians in many ways constitute the quintessential elite, at least insofar as political office still comes with unique resources, means and power, journalists and editors have traditionally been seen, and to some extent seen themselves, as non-elites or even anti-elites. This image is, however, no longer viable. In a society where influence on opinion formation and control over the form and content of the public debate are rivalling material and coercive resources, high-ranking journalists and editors have joined politicians and communication experts in the new elite configuration of the political communication elite.

This is not to say that journalists and editors have simply become part of the political elite in terms of their institutional position or overall logic of action. Rather, media elites have joined business elites, scientific elites, religious elites and other elites who may have significant impact on the process of political decision making from their position within their particular sector of society. Just as other sectoral elites have long been recognized as having potential influence on politics, high-ranking journalists and editors have become 'persons who are able, by virtue of their strategic positions in powerful organizations and movements, to affect political outcomes regularly and substantially' (Higley and Burton 2006), or simply persons who possess 'resources' that grant them power and influence in society (Etzioni-Halevy 1993, 95). Indeed, high-ranking media actors have privileged access to an increasingly scarce resource: public attention, opinion and acceptance in political decision making.

The fact that media actors can be seen as a part of the broader elite circles in society has certainly caught the eye of populist parties and movements. Indeed, the populist claim to incarnate the people against a distant, arrogant or even corrupt elite routinely includes a critique of mainstream media. According to populist arguments, mainstream media are part of the larger elite conspiracy against the common people involving lies, suppression and propaganda. Although there is precious little reason to mistake populist rhetoric for facts, and even less reason to consider alternative populist media proper journalism in any kind or form, the populist alignment of the media with the elite does to some degree hit a nerve: journalists are (also) elites, and the fact that they (or at least some of them) form part of societal elite circles and entertain relations with other elites will have consequences not only for the public debate of political issues but also for policy making, political culture and citizens' take on politics.

The book, secondly, focuses on elite cohesion. Although the individual features and composition of the political elite and the media elite are of course still a relevant issue, the particular nature of the political communication elite makes the question of cohesion within and across these sectoral elites more pertinent. Building on attitudinal research and the idea of elite 'belief systems', elite cohesion, understood more specifically as attitudinal consonance between different sectoral elites, is seen as the key entry point to a meaningful study of the relation between modern-day elites (Converse 1964; Putnam 1973; Sartori 1969). This is partly an analytical choice privileging attitudes over alternative dimensions of elite research such as interaction frequency, organizational ties and socio-demographic variables (Bürklin 1997; Christiansen, Togeby and Møller 2001; Hoffmann-Lange 1992; Ruostetsaari 2007).

The focus on elite attitudes places the book in the tradition of attitudinal research and the basic proposition that 'attitudes matter'. Although a matter of continuous debate and refinement, this proposition reflects a highly pervasive understanding that behaviour is shaped by situational conditions as well as the attitudinal predispositions people bring to those situations (Greenstein 1969 cited by Putnam 1973, 2–3). However, elite attitudes and the attitudes of the broader citizenry do not necessarily matter in the same way and to the same degree. For one, elite attitudes and belief systems are often assumed to be more coherent, more consistent, more structured and more democratic than mass attitudes (Converse 1964; Kuklinski and Peyton 2007; Peffley and Rohrschneider 2007). Moreover, elites are in a position to shape political actions and decisions directly. Hence, elite attitudes can be considered the key determinant of societal development and political regime stability – and indeed whether regimes are democratic (Dahl 1971, 124).

Mass attitudes, civic culture and political support are, as demonstrated with ample clarity by the recent upsurge in populism, an important part of the equation. Populism is, however, also a result of the fundamentally asymmetrical relation between elite attitudes and mass attitudes. The aim of the book is not to measure the assumed distance between the elite and the people so often alluded to. By focusing on the particular issue of elite cohesion, it does, however, shed light on the other half of the relation between elite attitudes and mass attitudes so central to current debate. Such an approach does not support the populist narrative of the people against the elites. It does, however, pose the following questions: What if the problem is that modern-day elites get along too well – not in terms of displaying openly undemocratic and corrupt behaviour, but simply by sharing a certain mindset? And would the alternative – an elite divided by ongoing struggle and characterized by mutual ignorance – be a better safeguard for democracy? The book does not pretend to provide a definitive answer to this question. Nevertheless, the empirical study of elite cohesion is deeply entrenched in broader issues concerning the current and future state of democracy. In order to get some bearing on this issue, a brief discussion of the democratic controversies that have always surrounded the existence of elites is in place.

WHY ELITE COHESION MATTERS

For proponents of more or less radical versions of direct democracy, the issue is rather straightforward: elites are fundamentally antithetical to democracy, and democratic progress is possible only through substitution of elites with the true role of the people. By contrast, liberal strands of thought such as pluralism and democratic elite theory take the existence of elites to be an important and necessary feature of modern democracies. Important as the general critique of elites may be, the issues raised in this book speak more directly to disagreements *within* the liberal tradition.

Although liberal theorists tend to agree that the existence of elites is not a problem per se, the issue of elite cohesion is the source of substantial disagreement. Whereas some advocate elite cooperation and integration, that is, a high level of elite cohesion, others advocate elite autonomy and differentiation, that is, a low level of elite cohesion. The former position reflects a *consensus theory* of society and democracy, emphasizing elite commitment to existing social institutions and rules as an integrative force in society and a source of societal stability. The latter position, by contrast, is embedded in a *conflict theory* of society and democracy, inspired by the central tenets of pluralism, identifying the balance of power between elites as the safeguard of democracy.

Within this overall span of debate, the particular case of the political communication elite naturally involves particular attention to the democratic role of the public sphere and public debate of political issues. In general, elites are often considered detrimental to the participatory and deliberative function of the public sphere. Remaining once again with the more liberal spectrum of debate, however, some liberal-representative strands adopt a less categorical approach to the question of elite cohesion and recognize elite struggle for attention and support as an important aspect within the political public sphere (Ferree et al. 2002, 291). Although liberal approaches thus place fewer demands on public participation and deliberation in the public sphere, they provide a more nuanced approach to the issue of elite cohesion in the realm of political communication.

The Case for Elite Cohesion: Stability

The most prominent claim for the necessity of elite cohesion in modern democracies has been put forward in the work of Higley and colleagues (Field and Higley 1980; Higley 2007, 2009; Higley and Burton 2006). Building on the concept of 'restrained partisanship' proposed by DiPalma (1973), they argue that a 'consensual unified elite' is a necessary condition for political stability, which in turn is a prerequisite of representative democratic government (Field and Higley 1980, 117). In addition to a tight and dense network structure, such a consensual unified elite is characterized by a voluntary, tacit consensus about norms and rules of political behaviour and the value of existing governmental institutions (Higley 2007, 252–253).

According to this line of argument, democratic stability can be achieved only when agreements can be reached among elites representing rival organizations and groupings which commit their respective group of followers to agreements on divisive issues (Burton, Gunther and Higley 1992, 10). A consensual unified elite is thus required to 'shape and contain issues whose open and dogmatic expression would create disastrous conflict' (Field and Higley 1980, 37). Elite adherence to liberal values and elites' 'tacit acknowledgment of their mutual dependency' (Engelstad 2009, 396) are seen as the two main stabilizing factors in the creation of democracy (Higley 2007; Higley and Burton 1989, 2006). Norms and rules established and shared by elites over time become engrained in political institutions and political culture and foster peaceful and enduring political practices (Higley 2007, 253).[1]

Although proponents of the consensus perspective take cohesion to be essentially beneficial to democracy, it is also acknowledged that elite cohesion may become democratically questionable when consensus takes the shape of ideological consensus. Such an 'ideologically united elite', defined by the 'coerced expression of a single belief system' (Higley and Burton 2006, 13) among elites, undermines democracy through the dominance of one elite group, which requires all who aspire or possess power to conform to its beliefs. As such, cohesion between elites may potentially also become problematic for advocates of elite consensus, depending on the origin and character of the values that make up the elite belief system. However, this distinction suggests that elite cohesion becomes democratically problematic only once it approximates that of state-party elites in totalitarian one-party systems. In a situation where one of the primary challenges to democracy comes from populist movements reacting to what is perhaps an excessively unified elite, however, the question of the limits to elite cohesion and the tipping point between the stability and instability of democratic institutions seems more paramount than ever, even if the basic relation between elite consensus and democratic stability is accepted.

The public sphere is rarely a key issue of concern from the perspective of elite consensus and stability. As Engelstad (2009, 396) points out, the public sphere is 'overshadowed' in this perspective by other forms of organization such as elite networks and committees (see also Sartori 1987). In general: 'An interaction structure, which provides all important elites with access to central decision-making is a precondition of any stable democracy' (Higley et al. 1991, 36). Such an interaction structure is not necessarily or even primarily located in the public sphere. Indeed, the efficiency of such an interaction structure can be assumed to increase the more it resembles forms of organization usually considered the exact opposite of the public sphere: networks with highly restricted access, bilateral consultations, working groups and so on.

In earlier work, Field and Higley state that the stability provided by elite consensus depends on elites 'co-operating tacitly to keep the public's consciousness of really divisive issues to minimal proportions' (1980, 72). Such limitation to the expression of controversial issues is claimed to be beneficial to the public because it gives the entire public – and not just a fraction of it – the sense of government responsiveness and thereby allows 'wide and reliable political freedoms' (Field and Higley 1980, 73). This view clearly does not amount to a democratic theory of the public sphere, but rather the opposite: a democratic theory that takes a highly restrictive view on open debate and places secrecy over publicity in the key phases of political decision making.

However, some liberal theories adopt a less antithetical approach to publicity where elite cohesion and commitments to the political public sphere are not necessarily seen as mutually excluding (Ferree et al. 2002, 290). Within the framework of the so-called arena model, Neidhardt (1994) argues that a stable 'generalized exchange' between media and political spokespeople is beneficial or even necessary to the public sphere. The stability of the communication flows required for generalized exchange in turn depends on the relationship between communicators and speakers (Neidhardt 1994, 7). Speakers, for example politicians and political spokespeople, expect publicity for their issues in exchange for information. Media actors in turn expect the delivery of issues and opinions, with which they can receive the attention and agreement of their audience (Neidhardt 1994, 15).

Speakers and communicators within the arena of the public sphere need some basic understanding on procedures, conditions and potentially also a shared value base to produce information rather than white noise. The basic understanding still allows for dissent but provides a common reference and anchor point to public communication (see also Kantner 2004, 43–60). To be able to reside in a state of respectful disagreement, a norm of civility is therefore key to liberal models of the public sphere (Dahl 1989; Ferree et al. 2002, 294; Strachan and Wolf 2012). Maintaining such a norm requires a basic level of cohesion among speakers.

The Case against Elite Cohesion: Autonomy

Whereas the case for elite cohesion is made, generally speaking, by linking the existence of elite cohesion with an overall societal consensus held to be necessary for social stability and efficient decision making, the case against elite cohesion is usually associated with a conflict theory of democracy, associated with the core pluralist idea of contestation between social interests and checks and balances. From this perspective, elite autonomy is seen to be absolutely crucial in functionally differentiated democratic societies. Elite autonomy is defined as sufficient control of (at least a significant share of) the resources on which the power of individual elite groups is based. Such resources include the means of physical coercion, material resources, administrative/organizational or symbolic resources (Etzioni-Halevy 1993, 98).

The concern for elite autonomy is the core of democratic elite theory, most prominently put forward in the work of Eva Etzioni-Halevy. For democratic elite theory, elite autonomy and the principles of democracy reside in a 'circle of mutual protection' (Etzioni-Halevy 1993, 104). If the independence and special position of elites are sustained by democratic principles, elites will have an interest in preserving those principles – as well as the power to do so. Elite autonomy is frequently manifested in conflict among elites. A pervasive consensus among elites would precisely preclude such elite conflict and eventually jeopardize democracy (Etzioni-Halevy 1993, 110–111). Correspondingly, the approach to the democratic limits of elite cohesion is reversed: the question is not when cohesion goes too far but rather under what conditions cohesion can democratically be acceptable at all.

Democratic elite theory acknowledges that radical and complete elite autonomy cannot, and probably should not, be implemented practically. The ability of individual functional elites to function properly according to the logic of their sector will more often than not require some level of interaction with other sectoral elites. Such interaction regarded as compatible with elite autonomy and thus as democratically acceptable is labelled elite cooperation: 'It is in fact chiefly elite cooperation (rather than elite consensus on rules or elite solidarity), which is necessary for the proper functioning of any political system, hence also democracy' (Etzioni-Halevy 1993, 109).

Such elite cooperation is essentially based on nothing but overlapping self-interests of different elites: 'Elites do not have to "agree to disagree"; it is sufficient that they cooperate so long as they find it advantageous to their individual group interests' (Engelstad 2009, 386). However, even elite cooperation presents us with the potential risk of infringing on elite autonomy. Two scenarios are possible: the *subjugation* of elites occurs, when a government elicits the cooperation of elites in a way that infringes on their relative autonomy in the control of resources. In contrast, *collusion* of elites occurs when elites develop close interconnections and cooperate with each other for the exchange of resources in a way that threatens their mutual autonomy. Both scenarios undermine democracy (Etzioni-Halevy 1993, 113).

From the perspective of elite autonomy and conflict, the public sphere essentially provides a site for contention and struggle between elites (Engelstad 2009, 399). In more general terms, the importance of the public sphere lies in its ability to maintain elite autonomy by granting elites access to symbolic resources, that is, information, ideas and knowledge, as well as the ability to construct reality for others (Etzioni-Halevy 1993, 94). Rather than a public sphere defined by standards of broad public participation and elaborate rules of deliberation, the basic concern associated with public sphere refers to the practical implementation of constitutional essentials such as freedom of speech and expression, without which an informed public debate cannot develop (Etzioni-Halevy 1993, 104).

Elite autonomy and a well-functioning arena of public debate are thus mutually reinforcing – while the degradation of elite autonomy threatens the public sphere and vice versa. Such degradation can also be understood in terms of subjugation or collusion. Subjugation occurs when political elites attempt to restrict freedom of speech and information in order to remain in control of symbolic resources, thus blocking the free access to such resources needed for other elites to remain autonomous (Etzioni-Halevy 1993, 183). Moreover, the relation between the political elite and the media elite presents a potential problem of (more or less voluntary) collusion: if cohesion between the two sides extends beyond elite cooperation, the two sides may gain a level of undue control of symbolic resources in conjunction (Etzioni-Halevy 1993, 113).

In addition to providing a site of elite contention, the public sphere con- stitutes a relation between elites and the public. In contrast to participatory democracy, the public is conceived largely as an electorate in need of suf- ficient enlightenment to make informed political choices (Dahl 1989). An informed public debate in turn requires an open flow of information. The key criterion applied to the relation between elites and the public is thus transpar- ency and plurality of information (Ferree et al. 2002, 291). In practical terms, such a flow can be provided to the public only when elites are sufficiently exempt from government control and political control. Thus, 'relative elite autonomy and the democratic role of the public go hand in hand' (Etzioni- Halevy 1993, 107).

From the perspective of democratic elite theory, the informational role of relatively independent oppositional elites required in the public sphere supplements the overall principle of elite autonomy by 'generating the type of adversary public discourse without which the electoral and other principles of democracy could not be implemented' (Etzioni-Halevy 1993, 93). Elite autonomy alone cannot guarantee elite responsiveness to public demands, but elite rivalry combined with an informed public at least increases the likeli- hood that public opinion will have some influence on the actions of the elites (Etzioni-Halevy 1993, 108).

Finding the Balance

Although the case for and against elite cohesion provides a helpful overview of the debate about the broader implications of elite cohesion, individual arguments are not always clearly polarized between the two extremes. Elite autonomy amounts to a balance of power that requires a level of stability, just as advocates of elite consensus accept that stability should not be maintained completely at the expense of autonomy – as in the case of ideological consensus. As such, there is little reason to support the case either for elite cohesion or against cohesion unilaterally. The point is rather that elite cohesion requires a balance between conflict and consensus, between autonomy and stability. If elite cohesion is partly to blame for the current challenges to democratic institutions and politics, then, it is because of missing this balance more than anything else.

This focus on the balance and compromise also pertains to the role of the public sphere. The public sphere depends not only on elite cohesion but also on elite autonomy if the struggle for attention and support among the (elite) actors of the public sphere is to provide sufficient political information to the audience (Neidhardt 1994). In this respect, the conceptualization of the public sphere as an arena for elite struggle that at the same time requires some form of stable generalized exchange based on elite cohesion points to the fact that media elites reside in a whole array of double functions: they are elite speakers *and* communicators of elite communication (Neidhardt 1994), they form part of (horizontally integrated) elite networks *and* challenge horizontal elite cohesion by enabling elites to observe each other (Hoffmann 2003, 63). As already hinted at, this has to do with the particular nature of the political communication elite.

BETWEEN ELITE RESEARCH AND POLITICAL COMMUNICATION STUDIES

The elite status of media high-ranking professionals and their role in emergence of a political communication elite have only recently begun to receive scholarly acceptance and interest. Moreover, such interest has been divided between two relatively independent research traditions: elite research and political communication studies. A key ambition for the book is thus to transcend the dividing line between these two traditions and combine their respective insight in a comprehensive and hitherto underdeveloped approach to the question of elite cohesion in the political communication elite. Whereas elite studies provide us with a basic understanding of media elites and political elites, their particular form of interaction and common dependence on the public fall under the province of political communication studies.

Following some initial hesitation to acknowledge journalists and editors as members of elite circles, elite research has gradually added the media to the list of important sectoral elites in current society (see e.g. Best and Higley 2018; Christiansen et al. 2001; Higley, Deacon and Smart 1979; Hoffmann-Lange 1992; Ruostetsaari 2015). Although the potential political significance of the media elite and the evolving relations with the political elite have also been recognized, elite research still lacks a more thorough understanding for the particular dynamics at play in the relationship between media and political elites, and in particular the role of the public sphere in the elite status of these two groups of elites. While political elites and media elites share a number of basic attributes with other sectoral elites in current society in terms of their hierarchical organization, patterns of elite circulation and recruitment, they set themselves apart from other elites through the particular dependence on the public sphere ingrained in their sectoral function and particular form of power.

Indeed, the public represents a crucial resource that grants both media and political elites power and influence in society (for a similar line of argument, see Bourdieu 2005). Both media and politicians are dependent on the existence of publics, and in the case of politicians also on public support. To create public attention and gain public support, political and media elites create, exchange and publicize political messages (Neidhardt 1994; Pfetsch 2004). Although general elite features remain important, the latter point merits a particular focus on media elites and political elites from the perspective of political communication: political elites and media elites can, in contrast to other sectoral elites, be denominated as political communication elites, given their dependence on a functioning (political) public sphere – and vice versa.

In the field of political communication studies, on the other hand, the political significance of the media and the relevance of analysing the particular interplay of media and politics shaped by their common relation to the public is well established. However, media actors have yet to be acknowledged as elites in their own right, providing a counterpart to political elites. In the field of political communication research, the term 'elite' is currently applied almost exclusively to politicians and others operating within the limits of political institutions and organizations. General theories and models of political communication sensitive to the importance of elites tend to apply the label of elite to the political side of the table rather than to the media (e.g. Bennett 1990; Entman 2003; Herman and Chomsky 2002).

Although it is acknowledged, at least indirectly, that media actors covering political issues and liaising with political elites often come from the top of their class, the media are not regarded as a distinct elite group in itself. In the specific area of journalism studies, some contributions have dealt more explicitly with the 'media elite' (e.g. Diezhandino, Bezunartea and Coca 1994; Lichter, Rothman and Lichter 1986; Rieffel 1984; Weichert and Zabel 2007). These studies are, however, focused on mapping the social background, political attitudes and work routines of leading journalists, rather than the role of media elites in the process of political communication and the interplay between media elites and political elites. Moreover, the term 'elite' is often applied to the media organization as a whole, rather than individual editors, journalists or media managers, thus conflating the media elite with particular outlets deemed to be 'elite media' (Lichter, Rothman and Lichter 1986).

A EUROPEAN PERSPECTIVE

Empirically, the book focuses on six European countries: Sweden, Denmark, Germany, Austria, France and Spain.[2] Rather than global differences between the major systems or traditions of political communication, then, the book is concerned with similarities and differences within the realm of European nation-states. On the one hand, these countries are clearly rather similar in terms of a basic commitment to party-based democracy, freedom of the media and economic development. On the other hand, the six countries do display significant variations once we look closely at the media system, the political system and the social structure. In more analytical terms, the six countries have been selected to represent varying cases based on two schemes of classification: Hallin and Mancini's framework for comparative analysis of 'media systems' (2004) and the typology of national elite structures developed by Hartmann (2007a). The former draws the following widely cited distinction between three distinct ways to organize the relation between media and politics:

> The Liberal Model is characterized by a relative dominance of market mecha- nisms and of commercial media; the Democratic Corporatist Model by a his- torical coexistence of commercial media and media tied to organized social and political groups, and by a relatively active but legally limited role of the state; and the Polarized Pluralist Model by integration of the media into party politics, weaker historical development of commercial media, and a strong role of the state. (Hallin and Mancini 2004, 11)

Within this distinction, the six countries under study in this book are associ- ated most directly with the democratic-corporatist and polarized-pluralist model, although some of the countries do display liberal traits in some respects. As will also become evident, individual countries rarely fall straight- forwardly within one of these traditions but tend rather to combine elements of all three models. Whereas Hallin and Mancini's distinction concerns media systems, including the relation of the media to the political system, Hart- mann's typology makes it possible to consider the variation in social structure of the six countries, in particular, the social homogeneity of elites, patterns of elite education and recruitment, as well as the degree of elite mobility between societal sectors (Hartmann 2007a).

Based on a combination of these two typologies, the six countries can be divided into three groups, each represented by two members (figure 1.1): Sweden and Denmark represent the Northern European country group,

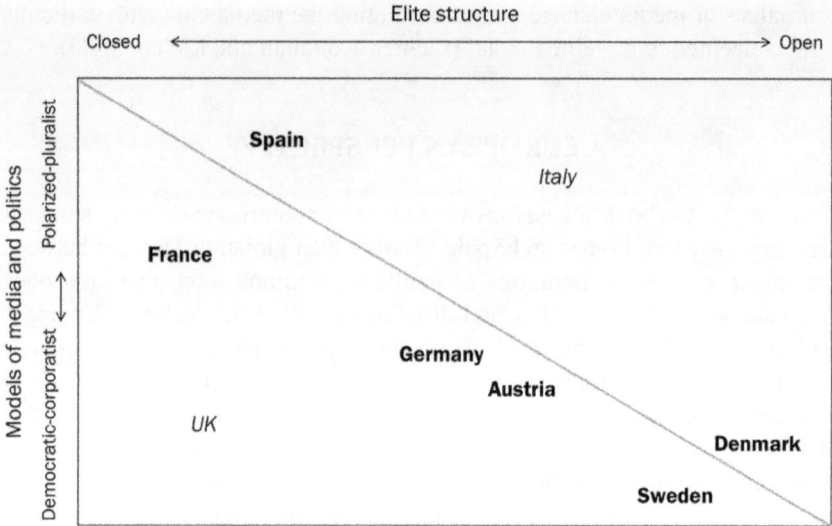

Based on Hallin and Mancini (2004, 70) and Hartmann (2007a)

Figure 1.1. Country Selection

Germany and Austria represent the Central European country group, and Spain and France represent the Mediterranean country group. Differences between the six countries are a matter of graduation rather than stark opposition. Moreover, a certain degree of historical co-evolution of social structure, the political system and the media system has to be taken into account. That said, the six countries distinguish themselves in the following way:

Countries adhering to the democratic-corporatist model are more frequently characterized by a relatively open or fluid social structure, in which elite positions are occupied by persons from different social backgrounds, while the opposite is true for polarized-pluralist countries. As displayed in figure 1.1, the six countries under study follow this logic. For purposes of contrast, two clear and notable exemptions to this pattern are also included: the United Kingdom has a liberal political media system but a social structure characterized by an extremely low social fluidity and upper-class-based elite structure, whereas Italy combines an archetypical polarized-pluralist political media system with a relatively open social and elite structure.

The inclusion of the six individual countries grouped along a European axis from north to south is the backbone of the comparative ambition of the book. Theoretically and empirically, the book highlights national variations in social structure, the media system and the political system, and remains committed to the systematic and comparative analysis of the effects of the national context on elite cohesion. In highlighting these national variations, it supplements the general categorization into a Northern European, Central European and Mediterranean country group with a detailed account of specific contextual conditions at play in each country. The task is thus to systematically discuss the conditions that can account for cross-national variation in elite cohesion in political communication, and not least to probe whether these differences can be retraced in the empirically observable attitudinal patterns of media and political elites.

Much more will be said on the included countries and the comparative approach of the book in later chapters. Here, a brief outline of the respective national debates on the topic of the book will serve as an introduction. In Sweden, the debate is primarily focused on the sustainability of the 'Swedish model' in modern-day mediated democracy (Nord 2007). The defining trademark of this model is the maintenance of collective public interest and societal balance through means of consensus and dialogue. A key instrument in this respect is centralized committees anchored in government, providing an institutional framework for elite cooperation and elite settlements (SOU 2000). Although comparisons between the two Nordic neighbours point to a similar consensus tradition in Denmark, the latter is also regularly characterized as having a more polarized and contentious style of political campaigning (see e.g. Strömbäck, Ørsten and Aalberg 2008). Moreover, the Danish academic and public debate is heavily preoccupied with the phenomenon of *spin*, which is routinely included in both electoral and routine political communication (Blach-Ørsten 2014; Dindler 2011).

In Germany, academic and popular discussion is predominantly occupied with the informal intermingling of journalistic and political elites, in particular in the form of so-called background circles and other quasi-institutionalized and organized forms of social interaction (Baugut and Reinemann 2013; Lesmeister 2008). In Austria, the discussion revolves around what is described as *Verhaberung*, a catchword describing the particular relation between media and political elites (Kaltenbrunner, Karmasin and Kraus 2010; Plasser and Lengauer 2010; Wörgetter 2007). In a similar fashion, the French public speaks of *connivence* (see e.g. Burgert 2010; Halimi 1997; Seggelke 2007). Whereas the Austrian term, which roughly translates to fraternization, implies a certain chumminess rather than evoking the image of a conspiring power elite, the French connivance refers to a tacit consent or acquiescence between elites that suggests more serious implications for social power structures. In Spain, finally, the lack of differentiation of partisan media and political elites and the ensuing political instrumentalization of the media are in the centre of attention. Here, the relationship between media and politics has been described as an 'umbilical cord that was never cut' (Papatheodorou and Machin 2003).

OUTLINE OF THE BOOK

The ensuing analysis proceeds in the following steps. Chapter 2 outlines why and how media and political elites can be understood as political communication elites. Existing elite definitions are reviewed and applied to the specific context of the study. Against this background, political communication elites are characterized as *sectoral elites*, defined by the functional orientation of their societal sector of origin, that is, the media sector and political sector. Moreover, political communication elites are defined as *strategic elites*, which entails influence on the collective conditions of society as a whole. The interplay between sectoral and strategic elites in political communication is then framed as a question of *elite cohesion*, defined as the *consonance of attitudes* both within and in between sectoral elite groups. In the second part, the chapter focuses on the ways political communication research has previously engaged the question of elite cohesion in political communication.

Based on the review of existing concepts and approaches to the study of elites and relevant approaches in the field of political communication research, chapter 3 develops a model of elite cohesion in political communication, specifying objects, levels, patterns, contextual conditions, as well as consequences of elite cohesion in political communication. The model combines three dimensions of attitudinal consonance: *value*, *procedural* and *epistemological consonance*, with three guiding principles of elite relations in political communication: *ideology*, *publicity* and *pragmatism*. Additionally, the model argues that attitudinal consonance can be defined in terms of *proximity* as well as *indistinction* of attitudes, based on which different patterns of consonance within and between the two sectoral elites can be observed. These patterns are, in turn, affected by the systemic environment of a country, in particular, the degree of sectoral autonomy and variety, as well as the level of social mobility. Moreover, these patterns of attitudinal consonance have important consequences for stability, plurality and civility in political communication.

Chapter 4 describes the pivotal factors that are suited to describe the specific systemic environment in political communication in European democracies. A key issue here is the question of how the more general factors of sectoral autonomy and variety within the media and political system, as well as of social mobility, can be broken down to the specific circumstances in the six countries under study. Moreover, the chapter describes who in the media sector and political sector of each country qualifies as political communication elite, and presents the elites finally surveyed in the empirical study.

Chapters 5, 6 and 7 present the results of the conducted elite survey. Whereas chapter 5 focuses on the level, principles and patterns of elite cohesion between sectors, chapter 6 switches the focus to an intra-sectoral perspective by analysing the level of cohesion among media elites and political elites separately. Chapter 7, finally, extends the analysis by focusing more broadly on elite cohesion among political communication elites as a social factor that is tested against competing sources of elite cohesion as well as in terms of the potential influence of elite cohesion on interaction patterns.

Chapter 8 concludes the study with a summary of main expectations and findings, as well as with an outlook with regard to consequences and limitations of findings, and implications for future research.

Chapter 2

Elites in Mediatized Politics

The concept of elites carries strong connotations to a single ruling class at the top of society. In contrast to this view, elites are defined by two key characteristics in this study. First and foremost, current elites are *sectoral elites*, which is to say that they operate within a particular subsystem of society and orient themselves to the functional requirements and institutions of their particular subsystem. Second, sectoral elites can attain the status of *strategic elites* exercising determinable and lasting influence on political decisions. The influence of a sectoral elite may extend well beyond its particular sector of origin and take on broader social and political significance. By the same token, political importance or power does not reside solely with politically elected or appointed elites. The political elite and media elite are in this sense both sectoral and strategic elites, exercising regular and substantial influence on the production of political messages, thereby ultimately affecting collective decision making.

TOWARDS SECTORAL AND STRATEGIC ELITES

The study of elites in social science is widely held to begin with the work of Vilfredo Pareto and Gaetano Mosca (Scott 1990, x). The former defined an elite as 'a class of the people who have the highest indices in their branch of activity' (Pareto 1935, 1422–1423). For Pareto, elite status simply means being among the best at one among a number of activities. However, Pareto's principal concern is the activity of government and hence the *governing elite*. Pareto is most renowned for the idea that history is an eternal 'circulation of elites', where ruling power continuously passes from elite to the next either through assimilation or revolutionary overturn. Non-governing elites and

17

non-elites, for their part, mostly play a role as would-be governing elites that may or may not play a part in the circulation of elites (1935, 1423). The emphasis on the ruling elite is also evident in Mosca's widely known concept of the *political class*. However, the use of class terminology also makes the distinction between elites and masses more explicit: 'In all societies . . . two classes of people appear, a class that rules and a class that is ruled' (Mosca 1939, 50).

The founding fathers of elite theory thus display a clear focus on a single governing elite ruling over non-government elites and non-elites: 'Both Mosca and Pareto, therefore, were concerned with élites in the sense of groups of people who either exercised directly, or were in a position to influence very strongly the exercise of, political power' (Bottomore 1993, 3). Neither Pareto nor Mosca displayed any empirical interest in the actual differentiation of elites; the distinction between the elite and the masses remained the central point of concern (Guttsman 1960, 139; Hartmann 2007). In principle, both of the founding fathers were aware of the heterogeneity of elites within the political sphere (Higley and Burton 2006, 6), recognizing 'that the "governing élite" or "political class" is itself composed of distinct social groups' (Bottomore 1993, 3). The general acceptance of elite heterogeneity, however, never translated into claims fundamentally challenging the idea of a single ruling elite. Subsequent development of elite theory has, however, been increasingly preoccupied with the existence of numerous and fundamentally diverse elites that may exercise considerable social influence, even if they are not members of the governing elite (Lasswell and Lerner 1952).

Sectoral Elites: Function and Organization

This development in elite theory is linked to a broader discussion about the transformation of society and the role of elites in relation to different forms of more or less dominant social organization. This discussion has not reached a settled compromise but can be largely divided in two schools. The first school of thought associates elites with the existence of a *ruling class*, that is, a more or less unified elite at the top of a predominantly class-based and hierarchically organized society. Another primary school sees elites rather as sectoral elites limited to functionally specific domains or systems in society (Hewitt 1974). The study conducted here takes the latter position and thus proceeds from the understanding that elites must be conceived first and foremost as sectoral elites.

The first school of thought is most prominently represented by C. Wright Mills and his seminal study of 'The Power Elite' (1956), as well as by the work of Pierre Bourdieu (1984, 1996).[1] Both authors insist on the existence of a tightly integrated power bloc on top of society that overrules functional differentiation (see in more detail Hartmann 2005, 2007b, 41–60). While Mills and Bourdieu do not deny the internal differentiation of the power elite or ruling class,[2] they oppose the basic view of the second school of thought: that society encompasses a number of interdependent sectoral elites of more or less equal standing (e.g. Dahrendorf 1965; Keller 1963; Stammer 1951). Such sectoral elites operated within the parameters of different societal subsystems and are united only through a 'shifting, roughly balanced power structure' (Higley et al. 1991, 35). Contrary to the notion of a unified dominant elite, these 'individual, functional subelites . . . compete with one another at the top levels of the key sectors of society' (Hartmann 2007b, 37).

Although the notion of diverse and competing elites is also central to democratic elitism and pluralism (e.g. Dahl 1961, 1967; Sartori 1987), the concept of sectoral elites is not inherently normative (Hoffmann-Lange 1992, 20). Rather, it reflects broader macro-sociological discussions about changes in the primary forms of social differentiation and organization. In contrast to the hierarchical and stratified model of society underpinning the idea of a single power elite or political class at the top of the social pyramid, the concept of sectoral elites reflects the proposition that current society is functionally differentiated before anything else: society is fundamentally and pervasively organized into a number of autonomous societal subsystems such as politics, law, religion, economy, and indeed the media (see Gerhards and Neidhardt 1991, 35; Luhmann 1977). From this observation it follows that elites arise and operate primarily within functionally distinct subsystems and sectors in society. In the words of a classical definition:

> Elites are the more or less closed social and political groups of influence, which by delegation and competition emerge from the broader masses of society and its various groupings to assume a specific function in the system's social or political organization. (Stammer 1951, translation by the author)

The primacy of functional differentiation in current society does not mean that hierarchy has lost its relevance as a societal principle of organization, but rather that such hierarchical organization takes place *within* specific sectors and subsystems. Elite status in sectoral elites is, as highlighted by Stammer, dependent on the internal organization of the sector or subsystem in question. Identifying a particular elite thus always involves an element of interpretation of the organizational hierarchy of the sector in question (Hoffmann-Lange 2007, 914; Putnam 1976, 8–12). The various sectors of society are occupied by a plethora of organizations, and membership of a sectoral elite usually requires a high-ranking position within organizations, and in particular the leading organizations of the sector in question (Bürklin 1997, 17). In this way, the organizational landscape of a sector produces its own elites, sub-elites and non-elites (Dahl 1961; Etzioni-Halevy 1993, 95).

Correspondingly, the concept of a sectoral elite can be 'used to describe those who occupy the leading positions in organizations or institutions' (Hewitt 1974, 45; see also Field and Higley 1980, 20). In a similar vein, Giddens proposes to use the term 'elite group' for 'those individuals who occupy formally defined positions of authority at the head of a social organization or institution', while the general term 'elite' 'designate(s) either an elite group or a cluster of elite groups' (Giddens 1972, 346). Sectoral elites are thus elites that, based on 'objectifiable criteria' (Bürklin 1997, 16), occupy the leading positions within different societal sectors (Field and Higley 1980, 20; Scheuch 1988).

Strategic Elites: Power and Influence

The existence of multiple and diverse sectoral elites in current society, in turn, raises the question of their political importance and influence in new ways. On the one hand, the solution proposed by the founding fathers is no longer viable: the power to rule cannot simply be inferred from elite status or vice versa. On the other hand, a sectoral approach runs the risk of assuming that all elites are equal, thus losing sight of the fundamental idea of power asymmetry in elite research: 'If elites are seen simply as all of those at the top of any hierarchy whatsoever, then the identification and analysis of elites is trivialized' (Scott 1990, xiii). Hence, the combination of functional orientation and organizational position required to identify sectoral elites must be supplemented by a criterion of societal influence: assuming the status of a politically relevant elite requires possession of resources that makes it possible to influence the course of development in society (Etzioni-Halevy 1993, 95).

In the words of Suzanne Keller, this issue can be framed as a question of whether sectoral elites also qualify as 'strategic elites', meaning elites 'whose judgments, decisions, and actions have important and determinable consequences for many members of society', in contrast to 'segmental elites' whose influence and impact are limited to their own sector (Keller 1963, 20). Whereas a segmented elite remains limited to its own sector, strategic elites extend their sphere of influence beyond their immediate sector (see also Scott 1990, x). The distinction between strategic and segmental elites thus recognizes the highly differentiated nature of current society and the various forms of power beyond political power relevant to such a society. However, it also makes the direct or indirect power over collective decision making a particular point of interest based on the proposition that political power is still a particular form of power that has the most fundamental and lasting influence on society (Hoffmann-Lange 2007; Moore 1979; Putnam 1976, 6–7).

Such influence cannot be inferred simply from taking political office: 'The decisive factor in distinguishing a political elite from nonpolitical elites and non-elites is the nature of the decision rendered – not the position held by the decision-maker' (Bachrach 1967, 68). In other words, the political relevance of elites pertains not to their position but to the strategic ability to influence decisions that impact on the societal course of development (see also Genieys 2010). This strategic ability provides an operational criterion of political power that resonates well with Higley and Burton's definition of members of an elite as 'persons who are able, by virtue of their strategic positions in powerful organizations and movements, to affect political outcomes regularly and substantially' (Higley and Burton 2006, 7). The definition also contains the empirically valuable clarification that such influence must be regular and substantial – otherwise the ordinary members of an electorate could be called an elite. The definition proposed by Higley and Burton is purposefully simple and flexible: 'Put most simply: elites are persons and groups who have the organized capacity to make real and continuing political trouble' (Higley and Burton 2006, 7).

Based on this criterion, it is possible to adopt a sectoral approach without trivializing elite research. On the one hand, the concept of strategic elites does separate political influence from the position of political office holders, thus including others than members of political organizations and actors operating within the political sector itself. Influence on political decisions is not limited to the political sector, but involves other elites 'based on a variety of resources located in different sectors of society' (Hoffmann-Lange 2007, 911). On the other hand, membership of strategic elites is afforded only to those who can exert 'influence on strategic (political) decisions that shape the living conditions of society' (Hoffmann-Lange 2007, 910). By implication, the strategic elite in most cases 'excludes a large group of individuals whom many people would spontaneously consider as belonging to the elite, for example, prominent athletes, artists, scholars, intellectuals, or the owners of large fortunes' (Hoffmann-Lange 2007, 910; see also Keller 1963, 20).

Although elite status does not follow automatically from political office, there is no doubt that high-ranking actors in the political sector are in a privileged position to influence decisions with determinable consequences for large groups of people. A more pertinent question for the study at hand is whether prominent journalists and editors can be said to constitute a strategic elite exerting political influence and power beyond the realms of the media system itself. The claim advanced here is clearly affirmative: the media play a crucial role in politics with important societal consequences (see also Mayerhöffer and Pfetsch 2018). This claim is supported by the many elite scholars who, based on the broader approach to political power and influence, consider media actors as elites (Bürklin 1997; Dahrendorf 1965, 247;

Etzioni-Halevy 1993; Hoffmann-Lange 1992; Keller 1963; Moore 1979) and even 'elites in politics' (Parry 1969, 13).

POLITICAL COMMUNICATION ELITES

Taking this claim a step further, it can be argued that members of the political elite and the media elite can also be designated as *political communication elites* under the conditions of mediatized politics, in which politics 'has become dependent in its central functions on mass media, and is continuously shaped by interactions with mass media' (Mazzoleni and Schulz 1999, 250; see also Strömbäck 2015). Mediatization of politics not only lends increased political importance to the media elite but also leads to a more fundamental process of mutual adaptation within the two sectors, which has come to define political elites and media elites alike (see also Hoffmann 2003, 13). Even if political elites retain a privileged influence on collectively binding decisions and access to means of physical coercion, the exercise of political authority has also been subjected to the demands of mediated communication (see e.g. Bennett and Entman 2001; Cook 1998; Meyer 2002).

Mediatization lends increased importance to the principal resource held by the media elite: control of access to the principal channels of public communication. However, mediatization is not simply putting more power in the hands of the media elite. Mediatization also changes the nature of politics, providing the political elite with new challenges and opportunities. Rather than producing a clear winner in a zero-sum power game, the process of mediatization links the political elite and the media elite closer together in the production of political messages. The result is the emergence of a distinct group of elites, operating at the intersection of media and politics.

This new elite draws together members from the established political elite and the media elite without questioning the continued existence of a separate political sector and a media sector within society. Correspondingly, political communication elites can be defined as sectoral and strategic elites, which by virtue of their organizational position exercise significant control over publicly communicated political messages and thus influence collectively binding decisions regularly and substantially. The implications of this definition for both sectors are further elaborated in the following sections.

Political Elites: Substantive and Symbolic Politics

Drawing on Easton's standard definition of the political system (Easton 1965), political elites can be defined on the most general level as those in a position to take collectively binding decisions. Referring to the understanding of political power and authority suggested by Max Weber, moreover, such a position implies legislative authority backed by the means of physical coercion (Hoffmann-Lange 2004, 30). The extent and limits of this legislative and coercive authority, as well as the kind of community it covers, thus appears as a fundamental question to the identification of political elites.

First and foremost, the privileged access to legislative and coercive authority includes government, which stands in 'decisive pre-eminence' over other elites based on 'legislative and coercive authority over the most general affairs of the community' (Parry 1969, 72). Government, however constituted, remains the core of the political elite, closely aligned with the idea of a governing elite introduced by the founding fathers of elite research. Second, the circles of the political elite can be expanded to include members of parliaments and constituent assemblies. Parliamentary and legislative studies, in particular, have invested significant efforts in mapping out the elected representatives of the national assembly under the assumption that they can be equated more or less directly with the political elite (Best 2008; Best and Cotta 2000).

Both government and most members of constituent assemblies must be considered members of the emerging political communication elites as well as the established political elite. Due to the dynamics of mediatization, membership of the political communication elite is premised on being in a position to influence or even control publicly communicated political messages. By this criterion, low-ranking members of parliaments and backbenchers are sometimes on the margins of the political communication elite, whereas government, opposition leaders, speakers, rapporteurs, committee members, chairpersons and often also assembly members with no particular role or responsibility fall within the ranks of the political communication elite. More generally, we can think of political communication elites within the political sector as elites of *symbolic politics* due to their particular influence on the formulation and delivery of political messages (Dörner 2004; Walgrave and Van Aelst 2006).

The emergence of political communication elites preoccupied with symbolic politics shaped by mediatization and what has been called 'media democracy' does not displace the traditional focus on *substantive politics* and 'negotiating democracy', located away from the public eye (Grande 2000). Indeed, many leading political actors are required to be both substantively and symbolically influential (Dörner 2004). Moreover, substantive influence is often the source of influence on the public debate: members of the governing elite thus regularly qualify as political communication elite due to the fact that their influence and 'officialdom' make them attractive to the media in a climate of mediated politics (Cook 1998). Nevertheless, the identification of political communication elites within the political sector involves a shift of focus from regular and substantial influence over the preparation, decision and potentially even implementation of political decisions to a regular and substantial influence over political communication and the political public debate. Consequently, the political communication elite can also include positions with less substantial influence, but which are particularly geared towards shaping and communicating political messages.

In addition to government and members of national assemblies, the political elite includes the so-called specialized elites basing their elite status on skills and competencies (Parry 1969, 74). Whereas government and assembly members, at least in democratic systems, are elected politicians, the specialized elite is composed of professional politicians (see also Weber 1948). Such specialized elites may correspond more or less to established professions, or they may simply bring specific 'trades and activities' to use in the political sector (Parry 1969, 74). Government and the specialized elites can of course overlap, as in the case of an elected minister, but are nonetheless relatively distinct. Specialized elites can in most cases be regarded as a support function to the governing elite. However, the support function should not be taken to imply less relevance or status of a sub-elite in relation to the governing elite: the specialized elite is an equally indispensable part of political decision making. Empirically, key examples of specialized elites are party leaders (see here in particular Eldersveld 1964, 1984) or state secretaries (Parry 1969, 74). Moreover, specialized elites include parts of the administrative branch of the executive that is sometimes excluded from the political elite (Dahrendorf 1965, 290).

The exclusion of the administrative branch of the executive is usually based on the traditional distinction between politics and administration, conveying an image of the administration as a politically peripheral organization charged with the implementation of political decisions or even a sector in its own right, distinct from the political sector (Aberbach, Putnam and Rockman 1981, 4–6; Bürklin 1997, 41; Hoffmann-Lange 2004, 30).However, scholars of public administration and bureaucratic politics have long since abandoned the notion of a clear distinction between politics and administration (Mills 1956, 231; Suleiman 1984, 2004). Correspondingly, top leaders in state bureaucracy must be considered part of the executive elite on par with elected or appointed members of the executive such as presidents, prime, state and cabinet ministers, as well as secretaries of state (Genieys 2010; Gulbrandsen 2008). They represent what Mills has called the 'political professional, whose career has been spent in the administrative areas of government, and who becomes "political" to the extent that he rises above the civil-service routine and into the policy-making levels' (Mayntz and Derlien 1989; Mills 1956, 228).

The political communication elite also draws members from the ranks of the specialized elites. For one, existing members of the specialized elites such as party secretaries and top bureaucratic leadership have been affected by the process of mediatization and the increasing emphasis on symbolic politics as much as elected members of the established political elite. Moreover, mediatization has produced a growing number of elite actors specializing solely in media relations and public messages, which make up a significant part of emerging political communication elites. This group, often taken as the most emblematic example of the new state of affairs in mediated politics and media democracy, consists of political communication professionals working within or for political parties and the administration. Although it is generally acknowledged that such communication professionals constitute the 'new elite of Anglo-American politics' (Blumler and Kavanagh 1999, 213),[3] it is still an issue of substantial debate whether political public relations (PR) professionals in Europe have reached a similar elite status (Sarcinelli 2004, 231; see also Negrine et al. 2007; Tenscher 2003).

Media Elites: Political Issues and Effects

While the term 'political elite' is applied more or less invariably to individual political actors, or a particular group of actors, the label 'elite' is often applied to entire media organizations or even branches of the media such as prestige papers and leading TV channels in media studies (Hachmeister 2002). Such an approach suggests that the term 'elite' refers equally to each journalist, correspondent and editor within the media outlet in question. This line of argument is demonstrated in exemplary fashion in the study of the U.S.-American media elite by Lichter et al., which assigns elite status to media personnel based on random sampling of employees in media outlets considered as leading news organizations (Lichter et al. 1986). The merits of the study notwithstanding, it conflicts with the criterion of organizational position associated with sectoral elites as well as the criterion of influence associated with strategic elites.

   Of course, many members of the media elite do indeed work for media organizations that are routinely considered elite media. Just like the power of a member of the political elite stems from his or her affiliation with a powerful political institution or organization, the elite status of an individual media actor is strongly linked to the status of his or her media organization. Nevertheless, membership of the media elite cannot simply be assigned to all those owning or working for elite media. Not all journalists working for a prestigious elite media outlet can be regarded as elite, as assumed by Lichter et al. (1986, 310). Conversely, the top hierarchy of second-tier media may qualify as members of the media elite (see also Hess 1981, 24).[4]

   Assigning elite status to individuals within organizations also comes with an additional caveat of particular relevance to the media sector: many

journalists work freelance for a number of outlets rather than being permanently employed by one media organization. In the case of Germany,
Hachmeister (2002) goes as far as to suggest that it is particular the small
number of prestigious freelance guest commentators that should carry the
name *Elitepublizisten*, comparable to so-called *éminences grises* within the
political sector. Such cases notwithstanding, regular and substantial influence
remains predominantly based on holding a permanent position within a media
organization (Pfetsch et al. 2004).

As was the case with the political sector, members of the political communication elite are drawn from the larger pool of the established media elite.
The main criterion for inclusion in the media side of the political communication elite is the direct impact on the political reporting of their media outlet,
that is, that those in question actively and regularly take part in shaping the
content of political reporting (for a similar definition, see Diezhandino et al.
1994, 49). This criterion implies a focus on active journalistic leadership
rather than ownership and administrative functions in the media. By implication, it also excludes a large number of actors who are considered relevant
or even essential in conventional approaches to the media elite, in particular
the leaders, owners and governing boards of the media (Dreier 1982). Conversely, actors who are not normally included in the general media elite, such
as leading political correspondents, may well be in the possession of substantial influence that would qualify them as political communication elites of
the media sector.

In general, it could be argued that the double-function of media as a pub-
licist organ and a business enterprise produces two somewhat distinct groups
of media elites (Kiefer 2005). Although the administrative and executive personnel, as well as the publishers and owners of media outlets, certainly also
have a general impact on media reporting (ranging from the effects of budget
cuts to the definition of an editorial line), they are not in charge of the actual
(political) reporting (Hoffmann-Lange 1979). Reflecting this point, the classical German elite study conducted by Ralf Dahrendorf distinguishes between
two communication elites: leading press editors and broadcasting directors
and, respectively, members of councils, supervisory boards or other control
organs of the media (1965, 285).

Membership of the political communication elite, moreover, requires focus
on political issues, in contrast to the many other types of areas covered by the
media such as business, finance, sports and culture. The political communication elite includes leading journalists of national media, who are close to
and have direct access to the political centre, that is, what Stephen Hess has
called the 'inner ring' of political news gathering (1981, 24). The inner ring
largely consists of journalists from a small number of topmost national media
organizations, supplemented by individual leading journalists of so-called

middle-ring organizations. These leading political journalists are media elites due to their influence on opinion formation in the political public sphere. This influence distinguishes them from leading journalists in other areas may carry the same rank from a strictly positional perspective. Together with the editorial level of political news production, the inner ring of political journalists makes up the strategic elite of the media sector (Bürklin 1997; Hoffmann-Lange 1992).

The very notion of a strategic elite within the media sector is premised on the assumption that the power to shape political reporting eventually transfers into political power. Elite research, however, primarily reduces the power of media elites vis-à-vis political elites to the normative control function of the press associated with the *fourth estate* and the journalistic role of the *watchdog* (see e.g. Etzioni-Halevy 1993). It does not pay much attention to the differentiated ways in which the political influence of the media has been described within communication studies and political communication research (for overviews, see Bryant and Oliver 2009; Nabi and Oliver 2009; Wolfsfeld 2011). While the control function of the media remains important, the potential political influence of the media exceeds such control through indirect effects on public opinion as well as direct effects on politicians who anticipate investigative media reporting.

Traditionally, the political power of the media has been associated with *indirect* effects, that is, the notion that media affect the cognitive orientations, emotions and judgements of citizens, which in turn affect political decisions, not least because of their potential impact on election outcomes (see e.g. Balmas and Sheafer 2010; Kepplinger 2007). Research suggests that these indirect effects take place primarily through cognitive processes affecting the issue priorities of citizens, such as agenda setting (McCombs and Shaw 1972),[5] as well as through the acquisition of political knowledge (Baum and Jamieson 2006; Delli Carpini and Keeter 1996; Dimock and Popkin 1997).

The extent to which media content shapes the opinions and judgements of citizens is a matter of debate due to selective exposure driven by the tendency to seek confirmation of existing views and avoid contradictory information (see e.g. Iyengar and Hahn 2009; Klapper 1960; Stroud 2007). Nevertheless, research on priming[6] (Iyengar and Kinder 1987), framing[7] (see e.g. Entman 1993; Scheufele 1999) and with some reservations also cultivation research[8] (Gerbner and Gross 1976; Shanahan and Morgan 1999) have indicated that cognitive effects may be followed by changes in orientations towards parties and candidates (see also Zaller 1992), as well as by long-term effects on political trust, political interest and political participation (Norris 2000; Xenos and Moy 2007). All of these effects may then bring about changes in election outcomes and result in adaptations within the policy-making process, as well as within the presentation and communication of political issues (Wal-grave and Van Aelst 2006).

In addition to such indirect effects, it has increasingly come into view how the media may affect politicians *directly*. Reasons for a direct reaction to media range from the so-called third-person effect, that is, that political actors assume their peers or citizens to be affected by media coverage (Cohen, Tsfati and Sheafer 2008; Davison 1983; Gunther and Storey 2003), to the fact that political actors originally communicate to the media to address their peers rather than the public. In this sense, journalists play a significant role in helping politicians, 'consciously or unconsciously, to reach agreed agendas and positions' (Davis 2007, 181). Kepplinger calls the direct media effect a reciprocal effect: 'Subjects of media coverage are directly influenced not only by media coverage but also by behavior of peers and reference groups who are aware of the media coverage and have changed their behavior toward the media subjects' (2007, 7).

Calling such influence direct does not imply that it outweighs the influence of media on public opinion but merely indicates that political actors alter their behaviour as a reaction to actual or presumed media reporting rather than as a reaction to changes in public opinion. Such effects are generally assumed to become more pronounced with the mediatization of politics (Mazzoleni and Schulz 1999; Meyer 2002; Street 2005; Strömbäck 2008), implying an adap-tation of politicians to the 'media logic' embedded in the criteria for selec-tion and presentation of news in different types of media outlets (Altheide and Snow 1979; Mazzoleni 1987; Meyer 2002). Indeed, indirect and direct influence may eventually become almost indistinguishable if we assume that political actors associate media reporting and public opinion:

> Whether the media really affect public opinion or not is irrelevant, what mat-ters here is that political actors believe that TV and newspapers determine the public's issue priorities. Whether media coverage is considered as a cause of public opinion, the media leading the public, or rather a consequence, the public leading the media, is not important either as long as political actors consider the media's issue attention as an indicator of the public's needs and wishes. (Walgrave and Van Aelst 2006, 100)

Combining elite studies with the insights of research on media effects in this way also provides useful input to the latter. In the majority of the political communication research, media and media reporting are analysed from an organizational or institutional perspective. Although some studies do take a more detailed approach, in particular when the focus lies on the effect of perceptions and interactions (Cohen et al. 2008; Davis 2007; Walgrave 2008), the elite perspective provides a more nuanced internal perspective on the media, distinguishing not only between elites and non-elites but also between the strategic elite of politically relevant journalists and editors vis-à-vis other groups sometimes considered part of the media elite. The main advantage of the elite perspective, however, lies in the ability to approach the media-politics nexus as a question of elite cohesion.

FROM INDIVIDUAL ELITES TO ELITE COHESION

Elite research can roughly be divided into three groups. The socio-demographic mapping of individual group characteristics is in many ways the most fundamental approach to the study of elites. Although the political elite may enjoy a particularly high degree of interest, the approach has been applied to the long list of sectoral elites, including business elites, administrative elites and cultural elites. A second approach is to focus on elite networks. Rather than the individual attributes of elite members, the object of study in this approach is the level of interaction and interconnectedness within and between sectoral elites. Correspondingly, particularly prominent members of elite circles are identified based on a criterion of centrality in observable networks. Third, and finally, we arrive at the approach adopted here: the study of elite cohesion.

In contrast to social background and involvement in networks, the study of *elite cohesion* implies an empirical focus on commonalities in the attitudinal patterns of elite actors. The roots of this approach are thus found in attitudinal research and studies of political culture. The merits of the socio-demographic approach and the network approach to elite research notwithstanding, the focus on elite cohesion is particularly well suited to the study of political communication elites. Building on this approach, the emergence of political communication elites can be equated with the degree of cohesion between political elites and media elites. More specifically, the broader idea of emerging political communication elites can be studied as a matter of *attitudinal consonance* within sectoral elite groups (intra-sectoral cohesion) and in between sectoral elite groups (inter-sectoral cohesion). Before elaborating on this in more detail, we need to briefly examine the broader idea of elite cohesion – and in particular how this approach is *not* applied in the study.

What Elite Cohesion Is Not: Integration, Consensus and Solidarity

One problem associated with the concept of elite cohesion is that it is often used interchangeably with elite integration, consensus or solidarity (Gulbrandsen 2008, 2012). In general, the concept of elite integration has been commonly used in elite research to refer to a range of aspects through which elite actors can be linked to each other (Moore 1979). In his widely cited framework, Putnam (1976) refers to elite integration as encompassing the conformity of elites in a number of different dimensions, such as socio-economic background, forms of recruitment, interaction and communication patterns, as well as norms and values.[9] In other cases, the term integration is reserved to signify the structural integration of elites, that is, the inclusiveness of communication networks among elites, while norms and value-based linkages between elites are referred to as value consensus among elites (Higley and Burton 2006, 9).

Whether deliberate or not, the term 'integration' evokes the fusion or amalgamation of separate entities into a coherent identity: 'Integration most generally thus refers to a relationship among parts through which they form a whole, so that the whole has its own distinct attributes, its boundary, and is thus recognizable as a separate structured entity' (Holzner 1967, 51). Analytically, this means that elite integration is, per definition, linked to the idea of a single and unified power elite (Mills 1956). The idea of elite integration is thus problematic, or at least empirically unlikely, under the conditions of sectoral elites that relate to each other through a complex combination of autonomy and interdependence (see also Dogan 2003). The same can be said for 'elite consensus', which applies the same logic specifically to attitudes as a subset of elite integration (Engelstad 2009, 393).

Moreover, elite cohesion is sometimes associated with 'elite solidarity' (Etzioni-Halevy 1993, 109). This interpretation of elite cohesion implies group consciousness as the feeling of belonging to a group (Thye and Lawler 2002) as exemplified by a standard socio-psychological definition of cohesion as the 'degree to which those who participate in a social system identify with it and feel bound to support it, especially its norms, values, beliefs and structure' (Johnson 1995). The notion that solidarity should be the benchmark for cohesion between sectoral elites is, however, rather limiting and highly improbable. If anything, sectoral elites are likely to display a functional orientation defined by their sectoral and organizational position and only in rare occasions show identification with the wider societal elite.

The improbable demands raised by the concept of elite solidarity not only concern cohesion between elites but also the internal cohesion of sectoral elites. Sectoral elites do not need to display solidarity or strong group identification in order to qualify as cohesive elites. Although Meisel's widely cited 'three Cs' (1958) – group consciousness, coherence, and conspiracy – suggest that group belonging and strong forms of group solidarity are a prerequisite of elite group formation, such demands are incongruent with the reality of sectoral elites. Indeed, the three Cs appear as an impediment to studies of elite groups and their role in processes of societal relevance, such as political decision making (Genieys 2010, 3; Pareto in Parry 1969, 48). Group solidarity is not a prerequisite for either inter-sectoral cohesion or intra-sectoral cohesion.

In a wider sense, the confusion of cohesion with integration, consensus and solidarity reflects a widespread interpretation of cohesion as a measure of social order and stability seen as necessary counterbalance to the functional differentiation and specialization in modern society. In this respect, elite theory and research draw on a normative juxtaposition of differentiation and integration deeply ingrained in social science. Suzanne Keller expresses this view in exemplary fashion:

> In modern industrial societies, each strategic elite represents both the common moral framework and a particular functional sphere. This poses some difficult problems. Ideally, the members of each elite must not only seek to align themselves with other elites, but also to retain their special identity; they must be knowledgeable of the duties and goals of all without over-valuing those of a particular elite. . . . Yet since the members of all strategic elites, to be effective, must keep sight of their common goals, they should have some knowledge of the concerns of each, a task becoming more difficult as specialization increases. (Keller 1963, 145)

Here, cohesion is essentially equated with the normative standard of a 'common moral framework' as a counterbalance to the individual goals of strategic elites operating within their particular functional spheres. A 'considerable degree of cohesion' is thus seen as an answer to the 'difficult problems' of current society (Keller 1963 146). This normative concern is further exasperated by Keller's use of the notion of a 'moral accord' as a shorthand for what she analytically refers to as perceptions, preconceptions, concerns, views and goals in the course of her argument. Keller's approach is not exceptional but reflects a deep-seated concern for social cohesiveness in the face of functional differentiation that goes back to the earliest sociological discussions of modernity (Durkheim 1984; Parsons 1951).

Hence, a more analytical concept of elite cohesion should be disassociated from integration, consensus and solidarity for reasons of empirical viability as well as implicit or explicit conflation with normative concerns. In sum, elite cohesion must be distinguished rigidly from elite integration, consensus and solidarity insofar as it (1) does not imply the amalgamation of separate entities, (2) refers to attitudes rather than all potential dimensions of elite interaction, (3) does not suggest the need for a moral consensus in the domain of attitudes and (4) does not entail group consciousness by members of elite groups.

Elite Cohesion as Attitudinal Consonance

In order to meet the aforementioned demands, elite cohesion is equated with the empirically observable level of attitudinal consonance in the ensuing study. Attitudes can, drawing on the broader tradition of attitudinal research, be understood as evaluations based on beliefs, feelings and past behaviour. These evaluations serve a knowledge function; they refer to cognitive categorizations rather than affect or emotions (Tesser and Shaffer 1990). In the context of political culture research, relevant attitudes are often referred to as value orientations and are of a 'profound and enduring nature' (Fuchs 2007, 163). Elite cohesion can thus be said to occur when such orientations are consonant, that is, synchronized and aligned among the members of a particular elite group.

Recent academic thinking on sectoral elites has thus begun to introduce the concept of elite cohesion more consistently (Dogan 2003; Engelstad and Gulbrandsen 2007; Gulbrandsen 2012; Pakulski et al. 2012). In his foreword to the volume Comparative Studies of Social and Political Elites, Engelstad uses the term 'elite cohesion' in relation to the competition and cooperation of elites across social sectors as well as to commonalities in elite orientations:

> The dynamics of political-economic systems cannot be well understood without taking into account the people that govern them from top positions, their goals, and how they compete and cooperate across societal sectors, i.e. the degree and form of elite cohesion. (Engelstad 2007, 7)

Dogan argues along similar lines when he states that modern democracies are characterized by 'interlocking' of separate elite groups, in contrast to the elite interchangeability of undifferentiated elites in feudal societies (2003, 5–6). This distinction highlights the fact that the notion of a homogeneous, undifferentiated elite must be seen as an empirical proposition that becomes increasingly unlikely with the transition from feudal to modern society. Elites in modern society are not interchangeable but rather loosely coupled through a 'common adherence to political game rules and the acceptance of each other's actions and roles as legitimate' (Dogan 2003, 2). The level of elite cohesion nevertheless remains an empirical question:

> In analytical terms, cohesion means interpenetration, overlapping, network. Here appears the concept of interlock as an essential factor of elite configuration. If the convergence and the overlapping between the functional elites are strong, we may perceive the shadow of a monolithic elite. If on the contrary, the osmosis between the various elite categories is relatively weak, if the separation generated by specialization and expertise is clear and solid, we may lean towards the pluralist interpretation of elite configuration. (Dogan, 2003, 5–6)

If the level of cohesion among different sectoral elites is very pronounced, the result may thus look a lot like a power elite or a ruling class in the conventional sense of the term. The more probable scenario is, however, that elites are interlocked without the loss of functional orientation or specialization. Elite cohesion thus refers first and foremost to the question of inter-elite relations in a context of distinct sectoral elites. This implies, secondly, that the question of cross-sectoral cohesion cannot be separated from the internal cohesion of such elites. In the context of sectoral elites competing as well as cooperating for social influence, cohesion is never one-sided but always split between cohesion within the individual sectoral elite and cohesion between different sectoral elites that are autonomous but nevertheless highly interdependent in modern and complex political-economic systems.

In a context defined by the existence of diverse sectoral elites, then, elite cohesion always has two intrinsically linked components: cohesion within sectoral elite groups (intra-sectoral cohesion) and cohesion between sectoral elite groups (inter-sectoral cohesion). The question of how to approach elite cohesion empirically as a matter of attitudinal consonance within and across sectors is further discussed and elaborated in the ensuing chapter. The remaining part of this chapter is dedicated to a brief survey of the contributions to this question from political communication research.

ELITE COHESION IN POLITICAL COMMUNICATION RESEARCH

To date, political communication research has largely failed to address the relationship between media and politics as a matter of elite cohesion. Whereas direct engagement with elite cohesion is rather limited, various approaches have touched on the issue in more indirect fashion by focusing on the relation between political and journalistic actors from the perspective of different research questions and interests. Such contributions can be divided into three main trajectories or perspectives, based on differences in their theoretical tradition and research questions. The three perspectives are not mutually exclusive. Particular research approaches may attempt to combine, reconcile or extend certain paradigms and thus not fall unequivocally into one of the three perspectives.

The first perspective can be designated as the propaganda perspective, drawing on critical media studies and the political economy of the media. Here, elite cohesion appears as an implicit concern in an overall focus on power imbalances in the relation between media and political actors. Typical research questions in the propaganda perspective are thus as follows: How do power relations between media and politics affect what is included and omitted in political news? Are media a propaganda tool of political elites? Are media part of society's power elite? How do media and political elites legitimize the current social order?

The second perspective, which can be labelled the social interaction perspective, approximates the question of elite cohesion insofar as it is preoccupied with the exchange of publicity for information between politicians and journalists, which is seen as a source of potentially enduring and close working relationship. Representative research questions include: What principles and mechanisms are the relationship between journalists and politicians based on? Which goals do political and media elites pursue in interacting with the other side? How do politicians and journalists work together in making the news? What determines who has the upper hand in this relationship?

Drawing its inspiration from political sociology and systems theory, the third perspective can be defined as cultural perspective. Rather than focusing directly on power or exchange, the cultural perspective approaches elite cohesion in terms of overlapping attitudes, belief systems and the potential development of shared communication culture creating a zone of interpenetration between media and politics. Correspondingly, key research questions within this tradition are rather closely aligned with the overall approach to elite cohesion proposed earlier: Do political and media elites share a common value basis? Which cognitive orientations frame the relation between media and political elites? Which societal conditions bring about a shared culture between media and political elites?

Other studies can of course also be said to invoke the cohesion between media and political elites. However, the discussion of the state of the art has been limited to approaches with potential analytical implications for the study of elites. Thus, a number of studies have been excluded from further elaboration given that the issue of elite cohesion is too peripheral to the applied approach. For one, studies dealing with political communication professions have been excluded. Such studies include investigations of socio-demographic background, work conditions or role perceptions of politicians (Aberbach et al. 1981; Best 2008; Genieys 2010; Kielhorn 2001; Patzelt 1997), political communication professionals (Hess 1984; Tenscher 2003) or political journalists (Clayman et al. 2012; Deuze 2005; Diezhandino et al. 1994; Hess 1981; Hoffmann-Lange 1979; Kramp and Weichert 2008; Mützel 2002; Pfetsch et al. 2004; Rieffel 1984; Weichert and Zabel 2007). Furthermore, general studies of elite demographics have been excluded (Bürklin 1997; Christiansen et al. 2001; Hoffmann-Lange 1992; Ruostetsaari 2007; SOU 1990). The elite demographics obtained from these studies are however an important point of reference when outlining the political communication context in the countries under study here (see chapter 5). Finally, agenda setting research has been excluded since it does not really deal with elite cohesion beyond rather general references to the 'interdependence' or 'symbiosis' of media and politics (e.g. Van Aelst and Vliegenthart 2013).

The Propaganda Perspective: Hegemony and Journalistic Deference

The propaganda perspective reflects a long-standing discussion in media studies about the tendency of the media to become a tool of government. Although the argument comes in more or less radical forms, the basic proposition here is that media content constitutes a form of propaganda insofar as it is biased towards governmental interests and perspectives and hence serves to manufacture, manipulate or distort public opinion. From such a perspective, elite cohesion is broadly associated with news bias and more or less clear-cut examples of propaganda in the media. More specifically, in cases where biased news content and propaganda output is not the result of direct political control of the media, assumed cohesion between political elites and media elites becomes a prominent explanatory factor.

Such cohesion can take the form of subjugation as well as collusion (Etzioni-Halevy 1993, 113). Subjugation borders on control insofar as it fundamentally threatens the autonomy of media elite, for example, through government 'flak' (Herman and Chomsky 2002). However, collusion based on a shared ideology is more commonly identified as the source of biased news content and propaganda in the media. Examples of latter includes cases such as patriotism (Bennett and Paletz 1994; Liebes 1997; Zandberg and Neiger 2005), the 'rally around the flag' effect (Mueller 1973), conflict-specific ideologies such as 'anti-communism' (Hallin 1986; Herman and Chomsky 2002) and the 'war on terror' (Domke 2004; Jackson 2005; see for an overview, Robinson et al. 2010, 35–38). More generally, the role of the media in times of war and conflict has been seen and studied as the paradigmatic example of media propaganda in the service of government interests (Bennett 1990; Bennett and Paletz 1994; Entman 2003; Hallin 1986; Herman and Chomsky 2002; Robinson et al. 2010; Wolfsfeld 1997).

Although the propaganda perspective is not committed to elite studies as such, the mechanisms of elite collusion thus play a vital part in explaining the deference of journalism to government. A crucial aspect of the propaganda perspective is that journalists in democratic societies based on constitutional and institutional autonomy for the media nevertheless may defer more or less freely to governmental perspectives and establish a cooperative relationship with the governing elites that potentially threatens journalistic norms and in a wider sense the democratic function of the media. Attempting to account for the democratic failure of the media, individual relations between high-ranking political and media actors come into focus. Thus, Entman points to this de facto elite position of high-ranking media actors:

> Elites concerned with foreign policy in Washington interact regularly, creating a networked community of active discourse and deliberation. . . . In this elite public sphere, individuals from different groups might have predictable policy

positions, cognitive and emotional biases, rhetorical strategies, and rules for how they interact with others, but violations, anomalies, intragroup disputes – and ambiguous stimuli – will crop up frequently and keep things interesting. The national opinion columnists, reporters, and editors are very much part of this elite public sphere. (Entman 2003, 164)

Given their position within an independent and influential societal sector, media elites would in principle be capable of maintaining distance to political elites and conducting critical journalism in accordance with more general ideas about the democratic function of the media. As such, the working relationship between political elites and media elites approximates collusion rather than subjugation, that is, a self-inflicted inter-linkage with government where 'journalistic deference to power is almost entirely voluntary' (Bennett, Lawrence and Livingston 2007, 179). Substituting such deference for an enhanced sense of accountability is thus seen as a remedy against the potential propaganda function of the media (Bennett et al. 2007). Media elites should ideally disconnect themselves more from political elites concentrating on poll majorities and cover public opinion in a more nuanced way (Entman 2003, 165).

Disconnecting in this way is, however, made difficult by the inherent journalistic reliance on officials as the main news source. Collusion is thus linked to the so-called indexing mechanism, that is, that media coverage and commentary is limited to the 'index' or range of viewpoints within the political elite (Bennett 1990), constituting a 'sphere of legitimated controversy' (Hallin 1986). This claim, originally developed with reference to media coverage of war and foreign policy, suggests that news content is seen as determined largely by the political state of affairs: if political actors are aligned around particular issues and frames, news coverage will follow. Only when political elites disagree internally, or events occur that are outside the control of elites, oppositional and truly independent media coverage is possible (Bennett et al. 2007; Entman 2003).

Adopting a more network-oriented approach, Krüger (2013) analyses the inclusion of journalists into elite networks as a potential driving force of the indexing mechanism, taking case of German foreign policy. The study, first, maps ties between journalists and politicians in established groups dedicated to informal exchange between journalists and politicians, in broader social and cultural organizations and in elite circles dedicated to foreign policy (e.g. the Bilderberg Group or the Trilateral Commission). Second, content analysis shows that the entire output of newsrooms populated with journalists included in such networks display a general elite orientation – in contrast to news outlets with no integration into elite circles. Whether these elite journalists have adopted the viewpoint of political elites through the participation in these circles or they were invited to the circles because of their foreign policy stance to begin with remains an open question.

Reverting the view to the journalistic use of sources in television programmes, the appearance of particular and limited constellations of expert sources has been taken as evidence for elite collusion as opposed to pluralism (Reese, Grant and Danielian 1994). Even if diverging and conflicting views are present in such source networks, the recurring encounters of politicians and journalists nevertheless lead to converging views or framing of the issues in question (see also Gäbler 2011). Based on interviews with elite news sources and top political journalists, Davis (2003) argues that the 'development of small elite communication networks which include top journalists' creates a situation in which 'elites are simultaneously the main sources, main targets and some of the most influenced recipient of news', leading to the exclusion of 'the mass of consumer-citizens [that] can be no more than ill-informed spectators' (Davis 2003, 673).

The most critical version of the propaganda approach is found in neo-Marxist media theory and studies of the political economy of the media focused on concerted power structures, class interest and hegemony. According to one straightforward formulation, this view suggests that the media serve as a 'guard dog' rather than a 'watchdog' of government and 'holds that media are not a separate or equal power, but that they provide a means by which the power oligarchy is maintained' (Donohue, Tichenor and Olien 1995, 122). Correspondingly, proponents of such criticisms tend to elite cohesion in more structural terms and question the value of remedies such as an enhanced sense of journalistic accountability. Journalists are rather seen as subjects of an ideological alignment within the given hegemony and more fundamental economic imperatives stemming from the capitalist nature of media firms (Herman and Chomsky 2002).

In his exemplary version of this critique, Gitlin describes the function of the media as systematic (but not necessarily deliberate) engineering of mass consent to the established order, which serves to maintain the hegemonic ideology of the ruling class and to extend it to the everyday ideas, assumptions and practices of the subordinate classes (Gitlin 2003, 253). The culture industry, in particular the media, is crucial to the creation of what Gitlin calls a complex hegemonic ideology. The complexity derives from the fact that hegemony involves an alliance of powerful groups rather than a unitary ruling class: the dominant economic class leaves the production and dissemination of ideology to the cultural sphere, including journalists and 'specialized bureaucracies within the State and the corporations' (Gitlin 2003, 257). Not unlike the internally differentiated ruling class of Pareto and Mosca, the notion of hegemony suggests an overarching power structure binding otherwise sector-specific elites together in a common power structure:

> By socialization, by the bonds of experience and relationships – in other words, by direct corporate and class interest – the owners and managers of the major media are committed to the maintenance of the going system in its main outlines. . . . The media elite want to honor the political-economic system as a whole; their very power and prestige deeply presupposes that system. (Gitlin 2003, 258–259)

Although media owners are identified as the principal actors of the media elite, the maintenance of the existing hegemony involves editors and reporters as well. Through the tools of editorial policy and control, as well as recruitment, rewards and promotion, media owners are able to incorporate journalists and editors in 'downward' flow of 'social osmosis', facilitated by the predominantly upper-middle-class origin and values (Gitlin 2003, 259–260). The relationship between journalists and their sources, correspondingly, comes to be defined and limited by the basic parameters of the hegemonic ideology: although disagreements and conflicting viewpoints may occur, these do not fundamentally 'overstep the hegemonic boundary' (Gitlin 2003, 263).

Although the propaganda perspective is mostly concerned with journalistic deference to government and hegemony resulting in biased news and propaganda, it can also be considered whether media content is determined by the ideology and hegemony of the journalists themselves. Reflecting this view, the study by Lichter et al. on the media elite as 'America's new powerbrokers' suggests that the media elite is capable of imposing a 'liberal bias' on media coverage that does not represent other elite interests than those of the media elite itself:

> Journalists at national news outlets . . . are a largely homogeneous group that is cosmopolitan in background and liberal in outlook. . . .[T]hey constitute an elite that competes for influence alongside more traditional leadership groups representing business, labor, government, and other sectors of society (Lichter et al. 1986, 53)

Rather than fundamentally questioning the propaganda perspective, however, this claim attests more importance and autonomy to the middle-class values and beliefs of the journalist. Whether this value system is in fact a more or less autonomous ideology or a subset of a broader hegemonic or ideological function, as suggested by Gitlin, remains a matter of debate. In a wider sense, the propaganda perspective is defined in large part by its commitment to a critical analysis of the media from the perspective of power and a more or less specific ideal about the democratic function of the media. Moreover, the approach is defined by a predominantly structural view on the relation between media and politics. Although this leads to a recurring focus on elites and elite cohesion, it also advances a structural perspective on elite cohesion rather than a discussion of elite cohesion as a matter of social interaction. The latter is the core of the second trajectory.

The Social Interaction Perspective: Interdependence and Institutions

The analysis of the media-source relation between political and media actors is perhaps the most established and homogenous approach to elite cohesion in political communication research. The centre of attention is the functional relationship between high-ranking journalists and politicians and their exchange of publicity for information (Fico 1984; Hess 1991; Tunstall 1970; Sarcinelli 1987). The various studies conducted in this tradition often refer explicitly to the political actors and media actors as elites. However, the tradition is not driven by theoretical interest in elite relations as such. The tradition can be defined rather as prevalent strand of media sociology, studying the media-politics relationship based on insights from the sociology of professions, the sociology of knowledge, symbolic interactionism and institutionalism. In this context, the interplay between media and politics is described as a 'symbiosis' (Miller 1978; Sarcinelli 1987), a 'tug of war' or a 'tango' (Gans 1979; Strömbäck and Nord 2006).

In his seminal study on 'Reporters and Officials', Sigal (1973) identified the interdependent relationship between politicians and journalists as a determinant of both news content and policy making.[10] News content is understood as the outcome of an organizational or even 'bureaucratic' process that consists of 'the bargaining interplay of newsmen and their sources' (Sigal 1973, 5). While news-making is a consensual process within the media, it amounts to a bargaining process between journalists and officials who 'use each other to advantage in their own organizations' (Sigal 1973, 181). This process ultimately shapes policies as well as the news (Sigal 1973, 185–187). In addition to the potential effects on news and policy, this approach raises the question of whether the interplay between journalists and officials can be described as 'a relationship governed by trust, norms, control, and balance' (Larsson 2002, 27), or rather as a struggle between journalists and their political sources, with both parts trying to keep the upper hand in the exchange relationship (e.g. Kepplinger 2009; Ross 2010; Strömbäck and Nord 2006).

A number of studies, most of them European, have focused more specifically on the quasi-institutionalized relationships between parliamentarians and parliamentary correspondents (e.g. Saxer 1992; for an extensive

overview, see Schwab Cammarano 2013). While some of these studies aim
to analyse the attitudinal basis of the interdependent relationship between parliamentarians and correspondents (e.g. Elmelund-Præstekær, Hopmann and
Nørgaard 2011), others choose a case-oriented approach to track its effects on
specific news outputs as well as policy making (e.g. Harmgarth 1997). While
such studies have provided important insights into the interaction between
officials and journalists in the processes of policy formation, they are generally 'more concerned with ad hoc variations in the relationship than with its
enduring regularities and structure' (Blumler and Gurevitch 1995, 30).

More general and enduring regularities have largely been conceived as a
process of institutionalization and institutional adaptation within the media-
source relationship: 'Relationships are institutionalized, intense and reflexive as both sides have come to incorporate the other within their everyday
thinking, decision-making and behaviour' (Davis 2009, 215). A widely cited
version of this argument can be found in the idea that the media-politics
relationship is defined by a 'negotiation of newsworthiness' (Cook 1998,
12). For Cook, the process of institutionalization is, however, less a matter of
continued reflexive interaction than imposition of institutional homogeneity
top-down: individuals, and indeed individual media organizations, are taken
to constitute homogenous units within the overall institution of the media (for
a detailed discussion, see e.g. Pfetsch and Adam 2008).

In more general terms, this tendency to subsume the level of concrete
interaction under the enduring regularities of institutions and institutionalization aligns the social interaction perspective somewhat with the theory of
social fields (Benson 2006). For Bourdieu, actors are merely 'agents' within
various social 'fields' (see Benson and Neveu 2005, 11–12; Meyen and Riesmeyer 2011). Social fields such as the political field and the journalistic field
constitute domains or sectors that lay claim to 'the legitimate vision of the
social world' (Bourdieu 2005, 36). Each field resembles a 'game', in which
the ongoing struggles 'for the power to impose the dominant vision of the
field' will always be based on a 'kind of fundamental complicity among the
members of a field' in that they accept certain general properties of the field:
'In order to fight one another, people have to agree on the areas of disagreement' (Bourdieu 2005, 36). Although struggles between individuals make up
a field, the interactions of 'visible agents' are seen to incarnate the 'invisible
relationships' or structures between these different fields:

> On an election night on television, for example . . . the political field, the social
> science field and the journalistic field are present, but they are present in the
> form of persons. . . . I postulate that when the historian addresses the journalist
> it is not a historian who speaks to a journalist . . . – it is an historian occupying a
> determinate position in the field of the social sciences who speaks to a journalist

occupying a determinate position in the journalistic field, and ultimately it is the social science field talking to the journalistic field. (Bourdieu 2005, 31)

The institutionalist approach, as well as field theory, seeks to establish a relation between enduring patterns and structures and the level of social interaction. Although the significance of media-source relations is pointed out, however, the notion of institutionalization, as well as established 'games' within and between social fields, tends to disconnect institutions and fields from the level of interaction and individual actors, or simply infer the latter from the former (Schudson 2002, 257). Bringing this issue to the fore, Cook states that the institutional quality of the media, and by implication the institutionalized exchange relationship with political institutions, is unrelated to the 'individual journalists and their individually held values and attitudes' (Cook 1998, 14). In effect, the internal cohesion within the media is taken for granted or simply deemed irrelevant (Cook 1998; Schudson 2002; Sparrow 2006). The last trajectory is preoccupied with a similar problem of connecting actor-level and macro-level observations but proceeds in a rather different direction.

The Culture Perspective: Systems and Interpenetration

The culture perspective draws its inspiration, on the one hand, from political sociology and studies of political culture (Blumler and Gurevitch 1995, 19–20), in particular the political culture model proposed by Almond and Verba (1963). Culture is seen as the key component in social organization in general and social cohesion in particular. In contrast to some versions of political sociology and studies of culture, however, this trajectory also draws considerable inspiration from the systems theoretical tradition developed in its classical sociological form by Parsons (1971) and later modified considerably by Luhmann (1984). In the field of political science, the work of Easton (1965) serves as the most important reference point. Consequently, culture is more or less consistently related to questions of systemic autonomy, reproduction and development. Although culture is viewed as a distinct phenomenon that cannot be inferred directly from systems, the analysis of culture is often discussed in terms of its degree of correspondence with formal or material systemic attributes. Applied to the media-politics relationship, the result is the idea of a distinct political communication culture:

Media-disseminated political communications derive from interactions between (1) two sets of mutually dependent and mutually adaptive actors, pursuing divergent (though overlapping) purposes, whose relationships with each other are typically (2) role-regulated, giving rise to (3) an emergent shared culture, specifying how they should behave towards each other, the ground rules of which are (4) open to contention and conflicting interpretation, entailing a potential for disruption, which is often (5) controlled by informal and/or formal mechanisms of conflict management. (Blumler and Gurevitch 1995, 32)

Political communication culture, in other words, consists of political and journalistic 'orientations toward specific objects of political communication, which determine the manner in which political actors and the media communicate vis-à-vis the general public' (Pfetsch 2008, 3684). In line with earlier studies of political culture, this concept has been used in comparative on national political communication cultures. The political communication culture of a country is seen here to include attitudes towards '(1) the institutions of exchange relations between politics and the media; (2) the input side of political communication, such as public opinion, (3) the output side of political communication, such as the agenda-setting processes that are triggered by political PR, and (4) the role allocations and norms of professional behavior' (Pfetsch 2008, 3684). While Pfetsch (2003) originally applied her concept empirically to the cases of Germany and the United States, it was later applied more extensively for the case of nine European countries (Pfetsch 2014).

The primary research interest lies in determining specific types of political communication cultures and their match with structural/systemic conditions. A crucial issue in this respect is whether the interaction between politicians and journalists gives rise to the formation of a distinct system of political communication. In general, the answer to the question resides in the analysis of the media-politics relationship as zone of 'interpenetration', applying a concept originally introduced by Talcott Parsons (1971, 1973), and further developed by Niklas Luhmann (1984) and Richard Münch (1991). The notion of interpretation, in contrast to integration, implies a distinct zone of interaction with a particular culture that presupposes rather than opposes the operational autonomy of the political and the media system (Choi 1995; Hoffmann 2003; Rinke et al. 2006; Wenzler 2009). Indeed, the zone of interpenetration presupposes rather than eradicates the autonomy of politics and journalism (see Plasser 1985). However, interpenetration also involves mutual adjustment and a significant degree of 'operative coupling between different functional systems' (Hoffmann 2003, 53).

Empirically, the interpenetration zone is manifested in mechanisms, cognitive orientations, interpretive frames and not least roles that guide specific actions and interactions. Focusing particularly on frames, Hoffmann shows that a wide array of commonly identified frames in political communication apply both to political and to journalistic action, thereby providing a cross-sectoral frame repertoire that stabilizes communication between the two parties (Hoffmann 2003, 123). These frames are flexible, that is, permit multiple (positive and negative) interpretations of identical actions. In the zone of interpenetration, elites use the professional norms of their home sectors flexibly to stage/dramatize themselves, thereby widening their scope of action, as well as constituting an independent structure of the political-journalistic zone of interpenetration (Hoffmann 2003, 161).

Hoffmann furthermore argues that such interpenetration primarily manifests itself in elite communication. Only when they occupy a sectoral top position, mutual orientations between members of different sectors (or functional systems) become likely. Thus, 'interpenetration as elite communication can be interpreted as an expression of stratified societal differentiation', although interpenetration and a shared culture do not suggest the re-emergence of a unified power elite (Hoffmann 2003, 63). Interpenetration is therefore a 'mixed blessing': on the one hand, it prevents self-referential sectoral elites from secluding themselves from each other, leading to the 'emergent shared culture' proposed by Blumler and Gurevitch (Hoffmann 2003, 161). On the other hand, it creates 'self-referential elite structures' (2003, 228) across sectors that detach the political-journalistic elite milieu from citizens/non-elites.

The idea of such interpenetration between media and politics resonates well with the policy-advocacy-coalition framework, which proposes that policy change is driven by a variety of actors united by a common (deep core) belief system (Sabatier and Jenkins-Smith 1993). Combining the notion of interpenetration with the advocacy coalition framework, Wenzler shows that cross-sectoral belief systems enable coalitions among elites in two different policy subfields (2009, 59). In a similar vein, Rinke et al. (2006) identify policy-specific media-source networks as a potential zone of interpenetration between the political and the journalistic system. Such studies connect the more abstract notion of a zone of interpenetration made up by communicatively compatible frames with specific policy coalitions between political and journalistic elites. These are neither short-lived nor (mainly) functional and pragmatic but the result of shared core beliefs.

Other studies focus on the emergence of specific communication cultures, in particular so-called informal communication cultures (Baugut and Reinemann 2013; Lesmeister 2008). Backstage relations or networks between media actors and political actors, according to this line of inquiry, bring about a distinct kind of communication culture in the form of a 'closed politics-media milieu' (Baugut and Reinemann 2013, 45). Burgert (2010) links policy networks to 'policy-specific communication cultures' and compares relations between journalists and politicians working in the field of economic and social policy. Being one of the few comparative studies in the field, her analysis furthermore sheds light on the context dependency of elite relations in political communication. While these studies are instructive in their own right, the question of elite cohesion must not be limited to the backstage of the

political public sphere to not pre-empt elite collusion and the notion of closed
elite circles. The full spectrum of operational and normative linkages between
media and politics becomes visible when taking all levels of inter-sectoral
elite interaction, as well as intra-sectoral relations into account.

In conclusion: while the attitudes and values of elites have been dealt with
in the propaganda perspective and the social interaction perspective, they
only come to the forefront of scholarly attention in the culture perspective.
In line with the earlier studies of political culture on which the perspective
builds, this approach assigns a prominent place to beliefs, attitudes and perceptions, thus paving the way for an attitudinal approach to the question of
elite cohesion. In other words, elite perceptions and attitudes move from a
secondary area of concern to the principal object of research. However, the
culture perspective also leaves a number of issues unresolved, in particular
with respect to the role and status of elites in the broader political communication culture.

SUMMARY: KEY CHALLENGES

While empirical research has been dealing with the relationship of media
and political actors, it has rarely done so within an explicit elite-theoretical
foundation. This becomes especially problematic when actors involved in the
relationship are denominated or described as elites without sufficient reflec-
tion on what this entails. Critical approaches associated more or less directly
with the propaganda perspective have often explicitly refused to treat media
actors as elites in their own right and failed to acknowledge that the subjugation or collusion of one elite group to/with another does not imply that the
status of elite must be revoked. Put differently: the autonomy of media elites
from other elites (political, business, etc.) may be undermined even in liberal
democracies with institutionalized press freedom, but this is not a reason to
deny leading media actors a strategic elite status in society (for a similar argument, see Robinson 2001). To study the relation between media and political
elites, a concept is needed that does not preemptively presume a dominance
of one elite group over the other.

If media are not by definition a tool of the political world, but rather a platform for *and* part of elite interaction, an elite theoretical perspective naturally
needs to include media actors in the actual sense of the word. While the institutional perspective on the media is fruitful in many respects, it falls short in
ignoring the degrees of cohesion and consistency within the media sector. If
the degree of consensus among political elites allows us to draw conclusions
for media performance (as is the case with indexing), couldn't the degree of

cohesion among media elites be decisive for the political process as well? And if – as it is basically assumed in all of the approaches mentioned earlier – elites of media and politics keep up frequent and close interactions, would the role of journalists in the political process not extend beyond the embodiment of media logic? An intra-sectoral assessment of elite relations is thus a necessary addition to the study of elite cohesion in political communication.

While much theoretical and empirical effort has gone into learning more about the consequences of elite cohesion, previous research has largely failed to address its contextual conditions due to the limited number of comparative studies. The comparative approach chosen in this study allows an empirical focus on the effects social and political environments have on the shape of elite cohesion. In contrast to cultural approaches, it does not seek to match certain types of political communication cultures with its systemic environment but asks which systemic conditions bring about elite cohesion. Put simply: there is always a culture, but not always cohesion.

The book takes up the challenge of providing an elite-theoretical foundation for political communication research by developing an analytical framework for the study of elite cohesion as attitudinal consonance. The framework, presented in the following chapter, provides new measures of assessing elite cohesion under the conditions of mediatized politics, as well as a nuanced conceptualization of the contextual conditions for and the consequences of different types and levels of cohesion in modern societies.

Chapter 3

A Model of Elite Cohesion in Political Communication

The chapter presents a comprehensive theoretical model for the study of elite cohesion as attitudinal consonance among political communication elites. As seen in the preceding chapter, the combination of elite studies with political communication research and the particular focus on attitudinal consonance introduce a number of additional issues and distinctions compared to the more established value consensus approach to elite cohesion. Hence, a new and more differentiated framework is needed in order to properly capture and analyse the *dimensions*, *context* and *consequences* of attitudinal consonance in political communication. Figure 3.1 presents an overall model developed to meet this need.

The chapter is organized according to the structure of the model, starting with the different dimensions of elite cohesion as attitudinal consonance. These include, first, the *sources* of elite cohesion. In this dimension, we can distinguish between three basic types of attitudinal consonance shaped, respectively, by values, procedures and epistemology. The second dimension encompasses the guiding *principles* of elite interaction in political communication, including ideology, publicity and pragmatism. These principles can be understood as more or less institutionalized compromises between the autonomy and mutual dependence of different elites. Correspondingly, elite cohesion in this dimension furthermore depends on the *stances* of elites, that is, whether they accept, reject or are ambiguous about the particular compromises involved in the different guiding principles.

The third dimension is the *pattern* of elite cohesion. Here, the proposed model introduces a new distinction between *proximity* and *indistinction* of attitudes in order to better gauge the extent of elite cohesion. In contrast to the presence of attitudinal proximity, indistinction signals the absence of a

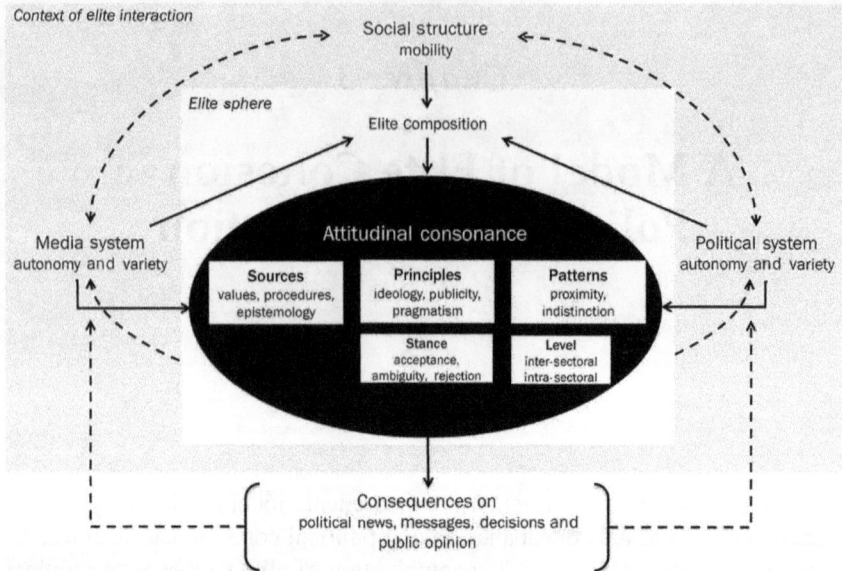

Figure 3.1. Modelling Elite Cohesion in Political Communication

clear line of demarcation between different elite groups. As such, indistinction denotes the inability to distinguish elite groups based on their attitudinal patterns. By combining the two measures of proximity and indistinction, four different patterns of elite cohesion can be distinguished at the *inter-sectoral* as well as the *intra-sectoral level* of analysis.

The latter part of the chapter elaborates on the consequences and context of elite cohesion. Here, the chapter offers a brief discussion of the potential *consequences* of the content, form and extent of elite cohesion for political news, messages, decisions and public opinion. The *context* of elite cohesion, finally, is seen to include the elite mobility and composition of the broader *social structure* as well as the attributes of both the *media system* and the *political system*. Building on this distinction, a number of more specific assumptions about the relation between context and dimensions of attitudinal consonance are developed.

SOURCES OF ELITE COHESION: VALUES, PROCEDURES, EPISTEMOLOGY

One effect of the older notion of a single and unified political class in elite research is a continuing tendency to see the basis of elite cohesion as a more or less pronounced consensus on inherently political or even democratic values. Even if the reality of functionally specific sectoral elites is acknowledged, the source of elite cohesion between such elites is still defined as a form of political value consensus on the basic institutions and rules of the political system, that is, 'the relative agreement among elites on formal and informal rules and codes of political conduct and on the legitimacy of political institutions' (Burton, Gunther and Higley 1992, 10; see also DiPalma 1973; Prewitt and Stone 1973). Thus defined, political value consensus is more or less indistinguishable from commitment to democratic institutions and rules of the game.

This is, however, a debatable approach if we accept the reality of society defined by the existence of different elites with specific orientations depending on the sector to which they belong. Elite cohesion is clearly not dependent on commitment to democratic values. Commitment to democratic values is of course an important normative issue but not a viable criterion for elite cohesion per se. The same can be said for political rules and codes of conduct in a broader (i.e. also non-democratic) sense. Generally speaking, cohesion between functional elites can never be intrinsically bound up with political rules and institutions.

Moreover, elite cohesion cannot be seen to depend solely on values. Not only is elite cohesion subject to the particular functional orientations of sectoral elites, but it is also subject to a more diverse set of attitudinal orientations within and across these elites. Although Putnam's work (1973, 1976) is geared towards the idea of integration and consensus, his classification of elite attitudes serves as a helpful entry point in this respect. Putnam distinguishes between normative orientations (assumptions about how society ought to work), stylistic orientations (e.g. partisan ideological commitments), interpersonal orientations (assumptions about other players in the political game) and cognitive orientations (assumptions about how society works) as basic elements of elites' belief systems (Putnam 1976, 79–92; see also Putnam 1973). Revising this distinction somewhat, in particular by integrating normative and stylistic orientations, we can distinguish between three basic types of attitudinal consonance based on *values*, *procedural requirements* and *epistemological assumptions* about the nature of society.[1]

Value Consonance

Most definitions of value consensus emphasize the importance of constitutive and fundamental values and ideals, such as the 'basic values' referred to by Etzioni-Halevy (1993, 109), and the 'legitimacy of political institutions' referred to by Burton, Gunther and Higley (1992). These ideals are commonly held to provide a basic foundation for the beliefs and actions of societal elites. Putnam refers to these as 'normative orientations of elites: everyday judgments about specific political objects . . . rest on commitments to more fundamental values – individual self-reliance, social justice, national independence, material progress and so on' (1976, 81). In a somewhat radical fashion, such values have been described as 'deep core beliefs that are . . . essential akin to religious convictions' (Sabatier 1998, 122).

Such beliefs are often equated with ideologies. When conceptualizing 'elite political culture' as a belief system, Putnam includes ideological orientations (or in his terminology: stylistic orientations) as a set of attitudes within elite culture in its own right. Likewise, Sigal includes a common 'forensic ideology' when outlining the media elites 'creed' as a prerequisite to group cohesion (1973, 65). Elite theorists, in turn, have insisted on a strict distinction between an 'ideologically united elite' based on a coercive, mono-lithic value consensus, which is characteristic of totalitarian regimes, and a 'consensually united elite' unrestricted by ideological orientations (Field and Higley 1980; Higley and Burton 2006). In order to be of value for empirical research, however, it is necessary to separate the question of value conso-nance from the idea of an all-encompassing and unifying ideology, as well as from the normative interpretation of ideological consensus as a demarcation line between non-democratic and democratic elites.

In addition to deep-seated beliefs, ideological conventions and constitu-tive norms, cohesion based on values pertains to the specification of more or less distinct roles guiding social action. In the widest sense, the importance of roles for elite cohesion goes back to Durkheim's observation that modern society is characterized by interdependence and complementary of special-ized functions and roles rather than a generalized commitment to general val-ues and kinship (1984). This is not to say that roles simply substitute values. Rather, values, norms and roles can be seen as increasingly specific guide-lines for social action linking overall orientations with specific behaviour.

In general, *values* primarily serve as 'more generalized ideological justifica-tions for roles and norms', whereas *norms* represent 'the general expectations of a demand character for all role incumbents of a system or subsystem' and *roles* can be seen as 'standardized patterns of behavior required of all persons playing a part in a given functional relationship' (Katz and Kahn 1966, 43). Role complementarity is thus the crucial condition for achieving consonance on substantive values among heterogeneous elites, providing a level of opera-tionalization to more general values and norms. As Blumler and Gurevitch state in their outline of what they call the political communication system:

> The degree of integration of a political communication system might be con-
> ceived in terms of the correspondence between its constituent parts. Thus, a
> highly integrated system would be one with high inter-correlations between

role orientations across levels, i.e. where all the participants in the communication process . . . consequently speak on . . . similar wavelengths. (Blumler and
Gurevitch 1995, 15)

Procedural Consonance

If attitudinal consonance is to provide guidance of interaction, however, it
must also extent to the domain of procedures. In contrast to value consonance, procedural consonance allows for the option of agreeing to (potentially) disagree by specifying rules and procedures that allow for cooperation
among elites when their norms and interests diverge. Correspondingly,
Etzioni-Halevy distinguishes between consensus on constitutive norms and
ideals and procedural aspects of how the elite game is to be played (1993,
110). Such procedural consonance becomes particularly crucial to the analysis of elite cohesion when we recognize the existence of competing sectoral
elites (e.g. Parry 1969, 94).

Procedural consonance corresponds more or less directly to the interpersonal type of attitudes identified by Putnam. In contrast to the general nature
of deep-seated values and their transformation to social identities through role
specification, consonance based on procedures amounts rather to 'operative
ideals' directly specifying how the various players are to play the political
game (Putnam 1973, 6). Elites may not share values or positions towards specific political decisions, but they share a 'code of conduct' on the appropriate
way to reach decisions and deal with their respective differences (Prewitt and
Stone 1973, 151). Albeit procedural, these rules or expectations still remain
of a general character. Thus, they refer to underlying predispositions guiding
and shaping elite interaction, rather than interaction processes as such (Putnam 1973, 3–4).

Within more or less liberal democracies, constitutional principles and the
basic architecture of political institutions are conventionally seen to provide
the key rules of the game. Or, reversing the argument: consonance on procedures, most importantly resolving conflict, is a necessary (pre)condition for
democracy (Sartori 1987). Correspondingly, democratic elite theory argues
for the importance of procedural consonance. It is evident, however, that
procedural rules are not necessarily democratic. It is hardly controversial to
state that even highly democratic systems provide an abundance of less than
democratic rules of the game that may serve as a basis for elite cohesion.
When looking at different sectoral elites in conjunction, this point becomes
even more pertinent: whereas intra-sectoral cohesion within the political elite
can perhaps be assumed to rely most on democratic procedures, such procedures cannot immediately be extended to the media elite and the inter-sectoral
level of analysis.

Epistemological Consonance

Finally, elite cohesion can also consist in consonance on the (assumed) context and structural conditions for elite (inter)action. While many authors recognize that the degree of cohesion among pluralist elites depends both value consonance and procedural consonance (or at least acknowledge this distinction), the importance of assumptions and ideas about the structural conditions that surround elite interaction is often treated more implicitly, if at all. In contrast to values and stances on procedural requirements, assumptions about structural conditions and the nature of the surrounding context are broadly epistemological in the sense that they represent a given knowledge and understanding of how the (common) world is structured.

Putnam describes such assumptions as 'cognitive predispositions' (1976, 80). This definition is, however, potentially misleading insofar as all value judgements and procedural stances can also be said to have a cognitive function. What sets such assumptions apart is rather that they are epistemological in nature; that is, that they provide a form of established knowledge of the social context. Such predispositions can be understood as the standardized interpretations of the social environment and the set of structural conditions it represents, including an understanding of key trends and developments (e.g. globalization and commercialization), challenges (e.g. increased competition) and solutions (e.g. specialization).

In terms of cohesion, common interpretations and perceptions of the structural conditions in which elites are embedded serve to align elites according to a shared world view in contrast to established truths and sedimented forms of knowledge within different societal sectors. As such, epistemological consonance can serve not only to avoid misunderstandings but also more fundamentally to overcome differences in perceptions of valid truths and arguments within political communication. Consonance of epistemological assumptions about the structural conditions facing different elites thus adds an important dimension to value consonance and procedural consonance insofar as it potentially imbues interaction with shared perceptions of the givens and truths that lie beyond the realm of values judgements and negotiation of procedural rules.

GUIDING PRINCIPLES OF COHESION: IDEOLOGY, PUBLICITY, PRAGMATISM

Constitutive values, procedural norms and epistemological assumptions about conditions and context constitute three general types of attitudes. Whether these attitudes lead to consonance, however, furthermore depends on the development of more or less established compromises between autonomy of individual elites and dependence on other elites in control of valuable resources such as information or access. Such compromises are defined here as guiding principles of interaction and negotiation between autonomous yet interdependent elites. Taking the nature and challenges of the interaction between specific sectoral elites into account, in other words, introduces a second dimension to the question of elite cohesion, making it necessary to view values, procedures and epistemology in the context of guiding principles of interaction between specific sectoral elites.

Concrete interaction between sectoral elites involves an ongoing negotiation between preservation of sectoral autonomy and acknowledgement of the rules and requirements of elites in control of other vital resources (Cook 1998; Etzioni-Halevy 1993; Gans 1979). Under such conditions of structural interdependence, which certainly applies to the relation between political elites and media elites, negotiation of a point of acceptable mutual interdependence becomes imperative. Guiding principles of interaction can, correspondingly, be considered more or less institutionalized trade-offs between sectoral autonomy (needed to pursue sectoral goals) and reflexive acknowledgement of other sectoral interests (needed to stabilize interaction) that both sides can agree on. The nature of such trade-offs may vary with the particular elites in question and their respective resources. In the case of political elites and media elites, we can identify three such guiding principles: *ideology*, *publicity* and *pragmatism*.

Empirically, the three guiding principles of cohesion become manifest in the attitudes of political communication elites (see appendix for details on how these principles have been translated into empirically measurable items). Each principle is subject to affirmation as well as rejection, meaning that cohesion based on each principle can take shape as (partial or full) positive commitment to the principle as well as (partial or full) rejection. Commitment to the principle of ideology involves acceptance of political stances and orientations as a legitimate sectoral interest, whereas rejection of the principle results in a mutual understanding that ideological stances must be set aside in order for interaction to work. The principle of publicity concerns the commitment to the political function of the media and the related standards of openness and access. Rejection of this principle, by contrast, acknowledges secrecy and limitations to publicity as a legitimate sectoral interest. The principle of pragmatism can be understood as a form of business logic, basing interaction on a mutual recognition of interaction as a business relationship where diverging interests and self-interested behaviour are tempered only by the mutual benefit of interaction. Rejecting this principle, in turn, maintains a more idealistic approach to the interaction between media and political elites.

Ideology (versus Neutrality)

The issue of ideology is the central question of the wider debate on the political parallelism of the media (Hallin and Mancini, 2004; Seymour-Ure, 1974). Historically, relations between media and politics can be said to rely on acceptance of ideology as a guiding principle of interaction. In modern democracies with a formally autonomous media system, ideology is less a matter of strict ideological alliances between politics and media than of a broad alignment of positions in the political spectrum and convergence on particular political issues, problems and solutions. Even though political parallelism far from always amounts to stable and all-pervasive ideological convergence, it remains a counterpoint to political neutrality.

Agreement on ideology as a guiding principle of interaction thus consists in a mutual commitment to alignment along ideological divides in a broad sense. Media and political elites face each other with the mutual expectation in mind that they will primarily act upon their ideological standpoint. While this may not always create pleasant encounters, it guarantees stability in interaction and reduces uncertainty. The rejection of ideology as a guiding principle, conversely, is integral to the process of de-alignment and results in a shared understanding of banning ideological alliances between media and political elites. As the political independence of the media increases, so does the scope of action for political elites, as potential points of contact within the media sector increase. Mutual expectations however remain equally high: both sides expect from each other to be politically neutral, that is, enter the interaction without ideological prejudices, biases and motives.

More specifically, the guiding principle of ideology is expressed in a particular constellation of values, procedures and epistemology, each of which can be either affirmed or rejected. In the domain of values, ideology as a guiding principle of interaction is expressed in a role match between the *editorial guide* in the media sphere and *gladiator* in the political sphere (Blumler and Gurevitch 1995, 15). Whereas the editorial guide perceives it as his or her role to present audiences with his or her own viewpoints and interpretations, the gladiator enters interaction with the media and the public as a representative of his or her party's political viewpoints. On the procedural level, this role match is complemented by the mutual acknowledgement that interaction between politicians and journalists is based on the political and ideological *convictions* of both sides. Ideology, finally, presupposes that media organizations are associated with a particular political position. A certain degree of political *parallelism* in the media system is here seen as primary structural condition of political communication.

Publicity (versus Secrecy)

In modern democracies, media and political elites need to negotiate not only the question of ideological alignment but also the media's function in a democratic society. The media's democratic role as a supervisory body or control agent within the political process requires a high level of publicity in the political system. This understanding is visible in the quasi-constitutional understanding of the media as *fourth estate* included in a system of checks and balances with the conventional branches of political power. The publicity principle places demands on openness and access to information in the political system but also propagates cohesion based on the acknowledgement of an adversarial media role and a state of more or less radical antagonism between politics and the media.

On the other hand, cohesion based on the rejection or only conditional acceptance of the principle of publicity does not preclude an understanding of the media as being impartial and objective. However, such viewpoint remains cautious about the media taking an active role as a control agent to politics, as well as about a political sector too preoccupied with transparency. In the last instance, the rejection of publicity subordinates political communication and media reporting to the political requirements of secrecy (Donohue et al. 1995; Mueller 1973).

More specifically, the guiding principle of publicity is expressed, first, in the complementary roles of the journalistic *watchdog* and the political role of the *information provider* on the value level (Blumler and Gurevitch 1995, 15). The mutual commitment to transparency in the political sphere requires acceptance of investigative journalism on both the media side and the political side of the table. On the procedural level, this takes its clearest form in a common stance on the legitimacy of *disclosure* of confidential political information by the media. To grant the media such a quasi-institutionalized monitoring role in the political process requires that elites have trust in the democratic role of the media. In terms of epistemological consonance, media's *impact on democracy* is thus a key aspect of the publicity principle. If political communication elites in turn jointly see media as an impediment to a well-functioning democracy, cohesion based on secrecy (as a safeguard against a potentially destabilizing media) becomes likely.

Pragmatism (versus Idealism)

The principle of pragmatism can be considered an entirely instrumental logic of interaction. Pragmatism conceives of interaction as the legitimate pursuit of sectoral self-interests harnessed only by the potential for a mutually beneficial outcome. This instrumental logic suggests that the interaction between media and politics is just business, where both sides agree that they each follow their own (sectoral) interests and acknowledge the right to do so for their counterpart as well. Consequently, mutual accommodation occurs only out of strategic consideration of the sectoral interest. The principle of pragmatism comes with a high degree of acceptance for conflict and self-interested behaviour on both sides.

The rejection of pragmatism can generally be said to involve a more idealistic stance towards the nature of interaction. Although the specific content of such an idealistic stance can vary according to particular circumstances, it will more or less invariably add a requirement of working together towards the common goal of guaranteeing political public debate and a common good, as well as social expectations such as treating each other with mutual respect or courtesy.

The constellation of attitudes specific to the guiding principle of pragmatism includes a match between the roles of the *mass communicator* and a *strategic communicator*. Whereas the former uses political actors, processes and issues as an instrument to reach a large audience, the latter uses the media and its elites as a platform to affect the outcome of political decisions. On the procedural level, the principle of pragmatism therefore requires that conflicts, which will necessarily arise in the confrontation of mutual interests, are not seen as an explicit violation of social norms but as an expression of a structurally given *clash of interests*. The primary structural condition implied by pragmatism is a certain degree of *commercial orientation* in the media. Whether operating within formally commercial media organizations or not, media elites are expected to be faced with commercial imperatives in their work and to follow economic indicators such as viewers' ratings and circulation numbers.

The three guiding principles are not mutually exclusive and can combine in different ways: the rejection of publicity does not by definition equal ideological alliances, just as the acceptance of ideology as a guiding principle does not preclude the acceptance of publicity, for example, in the form of partisan investigative reporting or *muckraking*. The principle of pragmatism, finally, invokes underlying motivations for cooperative or antagonistic behaviour in any form and shape. In that sense, ideological alliances may be kept up for mere reasons of mutual self-interest, just as well as for established social ties, while agreeing on confidentiality may result out of social and idealistic reasons, just as well as out of strategic considerations.

EXTENT OF COHESION: PROXIMITY AND INDISTINCTION

Having established the two basic dimensions of attitudinal consonance, the question of a benchmark of consonance across these dimensions arises. In other words: When are attitudes consonant? Traditionally, the answer to this question refers to the *proximity* of attitudes. However, the developed framework introduces the *indistinction* of attitudes as a second aspect of attitudinal consonance, making it possible to identify distinct *patterns* of inter-sectoral and intra-sectoral cohesion. Whereas the former measures cohesion based on a criterion of distance between attitudes, the latter associates cohesion with the lack of clear separation between attitudes. In a more technical sense, the two dimensions express, respectively, the degree of *dispersion* and *discriminance* of attitudes.

Cohesion as Proximity: Dispersion

Traditional attitudinal elite research has generally interpreted cohesion as the identity of attitudinal positions. Even if established concepts such as elite consensus and elite unity may differ on other accounts, they interpret cohesion as congruence, agreement and approximation to identity. Unless positions are measured strictly as choices between binary alternatives, however, complete agreement or unanimity remains an empirically illusive result. Consequently, the operational criterion applied in elite research effectively becomes one of proximity: elites are considered cohesive when their attitudinal stances are sufficiently close to each other. Technically speaking, proximity can be understood as the *non-dispersion* of attitudes: analysing cohesion in terms of proximity proceeds from the assumption that the default condition in any social grouping is a dispersion of individual attitudes. Complete dispersion is given when individual attitudes are scattered with maximum and more or less equal distance. Cohesion, correspondingly, appears when dispersion and distance are replaced by some level of proximity between attitudes.

Three basic conditions of proximity have to be considered, when analysing cohesion in these terms. The first issue concerns the fact that attitudinal patterns tend to be rather complex, as the notion of belief systems suggests (Converse 1964). They are (1) based on multiple stances and attitudes rather than on a single stance towards an isolated object or proposition and (2) often expressed through evaluations that are far more differentiated than the binary choice between confirmation and rejection. The more complex attitudinal patterns are, the more crucial it is to define a threshold of proximity, that is, a standard determining at what point attitudes are seen to resemble each other sufficiently to qualify as congruent attitudes.

A second issue that must be taken into account is the dual nature of attitudes. At the most basic level, attitudes can be analysed in dichotomous terms, which is equivalent to the use of a single binary measure (yes/no). More nuanced expressions of attitudes and their corresponding scales are, however, also essentially dual insofar as they express a continuum from negative to positive. In the final instance then, any attitude can be expressed either as a commitment to a particular stance or rejection of a stance – and potentially also by indifference, ambiguousness or neutrality. The distinction between proximity based on positive or negative commitment is fundamental but tends to be overlooked in the discussion of value consensus. However, proximity can be based entirely on rejection, for example, when a group of actors displays a common rejection of xenophobia without an active common commitment to multiculturalism. Consequently, the basic distinction between congruence based on commitment, rejection or shared neutrality/ambiguity must be included in any comprehensive study of attitudinal proximity.

A final issue to be considered is the distinction between correspondence and complementarity of attitudes. In most instances, proximity of attitudes expresses correspondence between two stances on the same attitudinal object. Proximity can, however, also be said to occur as complementary stances, that is, stances on different propositions and expressions that are seen to match each other on a deeper level of argument. When measured in terms of complementarity, proximity requires the specification of different propositions assumed to express an underlying relation of mutual recognition and division of labour between specific elites. As such, complementarity is particularly relevant for value consonance, in particular its role dimension: given that roles are assumed to be functionally specific to media elites and political elites, respectively, commitment to complementary roles remains the key indication of attitudinal proximity (Blumler and Gurevitch 1995, 15). Procedural consonance can involve instances of complementarity, in addition to instances of correspondence, whereas epistemological consonance is limited to assessments of similar external conditions and hence to correspondence.

Cohesion as Indistinction: Discriminance

Although the level of attitudinal proximity is an established and consistent measure of cohesion, it also lacks sensitivity towards the reality of functional differentiation in modern societies (Luhmann 1984, 2006). Under the conditions of pervasive functional differentiation, represented on the level of elites by the existence of sectoral elites rather than a unitary political class, the mere lack of differentiation between these elites must be considered a potential instance of cohesion in itself. The criterion of cohesion as *indistinction* accommodates this insight by introducing a measure of attitudinal consonance bound to an initial condition of complete separation.

Whereas cohesion is seen to increase the more it deviates from the initial condition of maximum dispersion and equal distance in the case of proximity, cohesion increases the more it deviates from the initial condition of complete separation in the case of indistinction. The more indistinct groups of (sub-)sectoral elites are in their attitudinal patterns, the higher the degree of cohesion among them. This is not to say that indistinction is a weaker form of cohesion. Indeed, indistinction can even be taken as evidence of cohesion that overrules functional differentiation insofar as it potentially points to other commonalities than those pertaining to the functional orientation of sectoral elites.

In technical terms, indistinction is based on a measure of *non-discriminance* between attitudes. In general, discriminance refers to the possibility to distinguish different groups from each other, based on the attitudinal stances of their members. Consequently, different groups of elites are discriminant if these groups can – at least to a large degree – be reconstructed based on the attitudes of their group members. The maximum level of discriminance refers to a scenario where two or more elite groups are divided completely. In practical terms, this means that individual elites can unequivocally be matched with their group of origin based on their attitudinal stances. In turn, under the condition of minimal discriminance, elites' individual attitudinal stances do not yield any information of original group membership. Formally speaking, such a state of indistinction occurs when the distinction between groups based on the systematic allocation of individual membership does not produce a better result than if membership was allocated randomly.

In sum, elite cohesion must thus be conceived both as the opposite of separation (*indistinction*) and as the opposite of distance (*proximity*). From this follows that cohesion can no longer be perceived as a matter of mere presence or absence. Rather, cohesion appears in different forms or patterns, depending on the degree to which it is based on indistinction and/or proximity, respectively. The various ways in how these two aspects combine empirically yield different patterns of cohesion that have particular implications for elite relations – both in between and within sectors.

PATTERNS OF INTER-SECTORAL AND INTRA-SECTORAL COHESION

The combination of indistinction and proximity applies to cohesion both within and between sectors. However, the particular patterns of cohesion also vary between the inter-sectoral and the intra-sectoral level of analysis. Inter-sectoral cohesion, on the one hand, refers to the cohesion between different sectors, that is, between the media sector and the political sector in the study conducted here. Inter-sectoral cohesion thus provides a measure of the extent to which the differentiation between the two sectors can indeed be observed empirically. As such, the issue of inter-sectoral cohesion provides an empirical operationalization of the larger question of functionally specific domains or systems and the level of coupling, interpenetration and co-evolution between them, not least in the case of media and politics (Luhmann 2009; see also chapter 2).

Intra-sectoral cohesion, on the other hand, refers to cohesion among elites within a societal sector. Elite studies often fall short of a systematic inclusion of factors associated with intra-sectoral cohesion, focusing instead on the differentiation and relations between different sectors. There are, however, good reasons for including the issue of intra-sectoral cohesion. For one, functional systems or sectors such as politics and the media are subject to further differentiation, resulting in groups or factions that may belong to the same sector, but are nonetheless competing through specialization:

> Elite persons in a given sector almost invariably have interests that elites in other sectors also have over resources and over priorities in their specific arenas. At the same time, there may be fierce competitive relationships within each sector elite. It is here that a central aspect of the Schumpeterian problematic is situated: democracy is competition between factions of sector elites. In politics conflicts are fought out between political parties, between interest groups that jockey for influence in each sector; in the economy between corporations competing for the same markets; and in the cultural sphere between numerous religious denominations, artistic styles, and voluntary associations. (Engelstad 2009, 395)

Second, the question of intra-sectoral cohesion brings up the question of hierarchical organization within sectoral elites. The primacy of functional differentiation does not suggest that hierarchical organization or stratification disappears altogether, but simply that it becomes a secondary principle of organization. In practical terms, this notion suggests that sectoral elites are still subject to an internal horizontal division between elites and sub-elites. The term 'sub-elite' refers to actors occupying the middle ranks of power structures and are seconds in command to the top echelons of the different sectors in society (Etzioni-Halevy 1993, 95–96; see also Hoffmann 2003).

In general, questions of inter-sectoral and intra-sectoral cohesion between elites are tightly interwoven when dealing with issues of horizontal and vertical division. The approach to this issue adopted here differs from the interpretation of elite cohesion as consensus in two rather crucial respects. First, intra-sectoral cohesion is not regarded as a prerequisite to inter-sectoral cohesion: even if sectoral elites in themselves are not entirely in agreement, they retain the ability as a group to be cohesive with another group. Second, intra-sectoral and inter-sectoral cohesion are not seen as mutually exclusive: even if sectoral elites form a unity, they will remain open to develop cohesion with other sectors. Put differently: intra-sectoral cohesion is not the result of the demarcation from other elite groups. Rather, this study proceeds from the proposition that inter-sectoral and intra-sectoral cohesion are independent forms of cohesion appearing in various constellations.

The nature of these constellations must be determined empirically in light of each other. It also follows that the implications of cohesion as proximity versus indistinction must be specified in relation to inter-sectoral as well as intra-sectoral cohesion. When seen in relation to the particular cases of inter-sectoral cohesion between sectors and intra-sectoral cohesion within a sector, different combinations of attitudinal dispersion and discriminance can be seen to produce different patterns of cohesion. In the case of inter-sectoral cohesion, the issue at stake in these patters is the relation between sectors. In the case of intra-sectoral cohesion, these patterns refer to the internal order or structure of a particular sector.

Patterns of Inter-Sectoral Cohesion

When applied to the issue of relations between sectors, the proximity (non-dispersion) and indistinction (non-discriminance) of attitudes combine to produce four possible outcomes. Two of these outcomes are rather clear-cut. The absence of proximity and indistinction constitutes a complete lack of cohesion. The presence of both proximity and indistinction constitutes the strongest possible form of cohesion. In addition to these two outcomes, the absence of either proximity or indistinction, combined with the presence of the other, constitutes more complex patterns of cohesion. In these patterns, cohesion emerges only in the form of indistinction *or* the proximity of attitudes, that is, attitudes of different elite groups are either non-discriminant but dispersed *or* non-dispersed but discriminant. Figure 3.2 outlines these four possible patterns of cohesion between two sectoral elite groups.

Each of the four possible outcomes displays a number of individual attitudes that can range from complete disagreement (X) to complete agreement (Z) to any given attitudinal object. Crosses and circles mark the different sectoral elite groups, respectively.

- Outcome A in the upper right-hand corner represents a case, in which attitudinal stances are dispersed as well as discriminant. In such a scenario where neither proximity nor indistinction can be observed, cohesion is entirely absent. Such absence of cohesion can also be described as complete separation of the two sectors: the sectors are clearly *separated* and distant to each other.
- Moving along the axis of proximity to the upper left-hand corner, outcome B describes a scenario where stances approximate each other but nevertheless remain clearly divided. This combination of low dispersion and high discriminance can be said to result in a neighbouring relation between the two sectors where both groups remain close to the borderline separating the two sectors without overstepping it. This relation can also be described

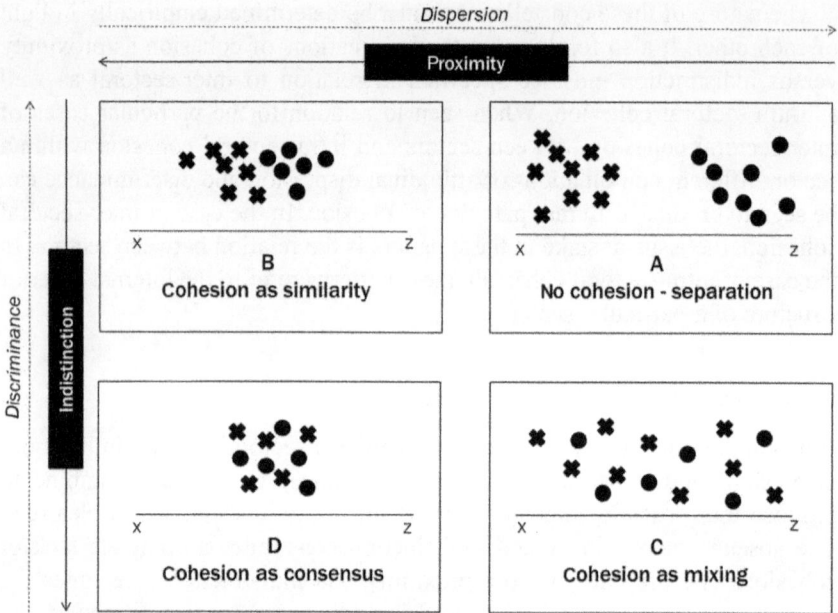

Figure 3.2. Patterns of Inter-Sectoral Cohesion

Stylized depiction – crosses and circles designate different sectoral elite groups and are spread out vertically for better visualization; to ensure visual comparability with the mode of displaying subsequent empirical results; type A is located in the upper-right corner.

as a tangential relation based on *similarity*: overall, attitudes are relatively congruent (non-dispersed), indicating that the stance of the different elites on a given object is similar. Despite this similarity, the two elite groups can still be distinguished based on their attitudinal patterns.

- By contrast, outcome C represents a scenario where stances are indistinct without being proximate. Or, put differently, the attitudes are highly dispersed but in a non-discriminant way. As in outcome A, individual attitudes are generally dispersed, but now cut across different elite groups. Consequently, the two groups can no longer be distinguished based on the attitudinal patterns of their members. One possible underlying mechanism may be that other (ideological or generational) groupings take precedence over differentiation between sectors. Correspondingly, this outcome can be described as *mixing* of the two sectors: the border between the two sectors is called into question or blurred by the intermingling of attitudes. In figure 3.2, cohesion as mixing is depicted as the result of high dispersion of attitudes among the elites of both sectors. However, such state of cohesion as mixing can also be the result of high intra-sectoral dispersion in only one sector.
- Finally, outcome D represents a case of full cohesion or cohesion as consensus, as individual attitudes in between two groups of elites are both

proximate and indistinct. Put differently: elite attitudes are so congruent that they are not only similar in stance, but at the same time indistinct for each elite group. As the name indicates, this case approaches the classical notion of an elite *consensus*: the two sectors have become so close and undivided that they can be considered, at least potentially, to constitute a coherent and integrated whole, that is, a unified elite.

But at what point are attitudes dispersed or discriminant? The distinct patterns of cohesion can be meaningfully identified empirically only if specific thresholds of discriminance versus non-discriminance and dispersion versus non-dispersion, as well as potential graduations, are defined. A relative threshold requires a point of reference that consists in alternative group divisions (based on ideology, seniority, etc.). Thus understood, attitudinal patterns of sectoral elites are then non-dispersed and non-discriminant if their degree of dispersion and discriminance is lower than in the benchmark distinction. An absolute threshold, on the other hand, establishes a fixed cut-off point that needs to be sufficiently justified and grounded in theoretical and empirical reasoning. For the purposes of this study, both absolute and relative thresholds will be defined in chapter 5.

Patterns of Intra-Sectoral Cohesion

Whereas dispersion and discriminance provide fundamental measures of cohesion between the media elite and the political elite in their entirety, the analysis of intra-sectoral cohesion adds the question of cohesiveness of individual elite sub-sectors, factions and hierarchies relative to the overall cohesiveness of the entire sector. Intra-sectoral cohesion pertains to cohesion in relation to the *internal patterns of differentiation* within the two sectors. Dispersion and discriminance of attitudes still provide the basic measures of cohesion in this second step of the analysis. In the case of intra-sectoral cohesion, however, dispersion and discriminance are seen in relation to the internal differentiation between individual subgroupings of the two sectors. The question is, in other words, how and to what extent the internal divisions along horizontal and vertical lines of differentiation contribute to the internal cohesiveness of the media sector and the political sector.

Due to the fact that the degree and patterns of internal differentiation are assessed in relation to attitudinal consonance on the level of the entire sector, the analytical framework in assessing patterns of cohesion must be adapted accordingly. Where the patterns of inter-sectoral cohesion directly emerged from the two dimensions of indistinction and proximity associated with low levels of attitudinal discriminance and dispersion, respectively, levels of discriminance and dispersion are now interpreted in terms of *order*, meaning the extent to which each sector is composed of equally cohesive subgroups, and in terms of *consistency* between the stance of individual subgroups and the overall stance of the entire sector.

The notion of order is based on the systems theoretical observation that most modern social systems are more or less specialized, that is, internally divided in a number of subsystems and groups that perform different tasks in relation to the overall function of the system. Modern systems do not require equally strong ties between all members of the system but allow a significant number of individual subsystems and groups to form, which are more strongly connected than the system itself. In more formal terms, this can be expressed by the principle that the level of coupling between individual elements increases with the division of the system into smaller units – and vice versa. However, this dynamic is not detrimental to the system, but rather a basic principle of ordering the system in a manner that is in accordance with the overall stability and function of the system. Based on this line of argument, a sector becomes increasingly ordered in attitudinal terms, if the dispersion of attitudes steadily decreases with every subdivision in smaller units. Or, putting it differently: the media sector and the political sector can be called ordered if each individual subgroup is as congruent as or more congruent than the sector in its entirety.

Whereas the level of order within the media and the political sector tells us something about the relative balance between the cohesiveness of individual subgroups and the sector as such, irrespective of the substance of this cohesion, the level of consistency pertains to the reproduction of particular stances within the sector. In general, a system can be said to be functionally consistent if the overall function of the system is reproduced by individual subgroups within the system. In attitudinal terms, this implies that each sector can be called consistent if individual groups within the sector reproduce the overall stance of the sector. However, completely identical reproduction of particular stances is of course almost impossible to attain empirically. The basic criterion for consistency is therefore that none of the identified groups within the sector deviate substantially from the overall stance of the entire sector, that is, that the stances of individual subgroups and the entire sector are non-discriminant. Figure 3.3 outlines the four possible patterns of intra-sectoral cohesion, based on the level of order and consistency of attitudes in a given sector.

The figure displays the example of two levels (the first level L1 referring to the level of the entire sector, the second level L2 to the sub-sectoral level) and two subgroups on the second level. In reality, any sector can of course be subject to more than two levels of internal differentiation, as well as a larger number of different subgroups. Both the entire sector (black arrow) and the two subgroups (dark grey and light grey arrow) are again placed on a scale that ranges from complete disagreement (X) to complete agreement (Z) to any

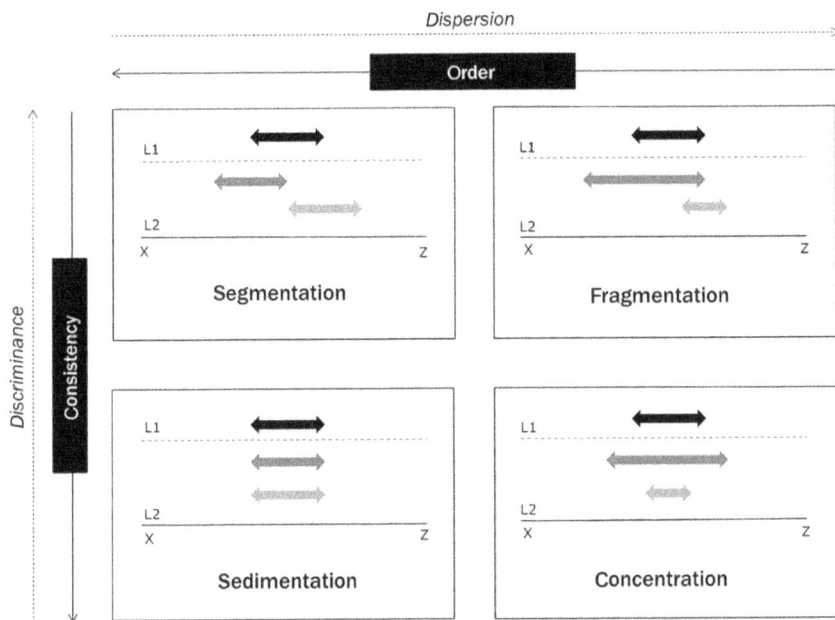

Figure 3.3. Patterns of Intra-Sectoral Cohesion
Stylized depiction for two levels and two subgroupings (dark grey and light grey) on level 2 (L2) – the length of each arrow indicates the degree of congruence within a given subgroup; the position of each arrow along the axis from *x* to *z* indicates the mean stance of each subgroup.

given attitudinal object. The position of each arrow along the axis from X to Z indicates the mean stance of each subgroup. The length of the arrow indicates the degree of congruence within each (sub)group. As outlined earlier, the level of order is inversely related to differences in dispersion between different sectoral groups, while the level of consistency in turn is inversely related to the degree of discriminance between sectoral and sub-sectoral stances.

- The pattern of *sedimentation* in the lower left corner occurs if attitudes between subgroups are ordered as well as consistent in relation to the overall stance of the entire sector. Thus, sedimentation refers to the consolidation of overall patterns within smaller subgroups. This means that the overall stance of the entire sector is the basis for equally or increasingly firm cohesion within the subgroups of the sector. For all subgroups, attitudinal congruence is not only as firm or firmer than overall sectoral congruence but also consistent with the overall stance of the sector.
- The outcome of *segmentation* in the upper left corner describes a pattern of cohesion that is also ordered, but inconsistent. This means that the individual subgroups are at least as congruent in their attitudes as the entire sector

taken together but that at least one of them clearly sets itself apart from the overall attitudinal stance of the sector.

• The outcome of *concentration* in the lower right corner depicts a scenario, in which individual subgroups replicate the sectoral attitudinal stance but differ substantially from the overall sector in the level of internal congruence. In contrast to the case of sedimentation, the consolidation of attitudinal stances does not occur even or symmetrical within the individual subgroups. Consequently, the individual subgroups of a concentrated sector centre around a common stance but do so with different levels of internal agreement in their respective subgroups.

• Finally, the outcome *fragmentation* in the upper right corner appears where sub-sectoral attitudinal patterns appear both disordered and inconsistent. A case of fragmentation essentially denotes a case of incomplete or unsystematic internal differentiation. Fragmentation is not a case of complete dissolution of a sector but rather indicates that the sector displays no identifiable pattern of internal cohesion. Although an overall pattern of differentiation is missing, individually cohesive subgroups may still appear in the shape of a cohesive outlier group.

As was the case for inter-sectoral cohesion, the empirical identification of these patterns of intra-sectoral cohesion requires that specific thresholds of discriminance versus non-discriminance and dispersion versus non-dispersion are specified. For the purposes of this study, both absolute and relative thresholds will be defined in chapter 6.

CONSEQUENCES OF ELITE COHESION

Before moving to the question of the contextual factors affecting the degree and shape of elite cohesion, a brief discussion of the consequences included in the theoretical framework is in place. As evidenced by the extensive body of literature discussed in chapter 2, elite cohesion is widely assumed to have effects on (1) political news making, (2) political message production and (3) the political decision-making process. These can in turn be linked to (4) the nature of public opinion and citizens' cognitive orientations. In normative terms, such effects are essential to the broader implications of elite cohesion discussed in chapter 1. In empirical terms, the analysis of such consequences links the study of elite cohesion with organizational studies of news making, the analysis of media content and finally with the entire research field of media effects studies.

The contribution of the developed framework in relation to such studies can be summarized in the propositions that (1) the extent and type of inter-elite cohesion, (2) the dominant guiding principles of cohesion, including the negotiated stance of the principle and (3) the extent and type of intra-sectoral cohesion all have effects not only on political decision making, message and news production but also on the public, for example, in terms of political knowledge, political interest or other political orientations. Although the empirical study conducted here is not designed to test such effects, it is worth spelling out in more detail how the proposed framework contributes to the broader debate on the effects of elite cohesion.

Correspondingly, the following sections introduce three general trajectories for a systematic assessment of effects empirically as well as normatively, based on the claim that attitudinal consonance of political communication elites has consequences for (1) *stability*, (2) *plurality* and (3) *civility* in political communication. The three categories do not constitute normative standards of assessment per se but rather potential empirical outcomes of attitudinal patterns and constellations before anything else. On the other hand, they also provide an entry point for normative reflections on the potentially pervasive effects on the political public sphere and democracy.

Stability

Attitudinal consonance can, first and foremost, be seen to affect the stability of communicative exchange in the public sphere and the production of political news and messages more specifically. Indeed, the assumed correlation between elite cohesion and stability is perhaps the most basic premise of the debate for and against elite cohesion. The idea that elite cohesion is positively related to stability leads to deep-seated conflicts over the acceptable trade-off with elite autonomy, that is, the extent to which stability is possible or acceptable without infringement of sectoral autonomy and the underlying division of power between different elite groups. Applied to the political communication elite, the case for elite cohesion will thus highlight the importance of stability in the communicative flows between politicians and media actors as a condition for a properly working public sphere and hence for democracy as such.

Sufficient informational input to the political public sphere requires ongoing and sufficient production of political news and messages, which in turn depend on stable interaction and exchange of information between politicians and media actors – and without elite cohesion, such stability will be endangered. On the other hand, the concern for elite autonomy warns against a one-sided emphasis on stability. This concern becomes all the more pronounced when the potential impact on political decisions is taken into account, that is, when stability reaches a point where decision-making elites simply co-produce political news and messages in order to cover the public flank and ensure the undisturbed adoption and implementation of collective decisions (Davis 2007).

The relation between attitudinal consonance and stability is deeply engrained in the interactional approach to elite cohesion in political communication as well as more systemic approaches (see chapter 2). Thus, Blumler and Gurevitch argue that the stability of political communication systems depends on the 'degree of correspondence between its constituent parts' (1995, 15), namely the orientations of media and political actors, as well as of the audience. If 'all the participants in the communication process share equivalent orientations and consequently speak on, or are tuned in to, similar wavelengths' (Blumler and Gurevitch 1995, 15), the level of communication conflict is low.

However, this approach also serves as a reminder of the critical role of the citizens as an active audience: the system does not only become more instable in case of a lack of consonance between the two groups of political communication elites but also if elite attitudes are merely consonant within and between elites while still failing to match those of the citizens and the general public. Consequences of such a mismatch of attitudes between elites and citizens are also discussed in terms of elite-mass-incongruence (see e.g. van Beek 2010). While contributions on this issue are many and diverse, they all highlight consequences of such incongruence for democratic and political stability: political alienation (Davis 2003), lack of diffuse political support, as well as disturbances in the input dimension of the political system (see Easton 1965).

The issue of stability applies most directly to the inter-sectoral level of analysis, where such consonance can be considered a critical factor for the smoothing of the exchange between the two sides, in particular, in form of cohesion as similarity or consensus. If consonance becomes too pronounced, however, it may also become detrimental to stability if it contributes to a widening gap between elites and the masses. Moreover, coherence in belief systems may also affect stability, in particular coherence on the underlying principles of cohesion. If stances and levels of cohesion contradict each other within specific guiding principles of interaction, the potential for ruptures in elite relations increases.

However, the stable and efficient production of messages and news can also be said to benefit from intra-sectoral cohesion. A certain level of intra-sectoral cohesion is necessary to ensure that individual subgroups within stay in tune with the overall goals and functions of each sector in relation to the public sphere. The pattern of intra-sectoral cohesion, moreover, indicates different degrees of differentiation and specialization within each sector. Here, fully consistent and sedimented sectors suggest a high degree of stability but also a potential loss of flexibility and division of labour, whereas segmentation allows for a more open balance between stability and flexibility in the production of messages and news. Disordered patterns of sector internal cohesion, such as concentration and fragmentation, in turn, indicate more volatile patterns of differentiation and thus a potential threat to sectoral and thus also overall stability in political communication.

Plurality

The issue of plurality is central to liberal variants of democratic theory linking diversity of viewpoints and availability of information with the ability of citizens to make an informed political choice and 'enlightened understanding' among citizens in a broader sense (Dahl 1989). Plurality, in this sense at least, means that all relevant viewpoints are publicly communicated and debated before any binding and authoritative decisions can be made. With respect to political news making, elite cohesion in political communication may affect the plurality and completeness of relevant information in ways that are often invoked as a common touchstone for the case against elite cohesion. Elite cohesion can thus be seen to restrict and limit the span of available news and messages by reinforcing mechanisms of 'indexing' and the privileged position of political sources in the stepwise flow of political communication (Bennett 1990; Entman 2003; see also chapter 2).

In other words, whereas elite cohesion is positively related to stability, it is generally seen to be inversely related to plurality and diversity in political communication. By extension, plurality often enters the equation as an extension of concerns about the trade-off between stability and sectoral autonomy, effectively pitting concerns for plurality in political communication against arguments in favour of stability. A lack of elite cohesion is, however, by no means a guarantee for presumably sound media coverage of political news, if it leads to an insufficient delivery of political information to the media. Moreover, a lack of inter-elite cohesion is also likely to impact on the plurality of (publicly heard) political messages, if it restricts the access of political elites to media coverage to a degree where politically legitimate voices are excluded.

The degree of plurality within the process of political decision making (i.e. the inclusion of all available viewpoints and relevant information) is also potentially affected by elite cohesion insofar as it involves the introduction of media elite actors into the preparation of political decisions. The main argument along these lines has been advanced by Aeron Davis (see also chapter 2): while earlier work by Davis points to the dangers of elite cohesion in marginalizing the role of citizens in the political process (2003), later work also alludes to the relevance of expertise brought into the decision making process by inner circle journalistic elites. In a more positive interpretation of

this phenomenon, media elites as expert sources of public opinion and sentiment can then contribute to the quality and responsiveness of the political
decision-making process (2009).

As with stability, the question of plurality invariably brings up the role
of citizens and mass attitudes. More specifically, the level of plurality can
be assumed to impact on formation of attitudes on political issues among
citizens. The *Receive-Accept-Sample (RAS) model* proposes that mass opinion, that is, individual citizens' take on political issues, is a response to elite
discourse presented in the media (Zaller 1992). Instead of regarding public/
mass opinion as an external factor (a view inherent to issues of elite-mass-
incongruence), the RAS model views the formation of citizens' political attitudes as largely elite driven. Elite cohesion on the norms and epistemologies
guiding political communication can thus be linked to mass attitude formation, and thus ultimately to the extent of political knowledge and political
involvement.

Plurality in political messages, decisions and viewpoints not only depends
on a level of inter-elite cohesion that is low enough to allow for a diverse and
open public debate but still assures that political communication elites cooperate in a way that guarantees that the diversity of political issues and opinions is made public. It is therefore particularly decisive which aspects and
principles of their relationship media and political elites are consonant on.
Arguably, the (conscious or unconscious) omission of information in news
reporting and political communication as a result of elite negotiations is most
directly linked to cohesion based on the principle of publicity, which entails
the question of how much information must and must not be made public,
and which sources and methods of investigation are regarded as legitimate.
Based on the principle of pragmatism, elite cohesion may however also be
associated with trends of 'infotainment' (see e.g. Jebril, Albæk and de Vreese
2013) and 'pop politics' (Ciaglia and Mazzoni 2014; Mazzoleni and Sfardini
2009) that both have been connected with a decrease in plurality in political
information.

The plurality of messages and news may be affected not only by the
absence or presence of inter-sectoral cohesion but also by patterns of intra-
sectoral cohesion. Intra-sectoral inconsistency is likely to result in different
communication styles, and thus in more multi-faceted, plural political messages and political news. While more ordered forms of sectoral inconsistency,
in particular in the form of a clear role specialization between different sectoral factions, contribute to plurality by establishing clear divisions of labour
among political communication elites, more disordered and fragmented attitudes will lead to plurality simply by preventing elites in both sectors from
relying all too much on established truths about which things should and can
be said and how.

Civility

The concept of civility in political communication has become an increasingly important topic of discussion regarding the tone of debate in the political public sphere. Particularly in the U.S. context, the question of incivility in politics has become an issue of substantial academic debate (Berry and Sobieraj 2014; Entman 2011; Herbst 2010; Mutz and Reeves 2005; York 2013). Although the political domain, particularly political campaigning and the use of smear techniques in the construction of political messages (Mutz and Reeves 2005), is often seen as the main driver behind increased incivility, the trend has also been associated with openly partisan news reporting (Entman 2011). Correspondingly, the ability of the mass media and their elites to either fuel or contain such incivility forms a crucial part of the debate on the assumed rise of incivility in political communication.

As Herbst points out, civility in a political context must be understood not only as a general behavioural norm but also as a strategic tool in elite interaction (2010, 7). A degree of incivility is thus an integral part of political life, debate and contestation. However, incivility may also develop to a degree where it becomes politically and socially destructive, hindering reasoned debate and decision making based on compromises between conflicting interests. Indeed, this is often assumed to be one of the more apparent effects of populist discourse on political debate and decisions. Reflecting this precarious nature of the balance between civility and incivility, the latter can and has been associated with various effects on citizens, ranging from political distrust and alienation at one end of the spectrum to higher degrees of political participation and interest at the other end (see also York 2013).

According to standard assumptions about elite belief systems, elite cohesion and civility are positively related. Building on the idea of a positive relation between elites and democratic stability, elite cohesion has conventionally been seen to strengthen and reinforce a form of common value base and fundamental commitment to political and democratic rules of the game that would certainly include those associated with proper public deliberation and civility in political communication. However, this is too simplistic with regard to the idea of elite cohesion as well as the status of civility itself. Hence, the idea of more or less direct correlation between elite cohesion and civility, modelled on the broader idea of elite consensus on democratic rules of the game, must be qualified by a more nuanced view on the relation between elite cohesion and civility, or perhaps more importantly the lack thereof.

For one, a strong acceptance of the principle of pragmatism can arguably contribute to incivility if it means that media and political elites agree that 'anything goes' and thus diverge from more idealistic conceptions about a

political communication elite working towards a common goal. Second, incivility as a pertinent element of political communication will arise only if there
are elites in both sectors who are willing to dispense with a civil and sober
tone in public debate, whatever their explicit motivation or cited necessity
to do so may be. Put differently, incivility in the political elite will result in
pervasive effects only if it spills over to news making and the public debate
and vice versa. The more patterns of cohesion challenge sectoral boundaries,
the more such a scenario becomes likely – even more so of course if the blurring or mixing of sectoral belief systems means that sectoral boundaries are
replaced by an ideological left-right split within the political communication
elite. Finally, incivility is likely to increase with the fragmentation of intra-
sectoral belief systems. Intra-sectoral cohesion as fragmentation means that
the sectoral belief system is in flux, indicating that the respective sectoral
elite is (at least for the time being) lacking a professional creed, one of the
strongest safeguards against incivility.

CONTEXTUAL CONDITIONS OF ELITE COHESION

Turning from the effects *of* to the effects *on* attitudinal consonance, the proposed framework emphasizes the importance of national structures, systems
and institutions. Although much elite theory has remained implicitly national
in its focus, the empirical study of elites has always been characterized by
a strong comparative tradition (Best 2008; Dogan 2003; Hartmann 2007a;
Ruostetsaari 2007; Sasaki 2008; van Beek 2010). Elite views or belief systems have traditionally been thought to vary due to a variety of structural
constraints that (for national elites) are rooted at the country level. Indeed,
the various institutional and cultural dimensions of the national context are
thought to supplement or even supersede individual childhood and professional socialization (Putnam 1976; Wasner 2004). In a broader sense, the
importance of national context and structural conditions for shared sets of
perceptions and attitudes has also been well established by political culture
research (Almond and Verba 1963) and consequently taken up comparatively
in political communication research (Blumler and Gurevitch 1995; Pfetsch
2001, 2014).

In his seminal study 'The Comparative Study of Political Elites', Robert
Putnam notes, upon the observation that Italian political elites show a markedly more ideological style in their belief system than British elites, that 'the
structure and style of elite belief systems vary cross-nationally' (Putnam
1976, 91). Although Putnam observes that factors such as childhood experiences, education, social origin and post-recruitment socialization can account

for differences in beliefs and views between the members of an elite group, national differences in historical courses of development, regime type and levels of economic development appear more dominant (see also Searing 1969). Putnam concludes: 'Members of an elite typically share many beliefs and values that distinguish them from their counterparts in other countries' (1976, 99).

Putnam's original observation that not only the 'style', that is, the values as such, but also the 'structure', that is, how the value base of different elite members within a country constellate to each other, vary cross-nationally is central also to this study. When being faced with remarkable differences between countries' elite belief systems, Putnam rather inductively looks for traces in political, economic and historical specifications. If one approaches this question more deductively, significant country characteristics can roughly be divided into two main factors. First, degrees of elite cohesion are a result of the *social structure* of a country, and resulting from it, its elite composition or configuration, which is determined by factors such as elites' social background, elite mobility and elite recruitment patterns (Hartmann 2007a, 17; see also Putnam 1976, 92). Second, elite cohesion among media and political elites is specifically shaped by the systemic conditions that make up the *political communication environment*, that is, characteristics pertaining to the *media system and political system* of a country (see also Putnam 1976, 122).

Although separate sets of structural conditions can be identified in each country, these are not independent from each other, neither theoretically nor empirically (see also Gulbrandsen 2012). Furthermore, contextual conditions (media system, political system and social structure) and attitudinal consonance are related through processes of mutual influence and co-evolution (Putnam 1976, 123). In a long-term perspective, elite cohesion may have repercussions on its contextual constraints through the consequences it has for the construction of political messages, political decision making and political public sphere.

The theoretical model outlined in figure 3.1 specifies basic ways in which context can impact on the consonance of attitudes: indirectly and directly. The key mechanism behind the *indirect* effect of contextual constraints, first, is the composition of elites in terms of their socio-demographic and professional background, as well as interactional ties. Thus, elite composition should be seen as a broad term that comprises factors like elite recruitment, elite communication and elite socialization, all of which translate social structure into elite attitudes (Parry 1969, 97). In the most general sense, social structure determines the circle of people that are eligible for elite positions, whereas the political and media system define the number and character of the particular elite positions within the political and media sector, respectively.

Second, characteristics of the media and political system impact *directly* on the consonance of attitudes by defining the immediate context of attitude formation. In other words, certain contextual conditions affect elite cohesion not only because they determine who occupies elite positions but also because they define the environment of the elites and hence the various reference points for attitude formation. Such reference points are also referred to as 'objects' of attitudinal consonance, including laws, regulations, institutions procedures and so on (Hunter, Danes and Cohen 1984). The indirect and direct mechanisms of influence on elite cohesion may finally vary over time and across national and cultural settings. The following sections discuss social structure, the media system and the political system as context in more detail and provide a set of general assumptions about the conditions shaping elite cohesion.

Assumptions about Social Structure: Vertical and Horizontal Mobility

The social structure of a country predominantly affects elite cohesion indirectly through elite composition. Pluralist and critical elite research have each dealt extensively with questions of elite recruitment (Hartmann 2007b; Keller 1963), elite socialization (Bourdieu 1996; Putnam 1976) and elite networks (Higley et al. 1991; Krüger 2011; Reese et al. 1994). While approaches and conclusions differ, these contributions all share the underlying assumption of a link between the structure of society and elite cohesion by subjecting people included in elite circles to similar elite socialization experiences (Searing 1969). More specifically, the various discussions converge around a general mechanism that may best be described as *social mobility*, a concept that includes both vertical and horizontal mobility (Sorokin 1927, 133).

Vertical mobility, turning to this issue first, refers to changing positions in the social hierarchy. Intergenerational vertical mobility is also referred to as social fluidity in the sense of the permeability of the social class structure (Breen, 2007). Social fluidity widens the elite composition in terms of its socio-demographic background, as it prevents persons from the same milieu, and in particular members of the highest strata of society, to one-sidedly occupy elite positions. The basic assumption established by the literature is that low levels of vertical mobility increase the potential for inter-sectoral cohesion.

In a fully class-based society, common childhood socialization and education among the members of the elite will soften up or even override sectoral boundaries and ease cross-sectoral elite communication (Gulbrandsen 2012). Correspondingly, inter-sectoral cohesion can be assumed to decrease the more a society departs from strict class divisions and social hierarchy. The more fluid, open and permeable a society is, the more attitudes are assumed to follow the societal position one moves *to* rather than one's social background (Parry 1969, 97; Turner 1992). Put simply, the primacy of functional orientation and decreasing importance of social background means that a leading politician remains a leading politician, whether he or she has been born a prince(ss) or a pauper.

At the same time as class-based homogeneity among elites decreases with vertical mobility, the more crucial it becomes for elites to negotiate acceptable forms of social conduct. Even though cohesion will generally decrease among elites in a fluid social structure, the principle of pragmatism versus idealism will therefore be particularly crucial to elite cohesion. The pattern of inter-elite cohesion produced by low vertical mobility can, in turn, be expected to be that of similarity: the common social background and orientation produced by rigid structures of stratification tends to make different sectoral elites alike but does not create alternative foundations for alignment that would fundamentally challenge sectoral boundaries. The main assumptions about the relation between vertical mobility/social fluidity and elite cohesion can thus be summarized as follows:

1.   Vertical mobility decreases the overall propensity for high inter-elite cohesion.
2.   A high degree of vertical mobility is furthermore expected to make pragmatism the dominant guiding principle of elite cohesion.
3.   Where inter-elite cohesion is present due to low vertical mobility, cohesion is expected to display a pattern of similarity.

Modern and functionally differentiated societies are generally assumed to display more vertical mobility and social fluidity than earlier societies based primarily on social stratification, although classes and hierarchy remain crucial (Bourdieu 1996). However, dynamics previously associated with a unified power elite in early modern and highly stratified societies may also be reintroduced in current society through elite mobility, that is, mobility between the top-echelons of different occupational sectors. Such elite mobility constitutes a particular case of horizontal mobility more broadly speaking, that is, changes between occupational sectors in the post-industrial economy, as opposed to the 'every man to his own trade' logic of industrial societies. Compared to horizontal mobility in general, elite mobility is also driven by particular factors such as the higher transferability of managerial skills vis-à-vis production-related skills and higher degrees of network capital facilitating changes between sectors.

Indeed, horizontal elite mobility is one of the most established factors consistently linked to the existence of a power elite in modern societies. As the concept of 'interlocked elites' suggests, horizontal elite mobility may account for substantial inter-sectoral cohesion of elites even in open and functionally differentiated societies (Dogan 2003). In settings where (political and media) elites commonly change between elites' position of opposite sectors, inter-elite cohesion is strengthened. Horizontally, mobile elites know and share attitudes and perceptions with their pendants in the other sector due to closer communicative ties, as well as cross-sectoral professional socialization. The type of cohesion emerging from high levels of horizontal mobility can, moreover, be assumed to gravitate towards consensus. The dynamics of horizontal elite mobility go beyond mere similarity, creating a potential for cross-sectoral bonds and more porous sectoral boundaries. Intra-sectoral cohesion is of secondary importance but can still be high, especially if it approximates consensus (see also Dogan 2003). The key assumptions about the effects of horizontal mobility on elite cohesion are as follows:

4.   Horizontal elite mobility increases the overall propensity for inter-elite cohesion.
5.   Where inter-elite cohesion is present due to horizontal mobility, cohesion is expected to display a pattern of consensus.

Assumptions about Autonomy in the Media System and the Political System

Turning to the context provided by the political system and the media system, the principal argument of the suggested model is that elite cohesion is subject to broad systemic features: the degree of *sectoral autonomy* and the degree of *sectoral variety*. The two terms are applied as analytical categories that capture how systemic factors can influence the separation and subdivision of sectoral elites in general and attitudinal consonance among and between media elites and political elites in particular. *Autonomy* from other sectors is a keystone of sectoral differentiation, thus countering inter-elite cohesion and strengthening intra-sectoral cohesion. In analytical terms, lack of autonomy can be the result of outside intervention, as well as co-orientation and mutual adaptation between sectors.

For political communication elites, autonomy is a key feature of the relationship between the political side and the media side of the table (e.g. media autonomy from state intervention), as well as the relation to third sectors and parties (e.g. the political sector's autonomy from patronage). Whereas general sectoral autonomy is a decisive element in the development of a sectoral creed and hence intra-sectoral cohesion, media autonomy from influence of the political sector and political autonomy from the media sector are likely to bring about less inter-elite cohesion between the two sides. The idea that

sectoral autonomy, as reflected in the various formal and quasi-formal institutions defining the media-politics relationship, will result in less inter-elite
cohesion is thus endemic to the very idea of distinct sectors.

The level of autonomy afforded in the politics-media relationship has
been shaped by specific institutions and traditions of state intervention and
broadcast governance that have a particular relationship to the principle of
publicity. Taking these traditions and institutions into account suggest that
inter-elite cohesion based on the principle of publicity can be expected to
be prominent in those cases, where sectoral autonomy is limited by a shared
commitment to the social and democratic function of political communication, also in otherwise-autonomous sectors of politics and media.

Where lack of sectoral autonomy results in inter-elite cohesion, we can
expect different patterns depending on whether infringement on autonomy
takes the form of *subjugation* or *collusion* (Etzioni-Halevy 1993, 113; see
also chapter 1). Subjugation implies that one sector is submitted to the overall
purpose and modus operandi of another sector due to the lack of control over
material, organizational or symbolic resources. A subjugated sector can thus
be said to become subject to outside intervention and thus be defined by an
outwards orientation and guidance in terms of purpose and a loss of individual purpose and resources. The result of such a scenario is similarity insofar
as subjugation by its very nature relies on the dominance of another sector
that does, however, remain a distinct sector. In contrast to subjugation, collusion involves the creation of common purpose, co-orientation and mutual
adjustment, making elites become increasingly indistinct and potentially
merge in groupings that overrule sectoral boundaries. Loss of autonomy as a
consequence of collusion thus primarily reduces the discriminance of sectoral
elites, leading to cohesion as mixing. The core assumptions about the effects
of sectoral autonomy can thus be summarized as follows:

6. High sectoral autonomy decreases the overall propensity for inter-elite
    cohesion.
7. A lack of sectoral autonomy based on models of social responsibility is
    furthermore expected to make publicity the dominant guiding principle
    of elite cohesion.
8. Where inter-elite cohesion is present due to low sectoral autonomy,
    cohesion is expected to display a pattern of similarity in the case of sub-
    jugation and mixing in the case of collusion.

Sectoral autonomy impacts not only inter-sectoral cohesion but also intra-
sectoral cohesion. In the most basic sense, intra-sectoral cohesion can be
expected to increase with sectoral autonomy. Sectoral autonomy involves not
only insulation from outside intervention and control but also development of

internal codes, regulations and standards, as exemplified by the notion of an independent *media logic* of an autonomous media system and the consolidation of a journalistic creed through professionalization. Such active development of internal logics, codes and regulations and professional standards not only increases intra-sectoral cohesion overall but also privileges procedures as a source of consonance. Where the creation of sectoral autonomy coincides with professionalization, in other words, procedural consonance is expected to be dominant.

With respect to the pattern of intra-sectoral cohesion, high sectoral autonomy can be expected to result in ordered attitudinal patterns, that is, sedimentation or segmentation, given that high level of autonomy insulates the sector from intervention or impulses from outside. As outside intervention is likely to affect subgroups differently, these different subgroups are also likely to differ in their level of internal congruence, leading to patterns of concentration or fragmentation in non-autonomous sectors. The key assumptions about the relationship between sectoral autonomy and intra-sectoral cohesion can thus be summarized as follows:

9. High sectoral autonomy increases the overall propensity for intra-sectoral cohesion.
10. A high degree of sectoral autonomy based on professionalization is furthermore expected to make procedures the dominant source of consonance.
11. Where intra-sectoral cohesion is present due to sectoral autonomy, cohesion is expected to display an ordered pattern, that is, sedimentation or segmentation.

Assumptions about Variety in the Media System and Political System

In addition to respective degrees of autonomy in the media system and the political system, elite cohesion is affected by the level of variety within each sector. In general, variety concerns the internal differentiation and specialization in media and politics, including *positional variety*, that is, the diversity of viewpoints, agendas and interests, as well as *institutional variety*, that is, the diversification between decision arenas and the plurality of different actors and stakeholders entering these arenas. Although the most immediate effects of positional and institutional variety in a given sector concern intra-sectoral cohesion, inter-elite cohesion is by no means unaffected, albeit mechanisms linking variety with inter-sectoral cohesion are somewhat more complex.

In general, one could assume that variety will lead to less intra-sectoral *and* inter-sectoral cohesion through overall dispersion of attitudes. However, sectoral variety may also increase inter-sectoral cohesion insofar as highly diverse sectors, in particular sectors with a high degree of positional variety make interaction and alliances across sectoral boundaries more likely. A prime example in this respect is when ideological proximity and alignment across sectors replace professional and sector-specific creeds due to political polarization. In this and related cases where positional variety approaches fragmentation, it becomes attractive or even vital for sectoral elites to seek relations outside their own sector, as finding alliances within their sector becomes increasingly difficult.

This mechanism is, however, most pronounced for positional vis-à-vis institutional variety. The link between positional variety and inter-elite cohesion is, moreover, dependent on the particular nature of positional variety in specific cases. An ideological outsider party in the political sector contributes to positional variety but may still lack ideological allies in the media elite. When positional variety does lead to inter-elite cohesion, however, it is likely to make ideology the key guiding principle due to the close connection with ideological polarization. This holds for both an affirmative and negative stance on ideology: elites from sectors with high positional and ideological variety can just as well compromise on leaving their ideological diversity out of their relationship.

In general, sectoral variety can be assumed to result in decreasing discriminance in the attitudinal patterns of both sectors. Inter-elite cohesion will be most pronounced when sectoral variety leads to cross-sectoral alliances that transcend professional and sectoral identities. The outlined importance of cross-sectoral alignment as a factor of inter-sectoral cohesion as a result of sectoral variety is in this sense clearly associated with cohesion through indistinction and thus suggests a pattern of cohesion as mixing. The core assumptions regarding the relation between variety and inter-sectoral cohesion can be summed up as follows:

12. Sectoral variety increases the overall propensity for inter-elite cohesion, particularly in the case of positional variety.
13. A high degree of sectoral variety is furthermore expected to make ideology the dominant guiding principle of elite cohesion, particularly in the case of positional variety.
14. Where inter-elite cohesion is present due to sectoral variety, cohesion is expected to display a pattern of mixing, that is, non-discriminant attitudes between sectors.

Within each sector, variety is naturally detrimental to intra-sectoral cohesion. Institutional as well as positional variety implies that a sector is split between additional groupings that make the maintenance of intra-sectoral cohesion

increasingly difficult. However, this inverse relation between variety and
intra-sectoral cohesion can be further qualified by looking at the various
sources of attitudinal consonance linked to institutional and positional variety. In sectors with low institutional variety, epistemological consonance
will be particularly pronounced. As the common sectoral surroundings are
structured in less complex terms, consonance on these common surroundings
will be easier to achieve as well. Cohesion based on value consonance will
in turn be particularly pronounced in sectors with low positional variety, as a
common sectoral take on the value and role fundament of each sector will be
easier to achieve with low levels of ideological diversity.

A lack of institutional and positional variety can, moreover, be expected
to result in consistent patterns of intra-sectoral cohesion. A consistent pattern
means that different subdivisions are not likely to display distinct attitudinal
patterns but may diverge in the level of congruence with which they adhere to
the overall sectoral position. The specific assumptions about the relationship
between sectoral variety and intra-sectoral cohesion can thus be summarized
as follows:

15. Sectoral variety decreases the overall propensity for intra-sectoral elite
    cohesion.
16. A low degree of institutional variety is expected to make epistemology
    the dominant source of consonance.
17. A low degree of positional variety is expected to make values the domi-
    nant source of consonance.
18. Where intra-sectoral cohesion is present due to low sectoral variety,
    cohesion is expected to display a pattern of consistency, that is, sedimen-
    tation and concentration.

SUMMARY: ELITE COHESION AS
ATTITUDINAL CONSONANCE

The chapter has, first, set out to develop a model of elite cohesion in political communication that can serve as a meaningful framework to empirically assess different level and forms of cohesion. Going beyond simplified
accounts of a presence or absence of cohesion, the model argues that elite
cohesion must be understood empirically as consonance in attitudes, which
allows for the specification of different sources, guiding principles, levels and
patterns of cohesion.

From this understanding of elite cohesion as attitudinal consonance follows
that any debate about the consequences of elite cohesion must go beyond
a crude, binary and normatively motivated opposition between sectoral

autonomy and societal stability. Rather, elite cohesion can be associated with a number of different consequences for stability, plurality and civility in political communication and the public political debate, depending on which sources, principles and patterns of cohesion are at work in a given setting.

Second, the chapter has dedicated a good deal of attention to the question of how these different nuances of elite cohesion are affected by the systemic context in which elites are embedded, summarized in an integrated model comprising the relevant attributes of the media system, political system and social structure. Based on this model, a series of assumptions have linked the level of vertical and horizontal social mobility, as well as the level of autonomy and variety in the media system and political system, to the extent and patterns of cohesion on the inter-sectoral and intra-sectoral level, as well as with dominant sources and guiding principles of cohesion.

These assumptions are general in the sense that they are not based on the actual conditions and experiences found in specific countries, but on theoretical reasoning. While this makes the model and its base assumptions applicable and transferable to a wide range of different types of countries and political communication regimes, it also means that the model works at a relatively high level of abstraction. The next chapter is therefore dedicated to applying the model to the specific case of European democracies.

Chapter 4

Political Communication Elites in the European Context

For the remainder of the book, the general model developed in the preceding chapter is applied to six specific cases: Sweden, Denmark, Germany, Austria, France and Spain. These have been selected based on their variation in the systemic conditions of elite cohesion identified in the model (see also chapter 1). In order to elaborate on this variation in more detail, the first part of this chapter is dedicated to a systematic mapping of the particular attributes of the countries included in the empirical analysis. Drawing on primary and secondary literature sources, and in some cases newly calculated measures, the vertical and horizontal mobility of social structure as well as the level of autonomy and variety in the media system and the political system of the six countries are systematically evaluated and scored.

In the empirical analysis, the data on the systematic context is combined with data on the attitudes of political communication elites based on a standardized quantitative survey. Correspondingly, the second part of the chapter explains the identification of political communication elites in each country and the composition of the final sample of the conducted study in greater detail. Moreover, the method and process of collecting survey data are briefly discussed. Taken together, the information on the systemic context and collection of survey data in the six countries prepare the ground for the comparative analysis of elite cohesion in the six countries in the ensuing chapters.

CONDITIONS FOR ELITE COHESION IN THE EUROPEAN CONTEXT

The model developed in chapter 3 and its underlying mechanisms are highly general and can be applied to various societies, political regimes or regions.

Narrowing down the focus to the six countries included in the study, the following sections discuss the attributes of these European democracies in relation to the overall model. The broader context conditions (degree of vertical and horizontal mobility in society, as well as the degree of autonomy and variety of the media and political sector) are broken down to specific context factors relevant in a European context, which are then systematically discussed for each of the countries under study.

Social Structure: Vertical and Horizontal Mobility

Social mobility is one key condition for the extent and patterns of elite cohesion in modern democracies, in terms of both vertical and horizontal mobility. While vertical mobility refers to the level of in particular upward mobility in society as a whole, horizontal mobility becomes in this context particularly relevant at the elite level. Vertical and horizontal mobility can be operationalized and measured in a variety of ways. However, not all measures are fit for comparative research, nor are they equally central to the question of cohesion among European political communication elites. For the purposes of the analysis conducted here, vertical mobility, also referred to as social fluidity, is best understood in terms of the permeability of the social class structure (Breen, 2007).[1] Such permeability can be equated with equal opportunities to reach elite positions independent of one's social origin, in opposition to a self-preserving cemented upper class (Hartmann 2007a; OECD 2012). Horizontal mobility, in turn, refers to elites shifting position between the media sector and the political sector, as well as other forms of horizontal elite ties between the two sectors.

In practical terms, assessing vertical mobility via the permeability of a society's class structure requires specific criteria based on which a person's *social background* can be assessed. Some of the more frequently used measures include material background (family wealth and income), educational background (parents' level of schooling), class origin (parents' occupation) or other measures of social status (titles, awards, inclusion in who-is-who lists, etc.).

By comparing the socio-demographic background of individual elites with the overall composition of society, it can be discerned whether people from the same milieu, and in particular members of the highest strata of society, hold an exclusive or disproportionate grasp on elite positions such as membership and leadership of government cabinets (Hartmann 2007a). Furthermore, different societal sectors can be compared based on the heterogeneity of their elites in terms of social origin. The more uniform the social background of elites across sectors is the more likely inter-elite cohesion becomes. This is particularly true if such uniformity refers to a small segment of the general population, that is, the upper and upper-middle strata of society.

A key factor playing into the relationship between social origin and elite status is *education* (Ishida, Müller and Ridge 1995). It has been argued that social background primarily affects individuals' opportunity to reach an elite position by determining their likelihood to obtain higher education, which in turn is seen as the sine qua non for the ability to reach an elite position in modern democracies (Hoffmann-Lange 1992; Putnam 1976; Schnapp 1997).

One of the more consistent ways to determine vertical mobility in terms of equality of opportunity in education is the calculation of *odds-ratios* for the likelihood for people from different social backgrounds to achieve similar levels of schooling (Breen 2010; OECD 2012). When comparing the proportion of students from a certain (low, medium or high) educational background who attend higher education to the proportion of parents with this level of education in the total parent population, equal opportunity is reached if the odds ratio of being a student in higher education is close to 1. In this case, people born into families with a low (less than upper secondary) educational background are as likely to attend higher education as those from more educated families. From an elite perspective, it is particularly interesting to focus on the odds ratios for students with parents with higher (i.e. tertiary) levels of education to attend higher education as well. The higher the odds for people with highly educated parents to attend higher education, the lower social fluidity and thus the better the conditions for inter-sectoral elite cohesion.

While access to education for all social strata is conventionally associated with social permeability, elite schools and universities may nevertheless serve as an extra layer of elite recruitment even as a larger part of the population obtains higher levels of education (Hartmann 2007a). Such elite educational institutions are defined by a clear focus on educating high-level generalists capable of serving in different sectors. The defining trademark of elite institutions of education, both on the school and university level, is that the focus of professional specialization is less rigid or follows relatively late in the course of education. Thus, they are about raising elites more than about raising professionals. Educational systems displaying this kind of elite orientation through the creation of designated elite schools and universities will tend to produce elites with a higher level of horizontal elite ties, and thus have a higher propensity of inter-elite cohesion.

Horizontal ties formed through training in elite schools and universities are, however, but one component in the larger issue of *horizontal mobility*. In its most direct manifestation, horizontal mobility is expressed in the professional cross-sectoral mobility of elites, that is, that elites switch from an elite or sub-elite position in one sector to an elite position in another sector once or more at a stage in their professional career. In general, horizontal mobility can be seen as the expression of the high level of career mobility and flexibility in current knowledge societies, as well as of a detached power elite whose members are pre-selected at a very early age. Either way, horizontal mobility will have consequences for the extent of inter-sectoral elite cohesion.

Professional mobility is best documented for the inter-linkages between the political, administrative and economic sector but has been increasingly discussed for political and media sector elites as well (see e.g. Fabris 1995; Plasser and Lengauer 2010). More broadly defined, professional mobility can also refer to cross-sectoral professional experience in another sector at an early career stage, that is, before having reached an elite or sub-elite position. This form of early career mobility is particularly relevant for the sub-elites in the field of political communication, who have traditionally gone through some level of journalistic training in many European countries (Sanders and Canel 2013). Moreover, horizontal mobility can be interpreted as a more general form of cross-sectoral movement and interchangeable positions not through career change but professional involvement in another sector through advisory positions, board memberships, membership in elite clubs and circles and so on.

Autonomy and Variety in the Media System

As is the case with the social structure and mobility, the emphasis on the autonomy and variety of the media system discussed in the preceding chapter is open to different measures and ways of operationalization. However, comparative media studies provide us with a relatively well-established set of factors that determine the autonomy and variety of the media system (e.g. Eberwein et al. 2011; Hallin and Mancini 2004; Humphreys 1996, 2014). Building on these sources, the autonomy of the media system can be associated with, respectively, the degree of journalistic professionalization and self-regulation, direct state intervention and political parallelism. Political parallelism furthermore pertains to the positional variety of the media system, whereas the institutional variety is linked with the development of a horizontal mass circulation press vis-à-vis a horizontal and elite oriented press.

A key component in the autonomy of European media sectors has been the development of journalism as a distinct profession. While *journalistic professionalization* is a broad trend ranging from the creation of journalism schools to the development and diffusion of journalistic culture and work routines, one of the more formal and clear-cut measures is whether national media systems are equipped with 'mechanisms of journalistic self-regulation' (Hallin and Mancini 2004, 37). Such mechanisms of self-regulation involve a more or less formal codification of journalistic standards and guidelines monitored by an appointed body and subjected to a variety of more or less strict sanctions (Eberwein et al. 2011). Journalistic professionalization, viewed in this way as structural context of elite cohesion, can thus be equated with the development, codification and supervision of common professional standards.

Even when mechanisms of journalistic self-regulation are present, however, the autonomy of the media system may be subject to *state intervention* through, inter alia, the establishment of public service broadcasting, state ownership of media outlets and news agencies (direct and indirect), press subsidies, as well as media regulation and media policy (European Journalism Centre 2014; Hallin and Mancini 2004, 41–44). We can distinguish broadly between state influence on the media in a *statist* sense (roughly equating the notion of *étatisme*), which means that the media are regarded as an integral part of government communication and thus subsumed under the overall demands of the state apparatus, and in a *public service* sense, in which the purpose of state intervention is to maintain the media as a key social and democratic institution. In this respect, state intervention has particular relevance for the guiding principle of publicity vis-à-vis secrecy. Where state intervention is based on a pure public service rationale for state intervention, acceptance of publicity is likely a crucial element for cohesion in political communication. More statist forms of intervention, by contrast, bind the media to political demands on secrecy and respect for national interests.

Excessive infringement of media autonomy through state intervention constitutes a rather clear-cut case of subjugation, in particular when combined with absence of journalistic professionalization and mechanisms of self-regulation. Even media systems with relatively strong safeguards against complete subjugation, which is generally the case in Europe, may however be subject to collusion in the form of *political parallelism*. Even if rigid press-party parallelism, as originally observed by Seymour-Ure (1974) based on the historical experience of the party press, is largely irrelevant in modern-day Western media systems, political parallelism in a broader sense continues to be highly relevant (Esmark 2014). Indeed, it still holds true that 'one of the most obvious differences among media systems lies in the fact that media in some countries have distinct political orientations while media in other countries do not' (Hallin and Mancini 2004, 27).

Political parallelism expresses itself in a number of ways, ranging from media content to political activities and career paths among journalists (Hallin and Mancini 2004, 28ff). However, two aspects of political parallelism are of particular relevance when focusing on the media system as context for the attitudinal consonance of political communication elites: the partisanship of media audiences, in particular in the case of print media, as well as the model of broadcast governance and regulation. Audience partisanship links media usage with party preferences and thus approximates the original concept of press-party parallelism, but crucially without measuring the alignment of parties and media directly (van Kempen 2007). As such, audience partisanship provides a viable measure of party-political parallelism in the media system as an external condition for elite cohesion.

A broader and more formal measure of parallelism in the media-politics relationship is found in the models of broadcast governance (Hallin and Mancini 2004; Humphreys 1996; Kelly 1983). The highest degree of parallelism is found in so-called politics-over-broadcasting governance where public broadcasting is directly controlled by the government or the political majority. This 'government model' can be seen to approximate statist subjugation, but nevertheless falls within the realm of collusion and parallelism insofar as parliamentary politics and competition serve as the basis for political control. The traditional counterpoint to politics-over-broadcast governance is the 'professional model', a formally autonomous media system substituting political control for professional control, archetypically represented by the BBC. Between the two ends of the spectrum we, find two models of 'politics-in-governance' that are based on political representation, either purely parliamentary representation or the wider inclusion of socially relevant groups such as churches, trade unions and professional associations. Summing up the four models of broadcast governance: 'In terms of political parallelism, the professional model is clearly toward the low end of the spectrum, the government model toward the high end, and the two other models – the politics-in-broadcasting systems – are in between' (Hallin and Mancini 2004, 32).

Logically and historically, the presence or absence of political parallelism is furthermore bound up with media pluralism and hence with the positional variety of the media system in general. The type of political orientation and audience partisanship found in older and newer forms of press-party parallelism tend to increase positional variety by increasing the overall degree of external pluralism in the media system.

In terms of institutional variety, the *structure of the media market,* in particular the press market, is a crucial factor in the media sector. Indeed, the development of a mass circulation press organizing the vertical flows of debate in the public sphere is one of the principal mechanisms of institutional variety and a key difference between media systems (Hallin and Mancini 2004, 22). Three aspects of press structure are particularly relevant for the question of elite cohesion: Circulation (i.e. the size of the [print] media market), concentration [of ownership] and centralization [i.e. whether media outlets are predominantly located in the capital], see Humphreys 2012). The lowest level of institutional variety is thus to be found in small, centralized and concentrated media markets.

The structure of the press market is not only informative in terms of institutional variety but raises another aspect highly relevant to the question of elite cohesion, as it provides a measure of the elite orientation of news organizations. While broadcasting – at least in industrial societies – is almost by definition a medium for the masses, newspaper circulation rates vary substantially across Western democracies. Where print circulation is low, print media are mostly a means of communication for the elite, and thus facilitate communication within or between elites rather than communication between elites and the masses, also referred to as a 'horizontal' process of debate and negotiation among elite factions (Hallin and Mancini 2004, 22). Consequently, print journalists are likely to become drawn closer to these elite circles. By contrast, high circulation rates turn media into profitable commercial enterprises, thereby making them more autonomous from the political sphere.

Autonomy and Variety in the Political System

In addition to the dimensions of the media system, a number of political system characteristics are particularly crucial to the relationship between media and politics (Hallin and Mancini 2004, 46). Although drawing on a number of key reference points from comparative politics, studies in political communication have traditionally focused on those aspects of the political system found to be of particular relevance for the evolution of media systems and political communication. The study conducted here adopts a similar approach insofar as it does not lay claim to a comprehensive survey of all dimensions of the political system but seeks rather to highlight factors of particular relevance to elite cohesion in political communication. These include the institutionalization of rational-legal authority vis-à-vis patronage and the broader structures of interest mediation in the case of political autonomy. As for variety, the key factors highlighted are polarization and concentration of power. Additionally, the professionalization of political communication is discussed.

Whereas the autonomy of the media system has developed from an initial condition of subjugation to political or other forms of control, the autonomy of the political system is rather a question of how the political system limits itself from the rest of society. Thus understood, the autonomy of the modern political system is intrinsically related to the development of *rational-legal authority*, expressed by 'a form of rule based on adherence to formalistic and universalistic rules of procedure' (Weber in Hallin and Mancini 2004, 55). In institutional terms, rational-legal authority can be equated with the creation of modern bureaucracies, that is, an administrative apparatus separated from political factions and other social interests, in order to serve the common good, maintains the rule of law and provide a factual basis for political decision making. In this sense, rational-legal autonomy is parallel to the role of journalistic professionalization in the media system insofar as it represents a professional creed emphasizing the notion of an autonomous institution committed to the common good (Hallin and Mancini 2004, 57; see also Max Weber's [1948] idea of 'politics as vocation').

The most clear-cut counterpart to political autonomy based on rational-legal authority and bureaucratic institutions is clientelism and patronage, that is, a system in which decision makers act as patrons providing services or favours to particular clients in exchange for support and loyalty. Influence of factional interests is of course endemic to party politics and democracy, but bureaucracy and rational-legal authority represent a limit to such influence meant to ensure the autonomy and stability of the political system. In this respect, clientelism implies a degree of factional influence where personal relations and connections involve subjugation of rational-legal authority, the public interest and bureaucratic neutrality to particular interests. Especially in systems with strong political parties, clientelism also appears in the form of party patronage, that is, scenarios where clients more or less directly draw on their party connection with officials in receiving public goods and services (Müller 2006). Lack of political autonomy and weak institutionalization of rational-legal authority can, on the one hand, be seen as an additional factor behind the subjugation of the media to political control. On the other hand, clientelism can also lead to subjugation in the reverse direction, that is, subjugation of political communication and decisions to media concerns and ownership: 'Private business owners will typically have political connections . . . and will often use their media properties as a vehicle for negotiation with other elites and for intervention in the political world' (Hallin and Mancini 2004, 58).

Political systems with a strong institutionalization of rational-legal authority can, however, still be subject to collusion. The archetypical expression of such collusion is *corporatist interest mediation*. Drawing on Lijphart's distinction between 'a competitive and uncoordinated pluralism of interest groups, in contrast with the coordinated and compromise-oriented system of corporatism', pluralism and corporatism can be seen as two basic principles for organization of the state-society nexus and the inclusion of socio-economic interests in the political process (Hallin and Mancini 2004, 53). The corporatist system reduces the autonomy of the political system considerably because it is based on the organization of social interests into pillars lead by peak organizations, which are then recognized by political institutions and incorporated routinely and pervasively into the political process through hearings, consultations, committees and so on. The pluralist system, by contrast, maintains a higher degree of autonomy for the political system due to its focus on competition between multiple factions and interests, neither of which are recognized as peak organizations nor incorporated into political decision making as such (Almond 1983; Schmitter and Lehmbruch 1979). When assessing the extent to which state-society relations are organized along corporatist lines in specific countries, it is, however, important to recognize the considerable scope for variation in the organization and incorporation of interest. As evidenced by the extensive literature on the matter, there are various modifications of the pure forms of pluralism and corporatism, including neo-pluralism, neo-corporatism, democratic corporatism and network governance (Molina and Rhodes 2002).

Whereas the degree of rational-legal authority and development of corporatist vis-a-vis pluralist systems of interest mediation represent conclusions to long and deep-seated historical trends, both dimensions of the political systems have been affected substantially in recent decades by the introduction of public sector reforms and managerial paradigms associated with so-called New Public Management (NPM) and New Public Governance (NPG) assumed to have had considerable, albeit differential, impact across the globe since the 1980s (Green-Pedersen 2002; Hood 1991; Pollitt and Bouckaert 2011). Both paradigms have a strong anti-bureaucratic stance and may thus serve to decrease the influence of rational-legal authority, even in political systems with an otherwise-strong tradition in this respect (Esmark 2017). Both paradigms also counteract corporatism, albeit for completely different reasons: whereas NPM involves centralization and strategic exclusion of interests, NPG aims to develop more flexible and variable inclusion through networks (Pollitt and Bouckaert 2011). Additionally, such reforms may increase diversity through a multiplication of career entry points and a performance-based reward system in contrast to the conventional seniority-based systems of political and bureaucratic recruitment (Haensch and Holtmann 2008; Schnapp 2004).

Political systems are characterized by varying degrees of *polarization* of the party spectrum. As such, party-political polarization in the sense of a diversity of viewpoints expressed by political parties constitutes the most fundamental aspect of positional variety in the political system. Broadly speaking, polarization of the party system is defined and measured in two ways: the variation in ideological distance between political parties (as expressed in their party manifestoes) and the electoral support for political parties on the extreme left and right. The former refers to substantial ideological polarization, whereas the latter can be designated as structural polarization (Lane and Ersson 1999). Consequently, party-political polarization and political parallelism of the media often go hand in hand since media elites tend to become 'participants in struggles among diverse ideological camps' (Hallin and Mancini 2004, 131). However, polarization does not translate directly to parallelism: even if ideological separation is a minimal condition for political parallelism, a polarized party landscape without media alignment cannot be ruled out a priori, for example, if an extreme outsider party is shunned by the media.

Whereas polarization indicates positional variety, institutional variety is determined by the *concentration of decision making*. In general, concentration of political decision making can be seen to reduce the institutional variety of the political sector, thus providing fertile conditions for intra-sectoral cohesion and reducing the probability of inter-sectoral cohesion. Drawing on Lijphart's seminal work on the executive-party dimension of political systems (1999) and Vatter's later addition of an executive-legislative power relationship (2009), the concentration of decision making constitutes one of the most established and widely used measures in comparative politics, including indicators such as the effective number of parties, the frequency of single-party governments, the average duration of ruling cabinets, the degree of electoral proportionality and the incorporation of interest groups. Such horizontal concentration is conventionally contrasted with vertical concentration or centralization, corresponding to Lijphart's federal-unitary dimension, including the constitutional design of the polity, procedures for constitutional amendment and bicameralism (1999).

Concentration of decision making determines the size and composition of the national political elite and thereby indirectly the degree and form of elite cohesion. For political communication elites at the national level, horizontal concentration is most decisive. The more de-concentrated the political system is along horizontal lines, the more variety in terms of party plurality, government composition and change of government. The overall level of diversity in the political system determined by the vertical level of concentration can also be assumed to play a role even if the focus of study is national elites. The vertical level of concentration refers, first, to the distinction between federal and unitary systems, according to which the former can be seen as more diverse or plural than the latter. However, the level of decentralization must be incorporated in specific assessment of variety on the vertical dimension (Vatter 2014). Decentralization can be very extensive within unitary systems and more or less absent in federal systems, meaning that the general relation between federalism and variety is modified or lacking altogether.

The previous sections highlight some of the more established factors of autonomy and variety in European democracies as developed in the field of comparative politics. However, another factor with particular importance for political communication must be taken into account: the professionalization of communication activities in the political sector. In general, professionalization includes political attempts to develop competencies, procedures and structures designed specifically for more efficient communication of political messages, including changes in organizational structures and procedures, use of specific techniques and instruments, as well as development of new roles, specialisms and skills (Donges 2008; Negrine 2008; Negrine et al. 2007, 35; Sanders, Canel Crespo and Holtz-Bacha 2011).

Although such professionalization is not an established focus point in comparative politics to the same degree as institutionalization of rational-legal authority, structures of interest mediation, polarization and concentration, it nevertheless has important implications for the autonomy as well as the variety of the political system. For one, the orientation towards media requirements and demands intrinsic to the professionalization of political communication implies that the sectoral autonomy of the political system decreases with the level of professionalization. The sectoral variety of the political system, on the other hand, rises with the professionalization due to the increasing specialization and emergence of distinct political communication roles, tools and procedures.

Professionalization of political communication is still an emerging field of research that has yet to yield universally agreed-upon measures or firm classifications of individual countries. On the regional level, there is some agreement that professionalization in Continental European (party-centred) democracies differs from the mode of professionalized campaigning and political PR in the U.S.-American context (Plasser and Plasser 2002, 78–86) Moreover, the form and degree of professionalization varies substantially between routine and electoral campaigns, between government and party-political communication, between different points in time and not least between individual governments, political leaders and political parties (Gibson and Römmele 2001; Strömbäck 2009). As such, differences within countries often seem to be more substantial than across countries, not least within the group of Western European countries.

In the party-political sphere, the quantitative and qualitative change in organizational structures and practices associated with professional(ized) communication has most consistently been linked to the creation and use of communication expertise, both in-house and from the outside (Plasser and Plasser 2002; Scammell 1998). In the sphere of government communication, Sanders and Canel (2013) distinguish between a strategic and a tactical dimension of professionalization. A strategic communication structure is defined by a clear link to the organization's long-term goals and includes 'defined functions that facilitate an organized and integrated communication activity undertaken by skilled and knowledgeable professionals who occupy positions at every level of the organizational chart' (2013, 279). Tactical communication structures are in contrast more disperse and fragmented, with little internal coordination and overarching activities.

A CLOSER LOOK AT THE CONTEXT OF ELITE COHESION: THE SIX COUNTRIES

Taken together, the various factors related to the social structure, the media system and the political system make it possible to provide a systematic assessment of the contextual conditions for elite cohesion in different countries. The second half of chapter takes on this task for the six countries included in this study. This is done in the following steps. First, a summary overview is provided, based on the most established sources comparing the six countries under study on the relevant factors (see table 4.1). Second, a more qualitative profile of the individual countries is included in order to deepen and elaborate the information provided in the summary overview, proceeding from the northernmost country Sweden to the southernmost country Spain. Based on this information, the individual countries are then scored based on their level of social mobility, sectoral autonomy and variety.

Sweden

Sweden is a comparatively egalitarian country with high social fluidity in terms of a permeable class structure. However, societal elites are still disproportionately composed of members of the nobility and upper classes. The combination of the monarchical tradition with the parliamentary dominance of social democracy throughout the better part of Swedish history has been said to result in a binary elite structure of a 'bourgeois' elite on the one hand and an elite centred around the working-class movement and the social democratic party on the other (SOU 1990). Members of the Swedish media elite are drawn disproportionally from the bourgeois fraction compared to the general population as well as other sectoral elite groups, in particular political elites (SOU 1990, 317, 329).[2] Although inter-sectoral mobility in Sweden has not been the subject of extensive research, Sweden has an outspoken elite consensus on 'the belief that society can be changed – or problems managed – through a centralized and rational reform and planning process' (Ruostetsaari 2007, 173), archetypically expressed in the Swedish tradition of cross-sectoral government commissions. Although this model of social steering may be somewhat in decline, Swedish elites, so the argument goes, share a 'significant homogeneity with respect to the way of thinking' (2007, 172) despite wide differences in opinions and ideological positions.

Sweden has a long tradition of journalistic self-regulation and safeguards ensuring media accountability are in place. State intervention to support the media as a social institution is strong and includes a government body issuing direct subsidies to the press. In all state interventions, the notion of public service takes clear precedence over the statist approach to intervention. Public broadcasting is traditionally strong, although not as dominant as in Denmark. Although formally also characterized by civic elements of broadcasting ownership and regulation, the Swedish broadcasting system has a high degree of political autonomy similar to the BBC's professional model. An *arm's-length-principle* keeps political intrusion in operational decision to

Table 4.1. Systemic Characteristics by Country

	Sweden	Denmark	Germany	Austria	France	Spain
Vertical Mobility						
Social and elite structure — Social recruitment of government cabinets 2006 (% upper and upper-middle class)[a]	N/A	47	63	36	85	71
Social recruitment of government leaders since 1945 (% upper and upper-middle class)[a]	33	15	31	13	80	60 (since 1976)
Social background of media elites[b]	Comparatively high	Diverse	Mostly middle class	Comparatively low	Mostly upper class	Mostly middle class
Odds ratio to obtain higher education for persons with highly educated parents (% of parents with high education in total)[c]	1.43 (33%)	1.26 (49%)	1.69 (31%)	2.04 (18%)	1.99 (21%)	2.26 (15%)
Horizontal Mobility and Elite Ties						
Elite orientation in educational system	No	No	No	No	Yes	No
Relevance of elites' professional mobility and communicative elite tiesa,[c]	Rather low	Low	Traditionally low, but increasing	Relatively high	Generally high	Less relevant for media and political elites

(Continued)

Table 4.1. (Continued)

Media system	Sweden	Denmark	Germany	Austria	France	Spain
		Autonomy: Journalistic Professionalization				
Journalistic self-regulation (Code of Conduct and Press Councils)[d]	In place, extensive	In place, established by law	In place	In place, but weak and suspended	Only of limited reach	None at the national level
		Autonomy: State Intervention				
Per capita public funding of public broadcasting in EUR thousand/% of total revenues, 2006[e]	45 (91%)	78 (92%)	82 (86%)	56 (50%)	23 (60%)	13 (44%)[c]
State intervention: Press subsidies[f]	Direct	Indirect; low-interest loans	Indirect only	Direct	Direct	Government advertising only
World Press Freedom Index, 2014 (0–100)[g]	8.98	7.43	10.23	10.01	21.89	20.63
		Autonomy and Variety: Political Parallelism				
Broadcasting regulation models[h]	Formally autonomous (arms-length)	Politics-in-broadcasting			Politics-over-broadcasting	
Media-party parallelism index, based on audience patterns, 1999 Total (print/TV)[j]	6.8 (6.0/0.6)	9.1 (8.3/0.6)	1.0 (0.7/0.2)	5.3 (4.4/1.0)	7.5 (5.4/3.2)	10.5 (8.0/3.5)
		Variety: Structure of the Press Market				
Circulation of paid-for and free dailies per 1000 adults 2012[l]	365	271	253	418	177	79

Media system						
Newspaper reach in % of the population, 2012[i]	76	64	67	73	50	36
Number of titles, paid-for and free dailies, per 1000 adults (total number), 2012[j]	11 (89)	7 (32)	5 (350)	2.5 (18)	2 (120)	3 (125)
Concentration: Market share of four largest publishing houses (CR4), based on circulation of paid-for and free dailies 2012[k]	66%	43%	42%	77%	45%	66%
Political System						
Parties in government (2008)[l]	Coalition Centre-right	Minority coalition Centre-right	Grand coalition	Grand coalition	Coalition Centre-right	Single Party Minority (Leftist)
Autonomy: Rational-Legal Authority						
Corruption Perception Index 2008 (0 highly corrupt to 10 highly clean)[m]	9.3	9.3	7.9	8.1	6.9	6.5
Party patronage[n]	None	None	Medium	High	Medium	Medium
Openness of civil service recruitment (0 = open to 6 = closed)[o]	0.0	1.3	4.7	4.9	5.6	4.7
Politicization of civil service leadership[p]	Partly	None	Fully	Partly	Fully	Fully
Autonomy: Corporatism						
Siaroff's (1999) corporatism scale (0–8)[q]	4.625	4.250	4.625	4.125	2.250	2.000

(Continued)

Table 4.1. (Continued)

	Sweden	Denmark	Germany	Austria	France	Spain
Variety: Polarization						
Electoral support for left- and right-wing parties in % (1990–1997)[r]	9.3	17.5	6.0	21.1	25.5	10.1
Left-right index, based on party manifestoes (−100 to +100) total range | mean deviance from 0[s]	50.5|13.7	52.0|17.5	57.7|17.5	17.1|9.2	76.5|23.9	24.4|9.8
Variety: Concentration of Decision Making						
Political centralization[t]	Unitary-decentralized	Unitary-decentralized	Federal-decentralized	Federal-centralized	Unitary-centralized	Semi-federal
Horizontal power concentration (z-scores; lower values indicate high concentration)[u]	1.04	0.77	0.69	0.67	−1.21	0.06
Effective number of parties (Laakso–Taagepera index)[v]	4.18	4.58	3.35	3.19	2.92	2.56

(Left margin label: **Political System**)

Sources and notes: [a]Hartmann 2007; [b]SOU 1990; Christiansen et al. 2001; Christiansen and Togeby 2007; Hoffmann-Lange 1992; Bürklin 1997; Kaltenbrunner et al. 2010; Rieffel 1984; Diezhandino et al. 1994; [c]OECD 2012; an odds ratio of 1 means that people from academic and non-academic homes are equally likely to enrol in higher education; Odds ratios equal to 2 mean that people with academic parents are twice as likely to attend higher education as those from non-academic homes; [d]Eberwein 2011; [e]European Audiovisual Observatory Yearbook 2007; until 2005, the share of public funding in total revenues has been closer to 10 per cent in Spain; [f]EJC, 2014; [g]www.rsf.org; [h]Hallin and Mancini, 2004; [i]Van Kempen 2007 – Index ranges from 0 (no parallelism) to 100 (maximum parallelism). The upper end of the scale is a theoretical one. Greece as the EU country with the most pronounced political parallelism in the media system has a value of 20; [j]World Press Trends 2012; [k]own calculations, based on World Press Trends 2012 (Sweden 2013) and own research; [l]at time of data collection, last parliamentary elections had been held in 2005 in Germany, in 2006 in Austria and Sweden, in 2007 in Denmark and France, and in (early) 2008 in Spain; [m]Transparency International, 2014; [n]Müller 2006; [o]Schnapp 2004; [p]Indicator is based on Schnapp 2004 and Alba 2001 for Spain; [q]refers to the appointment (and release) of leading bureaucrats by the minister/government, as well as replacement of bureaucratic leadership with a change in government; Siaroff 1999, based on eight indicators; mean across twenty-four countries: 3.271; [r]Lane and Ersson 1999, 145; [s]Volkens et al. 2014; based on manifestoes of parties represented in parliament for the last election at time of data gathering; [t]Vatter 2014, 465; [u]Vatter 2009.

a minimum. Sweden represents a classical European *newspaper country* with a print circulation that is among the highest in the world. Historically, newspapers had been tied to parties, unions and other social organizations (Hallin and Mancini 2004, 153). The important role of regional and local papers, as well as of free sheets, further contributes to the mass-orientation of the Swedish print market. At the same time, media concentration is comparatively high, with the family-owned Bonnier group accounting for about a quarter of the print circulation, as well as owning the main private TV broadcaster TV4 (European Journalism Centre 2014).

Rational-legal authority is a strong part of Swedish political and bureaucratic culture. Clientelism is virtually absent in Sweden, reinforcing the central idea of democratic corporatism that incorporation of societal interest is countered or balanced by a strong commitment to the rule of law and the common good. Recruitment within the political administration is very open, based on performance criteria rather than in-house seniority. Moreover, Sweden is also considered one of the exemplars of democratic corporatism, suggesting a rather open and permeable political system. Traditionally, electoral support for left- and right-wing parties has been rather limited in Sweden. Yet, the Swedish consensus culture is by no means based on a lack of ideological differences between parties. In contrast to Denmark, however, the political balance of two main ideological blocs is not based on wing parties.[3] The Swedish state is unitary, albeit with a considerable degree of decentralization to the local level. On the national level, concentration of decision-making power is further reduced by the strong role of corporatist and other interest groups, the multi-party system, as well as a particular division of labour between cabinet-like departments and free-standing agencies. The latter model also results in a considerable degree of politicization of the civil service: whereas the political administration is strictly neutral, the ministerial leadership is politically appointed. Professionalization of political communication in Sweden has been described as 'professionalization light': an increasing trend to professionalize political communication activities is confined by political parties with strong ideological profiles (Falasca and Nord 2013; Nord 2009).

Denmark

In many ways, the permeability of Danish class structure supersedes Sweden, in terms of both education and the openness of elite positions. Political elites in Denmark are quite heterogeneous in terms of their socio-demographic background, not only in the party-political and parliamentary sphere but also in the administrative sphere (Christiansen et al. 2001, 86). The number of politicians with an upper- or upper-middle-class background is traditionally low, although a certain trend towards 'embourgeoisement' has been noted

(Hartmann 2007a, 171, 2001, 52–53). Although recruitment within the political sector is comparatively open, it does not lead to high inter-elite mobility. Rather, the integration of political and administrative elites into inter-elite networks has been in continuous decline (Christiansen and Togeby 2007). Less information is available for the social background of media elites. Like parliamentary and executive political elites, media elites are, however, decidedly not from a high-status background (Christiansen et al. 2001, 217). Danish elites are characterized by a low degree of horizontal mobility (Christiansen et al. 2001, 224). This is especially true for the media sector: most members of the journalistic elite have never worked in another sector or assumed a high-ranking political position within parliament, political parties or the administration (2001, 68).

Although the media system environment in Denmark shares a number of similarities with Sweden, some important differences remain. Most noticeably, despite the formal principle of arm's-length, the actual political intrusion in broadcasting is considerably higher than in Sweden, shading more towards a parliamentary model of proportional representation (Hallin and Mancini 2004, 170; Nielsen 2010). Like in Sweden, the Danish press sector has historically been characterized by strong political affiliations, most clearly manifested in the four-paper party press on the local level. Already since the first half of the twentieth century, it continuously evolved into a more consolidated and commercial press sector, corresponding to a shift from a partisan to an independent news regime (Blach-Ørsten 2014). The dominance of public broadcasters is far more pronounced than in Sweden, in terms of both audience shares and public revenues. Political news making is more or less exclusively the domain of the publicly owned broadcasters DR and TV2, the latter however being de facto a private TV station in state ownership. State subsidies to the print market only exist indirectly (e.g. VAT tax exemption and reduced postal fees). While still a newspaper country with broad popular readership, circulation and newspaper are somewhat lower than in Sweden. Tabloids exist, but circulation rates are in stark decline, in part also due to the high circulation rates of free sheets.

As in Sweden, party patronage and clientelism have historically been rebuffed more or less completely by a strong commitment to rational-legal authority and bureaucratic institutions. Furthermore, Denmark is one of the few European countries in which top-level bureaucrats are not recruited politically (Blondel and Müller-Rommel 2007). Unlike in Sweden, the minister remains the only politically appointed figure, acting in a double role as cabinet member and sole leader of the administration within the policy domain. However, Denmark has also been one of the most ardent adopters of NPM, making performance orientation and recruitment in the civil service a solid trend (Green-Pedersen 2002). As in Sweden, a high number of political parties, and a multitude of stakeholders and veto-players characterize the national level of decision making. However, Denmark is more polarized than Sweden insofar as left- and right-wing parties have high levels of electoral support and constitute an established force in Danish politics. With regard to vertical concentration, the political structure in Denmark is even more decentralized than in Sweden, leaving both decision-making power and delivery of welfare services to the local level. Nevertheless, the lack of a federalist structure, the size of the country and the concentration on the larger Copenhagen area in terms of both population and socio-cultural relevance still makes Denmark a relatively centralized country. In contrast to Sweden, professionalization of political communication in Denmark has been rather extensive, also leading to a self-reflexive preoccupation with *spin* in public and media debate (Blach-Ørsten 2014; Dindler 2011, 8–9).

Germany

In its societal structure, Germany sets itself clearly apart from the more egalitarian states in Northern Europe. Upper and upper-middle classes are clearly overrepresented in the social composition of the entire elite, including media and political elites (Schnapp 1997, 77). Although a substantial part of the political elites traditionally also comes from a lower- and lower-middle-class background, the social background of ministers is becoming increasingly 'bourgeois' (Hartmann 2007a, 134). The classical career path of 'climbing the greasy pole' is giving way to social and educational background. This also fosters increased horizontal mobility between sectors, traditionally limited by the lack of elite schools and universities (139). Although examples of political elites that have only had a career in politics become more frequent, elected office is both preceded and followed by professional work in other sectors in most cases (154). A comparable development can be found in the German media elite. The traditional image of an immobile elite of university dropouts (Hoffmann-Lange 1979) is rapidly dissolving. Already by 1995, the vast majority of media elites had a university degree, although not primarily in journalism, but in social sciences more general (see also Weischenberg, Malik and Scholl 2006). Additionally, previous work experience in another sector, including the political sector is becoming more common, albeit not the rule (Bürklin 1997, 177).

Journalistic professionalism in Germany is high. The key entry point into the journalistic profession remains the Volontariat, that is, training on the job, although journalistic elites have traditionally also been educated in one of the leading professional journalism schools. Professional self-regulation is in place, although its key elements; that is, the Press Council and the German Press Code are frequently subject to criticism for lack of clarity, efficiency and real sanctioning power (Eberwein 2011). In contrast to many other European countries, direct press subsidies do not exist, which can be seen as an expression of a certain hesitance towards direct active state intervention in the media sphere (Hallin and Mancini 2004, 161). Press-party parallelism is low: tabloids and regional papers in particular are read across partisan lines, even if their content is at times quite partisan (van Kempen 2007). By contrast, the public service broadcasting regulation model in Germany is a prime example of politics-in-broadcasting with representation of parties and civic groups, which may nevertheless have implicit party alignments (Humphreys 1996). Although circulation rates have traditionally been somewhat lower than in the Nordic countries and influential quality newspapers with national circulation have a more educated readership, Germany must still be counted among the group of classical newspaper countries in Europe. Overall elite orientation is furthermore counter-acted by the particular role of the tabloid BILD, in terms of both circulation rates and agenda setting power.

Bureaucracy and rational-legal authority are thoroughly incorporated into the German political system and seems more resilient towards performance-orientation than in the Nordic countries. Ministerial leadership is highly politicized in Germany, coupled with a commitment to bureaucratic standards for regular civil servants. A main dividing line between Germany and the Scandinavian countries is the lack of a strong corporatist tradition. With respect to positional variety, the German party-political spectrum is traditionally non-polarized, and the different wings of the two big parties historically absorbed a great deal of more pronounced political cleavages, albeit the effective number of parties has risen.[4] Having been a three-party-system for a long time, firm party blocs do not exist, and coalitions between the two main parties are not uncommon, if other majorities cannot be found. On top of being a federal system, concentration of decision making on the national level is almost as low as in the Nordic countries. In Germany, U.S.-inspired professionalization of electoral campaigning had its heyday in the late 1990s and early 2000s, when political parties very overtly established so-called war rooms and hired spin doctors (Negrine et al. 2007). This trend appears to have ebbed since. However, professionalization in the government sphere vis-à-vis the party-political sphere remains significant, and government communication is rather centralized and well coordinated (Sanders and Canel 2013).

Austria

Austria's societal structure is a somewhat peculiar case. On the one hand, the permeability of its class structure (in terms of education) is far lower than in the Nordic countries and Germany. On the other hand, the upper or upper-middle class holds even less of a grip on the political domain than in the

Scandinavian countries. Social and educational backgrounds, which significantly determine elite status in other sectors in Austria, are less decisive for elite status in the sphere of political communication. In contrast to Germany, the share of political elites with an explicit working-class background is decisively higher, reflecting how engrained the principle of *Proporz* (patronage based on party proportionality) is in Austrian politics (Hartmann 2007a, 128). Furthermore, the number of university graduates among the journalistic elites remains comparatively low (Kaltenbrunner et al. 2010). All in all, Austria's elites in media and politics draw membership from a broad base in the population rather than the top echelons. The degree of horizontal mobility is equally ambiguous in Austria. General horizontal elite mobility is not particularly high (Hartmann 2007a, 143), but media and political elites seem to provide an exception in this respect. High-ranking journalists who make their way into politics (and in some cases back) are a well-known phenomenon in Austria (Fabris 1995).

Journalistic professionalization is less pronounced than in the other democratic-corporatist countries under study (Blum 2014, 231). The Austrian Press Council was suspended between 2002 and 2010, and 'existing codes of ethics need updating and are not well known by journalists; neither is there self- or co-regulation for private and public broadcasting' (Karmasin et al. 2011, 22). State regulation and intervention are comparatively high, and press subsidies – founded both in public service and in more political motivations – are substantial (Murschetz and Karmasin 2014). Political parallelism in the press is comparatively low, and party-owned newspapers nowadays only account for a fraction of the Austrian press market (Blum 2014, 226; Plasser and Lengauer 2010, 20). As in Germany, the Austrian broadcasting system is a civic one, albeit based on the particularities of the *Proporz* principle (Hallin and Mancini 2004, 169). Within the relatively broad parameters of the politics-in-broadcasting model, party-political intrusion in operational decisions of public broadcasting is substantial and on the rise. The most characteristic feature of the Austrian print market is the dominating market position of the tabloid Neue Kronenzeitung, which, together with the strong regional newspapers, contributes to the broad reach of newspapers and generally non-elitist character of the print media in Austria. At the same time, concentration of ownership is very high (Huber 2012, 116–117; Plasser and Lengauer 2010).

Austria's political system is defined by early bureaucratic-professional state formation and sound regulatory quality and rule of law. Moreover, Austria is routinely included in the group of countries with well-established corporatist structures of interest mediation. Clientelism (more or less formalized), however, presents a substantial factor in Austrian politics in the domain of civil service patronage, political dealings with public and private businesses as well as social policy benefits. With the erosion of the two-party coalition

hegemony and the surge of the right-wing populist parties, the two main parties SPÖ and ÖVP have however been forced to reduce their clientelist linkage
techniques (Kitschelt 2007). Until the emergence of the right-wing populist
parties FPÖ and BZÖ, Austria was almost exclusively governed by a grand
coalition consisting of the two main parties to the left and right of the political
middle, contributing to very low levels of polarization. Substantial polarization on the structural level, as well as a redefinition of the political landscape,
has occurred as a result of the establishment of the right-wing populist parties.
Austria is frequently described as a centralized federal state, as despite its federal structure, vertical centralization is much more profound than in Germany.
U.S.-inspired campaigning practices received a lot of attention at the turn of
the millennium (Hofer 2005; Plasser and Plasser 2002). The substantial professionalization of campaign management has however been largely restricted
to electoral campaigns, whereas the strategic orientation of routine party-
parliamentary and government communication remains rather limited.

France

It is certainly no coincidence that the French social structure has served as
the point of departure for Bourdieu's idea of an upper class or 'state nobility' that reproduces itself through education (Bourdieu 1996). More than in
other European countries, reaching an elite position is connected with having
visited the 'right' preparatory school, university and post-graduate institution.
Despite the fact that these institutions are mostly public, as well as strictly
performance-based, the odds for students of a lower-class background to
enter higher or even elite education are very low. The Grandes Écoles, which
provide distinct elite education tracks set apart from the remainder of regular universities, are by and large populated by students from an upper-class
background (Hartmann 2007a, 43). Consequently, political elites almost
exclusively have an upper-class background. The same can be said about the
media elite, not least since journalism has traditionally been seen as an elite
occupation that served as a stepping-stone to a literary or political career
(Rieffel 1984). The French educational system furthermore leads to high elite
mobility, especially in between politics, administration and the private sector, which recruit their elites predominantly among graduates from the École
nationale d'administration (ENA), either directly or through the successive
Grands corps de l'État (Hartmann 2007a). With respect to the relationship
between political and media elites, a degree from the Institute d'études poli-
tiques de Paris (Sciences Po) is the silver bullet for entry into ENA and a
successive career in politics and administration, and – in connection with a
degree of the few renowned journalistic schools – for a high-profile career in
journalism (Burgert 2010, 191).

Journalistic professionalism in terms of a common professional culture and ethical codes is still rather underdeveloped in France, despite the fact that the National Union of Journalists (which has only limited membership among journalists) has adopted a code of conducted already in 1919 (European Journalism Centre 2014; Hallin and Mancini 2004, 111–113). A national press council does not exist, and common professional standards are largely confined to individual newspapers (Hallin and Mancini 2004, 112). Media accountability and journalistic self-regulation, although 'constantly proclaimed to be a reality . . . remains (today) merely as an idea which hardly influences journalistic practices' (Baisnée and Balland 2011, 75). Not surprisingly, a statist approach remains dominant, making both public television and the national daily press 'national institutions' subject to heavy state intervention and subsidization (European Journalism Centre 2014). The statist approach carries over to the French model of broadcasting governance, which constitutes a rather overt case of political parallelism. For many years, the French model of broadcast governance has been heavily dominated by executive power and a clear example of party-politicized politics-over-broadcasting. More recently, the establishment of the state-funded and politically appointed Conseil supérieur de l'audiovisuel (CSA) as a formally independent control authority has weakened the executive grip over public broadcasting somewhat (Katsirea 2008; Neveu 1999, 383). However, political influence over the CSA remains substantial (Burgert 2010, 105).

Political parallelism in the press, by contrast, is moderate and mostly a result of its historical emphasis on commentary journalism in the elite dailies, rather than of a political segmentation of mass audiences like in the Nordic countries (see Hallin and Mancini 2004, 98–99; van Kempen 2007). A mass-circulation press following the model of Northern Europe has never fully developed. The national daily press, in particular, is characterized by a pronounced elite orientation (Burgert 2010, 110). In contrast to other Mediterranean countries, the French landscape of political news does, however, include tabloid newspapers (though to a lesser degree than in the Central European countries) as well as a regional press, both of which are far less elitist in nature (Baisnée and Balland 2011; Hallin and Mancini 2004, 97).

On the one hand, France is clearly aligned with the Nordic and Central European countries in its high degree of rational-legal authority, in many ways even being the epitome of a strong bureaucracy and professional administration (Hallin and Mancini 2004, 136). On the other hand, *étatisme* also means that autonomy tends to approximate closure of the political system in France, not least expressed by the fact that France lacks a corporatist tradition, or a tradition for widespread inclusion of social interests altogether. Due to the corps structure, recruitment to and career paths within the administration are rather closed, although government has a strong say in how the administrative leadership is composed. With respect to positional variety, the French party system is highly polarized in terms of both the support for left- and right-wing parties and the range of political viewpoints manifested in party manifestoes. As for institutional variety, France sets itself clearly apart from the four Nordic and Central European countries: due to the combination of a semi-presidential majority system and a unitary state, concentration in decision making is the highest among the countries under study.[5] The French semi-presidential system also provides comparatively fertile grounds for the professionalization of political communication, but increasing professional- ization has also lead to larger discrepancies between the executive (in par- ticular the presidential) and party-political sphere. The professionalization of the presidential communication assigns the president an even more elevated position and degrades political parties to 'electoral machines' (Maarek 2007). The central government information service (SIG) mostly plays a technical role in the routine communication of government actions (Maarek 2013).

Spain

Despite the absence of elite educational institutions, a long history of social disparity continues to have its effects in Spain, as upper and upper-middle classes still have a far higher likelihood to obtain both higher education and political elite positions. In contrast to France, the Spanish media elite has a more middle-class background (Diezhandino et al. 1994). About two-thirds of the journalistic elites, on the other hand, have a journalism-related degree, far more than, for example, in the Central European countries, and virtually all of them have a university degree (Diezhandino et al. 1994, 67). Similar to the grands corps d'état in France, the administrative corps structure rep- resents an influential system of elite education and political recruitment (Hartmann 2007a, 102–107). This contributes decisively to a high degree of horizontal elite mobility, as corps members very frequently occupy elite posi- tions not only within the administration but also the political and economic sphere (Alba 2001). Such horizontal mobility, however, does not include the media sector.

Similar to many other Southern European countries, the Spanish media system lacks a national press council and formalized code of conduct or a consensus on journalist ethics (Alsius, Mauri and Rodríguez Martínez 2011; Hallin and Mancini 2004, 112). State intervention is exercised more as a mechanism of political pressure rather than pursuit of public service (Arriaza Ibarra and Nord 2014). State subsidies exist only in the form of (volatile and pressure-prone) government advertising. The interventionist role of the Span- ish state often collides with clientelist relationships with the private sector, fostering further market deregulation (Hallin and Mancini 2004, 134–137).

As for political parallelism, 'It is reasonable to argue that it has increased in the new Spanish democracy, resulting in a division of most of the media into two rival camps', setting Spain markedly apart from the decline of parallelism in most of Europe (Hallin and Mancini 2004, 104). This trend includes newspapers as well as private broadcasting (Canel 2013; Hallin and Mancini 2004, 104–105). Moreover, the political majority has effective control over the public broadcaster RTVE (Sampedro and Seoane Pérez 2008). The government model of broadcast governance is, however, mixed with a parliamentary model insofar as appointment of the key governance board requires a two-thirds majority in parliament (Hallin and Mancini 2004, 107). Not least due to periods of dictatorial rule, a true mass-circulation press has never developed in Spain. Newspapers are traditionally directed towards an educated elite interested in politics. Furthermore, the elite-managed transition to democracy included the media as an integral part, consolidating its elite orientation (Hallin and Mancini 2004, 103).

Clientelist structures still remain present in Spain, albeit less tied to a model of party patronage than in Austria (Hallin and Papathanassopoulos 2002). The corps structure and a corresponding career system create for a relatively coherent administration. At the same time, the career paths of Spanish civil servants are highly politicized (Alba 2001). Moreover, the Spanish political system lacks democratic-corporatist structures of interest mediation. The level of polarization in Spanish politics is comparatively low, and the two main parties do not differ as substantially in their policy views, as the tone of the political debate suggests (Hallin and Mancini 2004, 130; Sampedro and Seoane Pérez 2008). In the first decades after the transition to democracy, Spanish political (and other) elites shared a profound consensual unity that was the product of the elite-driven democratic transition and consolidation after Franco (Gunther 1992, 40). More recently, however, and in particular after the 11 March bombings in Madrid, 'antagonistic bipolarization' between the two big parties increasingly replaces the formerly restrained partisanship (Sampedro and Seoane Pérez 2008). Spain is a majority system with substantial concentration of decision making on the national level. At the same time, it is one of the most decentralized countries in Europe, due to the structural division in autonomous communities with a distinct cultural and historical identity. Although a two-party split (PSOE, PP) essentially dominates Spanish party politics, regional parties also play a significant role in national politics, which often supersedes their quantitative representation in parliament.

In the party-political sphere, the Spanish model of professionalization of political communication is less concerned with garnering media attention and support (being regarded as largely fixed in partisan news making), but with tailoring professionalized (permanent and electoral) campaigns in relation to the political competition (Aira 2009; Sampedro and Seoane Pérez 2008).

Professionalized and systematized structures and procedures are only slowly emerging in Spanish government communication and have undergone several reformulations since the transition to democracy. Moreover, structures and resources remain highly dependent upon the prime minister's sensitivity and attention to communication matters (Sanders and Canel 2013, 137). Structural deficiencies also result in diffuse or lower-ranked communication positions, a fact that is also reflected in the comparatively low number of communication elites sampled through the positional approach applied in this study. Government communicators are mainly in charge of arranging the politicians' media encounters and rarely brief the press themselves. Media exposure resides almost entirely with the political leaders (146).

The Six Countries Compared: Summary Measures of Context Factors

Based on the comprehensive analysis of the degree of vertical and horizontal mobility, as well as of sectoral autonomy and variety in the six countries under study, table 4.2 gives a summary overview of the context factors related to elite cohesion in the six countries. The summary table represents qualitative measures of the individual country on the key conditions, taking the individual circumstances elaborated earlier into consideration within the general framework of the model presented in chapter 3.

Table 4.2. Context of Elite Cohesion in Political Communication

			SWE	DEN	GER	AUT	FRA	SPA
Social structure	Mobility	Vertical	+/o	+	o	+/o	–	–/o
		Horizontal	o/–	–	o	+/o	+	o
Media system	Autonomy	Absence of subjugation	+/o	+	+/o	o	o/–	o/–
		Absence of collusion	+/o	o	o	o/–	o/–	–
	Variety	Institutional	o	+/o	+/o	–	o	o/–
		Positional	o	+/o	o/–	o	+/o	+
Political system	Autonomy	Absence of subjugation*	+/o	+/o	+	+/o	+/o	o
		Absence of collusion+	o/–	o/–	+/o	o	o	o/–
	Variety	Institutional	+	+	+/o	o/–	–	o/–
		Positional	o	+/o	o/–	o	+	o

Notes: – weak presence, o medium presence, + strong presence; *includes absence of subjugation by third parties in terms of strong-rational legal authority, as well as of subjugation by media (in terms of a 'colonization' of the political sector by media and communication logics); +with third parties in general; for collusion between media and political sector see collusion in the media system.

The summary measures of context factors also provide a foundation for the assessment of the commonalities between the three country groups. Although the three country groups do indeed share a number of systemic patterns, some divergences remain: Sweden and Denmark differ in the degree of sectoral variety, Germany and Austria part ways in the autonomy of their media sector, as well as in their level of institutional variety, while France and Spain at forehand represent the most heterogeneous group, not least due to the differences in horizontal elite mobility and autonomy in the political sector, as well as a stronger public service orientation in France. Based on this assessment of the decisive features of the social structure, media system and political system in each country, more specific expectations about the extent and patterns of both inter-sectoral and intra-sectoral cohesion will be presented and tested in the empirical chapters.

POLITICAL COMMUNICATION ELITES: OPERATIONAL DEFINITION AND OVERALL SAMPLE

Political communication elites are defined as actors within political organizations and media organizations, who regularly and substantially influence collectively binding decisions through their capacity to determine publicly communicated political messages. Inclusion in the political communication elite is thus based on actor positions in the hierarchy of political organizations and media organizations, as well as the role of these actors in the process of political communication (see chapter 2). This logic follows a *positional approach* to the identification of elites, that is, the proposition that individual elites can be identified via their positions at the top of hierarchy within an organization based in a particular societal sector (Bürklin 1997, 16). A positional approach typically proceeds top-down in the organizational hierarchy, aiming at a *full survey* of elites from the topmost positions downwards until a specified cut-off point (Hoffmann-Lange 2007).

With respect to media organizations, political communication elites are generally found in media outlets covering domestic affairs and international politics based on independent journalistic and editorial activities in-house. Elite positions in reporting of national affairs are hereby not limited to so-called elite media but can also be found within second tier media such as leading regional newspapers or private broadcasters. The media outlets chosen for the elite sample thus include TV and radio broadcasters, daily and weekly newspapers, including tabloids and free sheets, political magazines, as well as news agencies. Online news outlets are not included as a category of their own. The significant consumption of political news via online media notwithstanding, the online news segment is still dominated by websites linked to

established offline media and editorial positions within these online spin-offs
are still not regularly included within the topmost positions of the respective
media outlet. Given that online elite positions are thus relatively few, they
are subsumed under the respective offline media outlet or else included in the
print category to guarantee respondents' anonymity. Table 4.3 provides an
overview of all media organizations included in the study.

Given the focus on direct, regular and substantial impact on publicly
communicated messages, the criterion for inclusion in the political communication elite of the media sector emphasizes active journalistic leadership
and proximity to the actual journalistic output, rather than overall control,
ownership and management of media organizations. As such, the applied
criterion excludes a large number of actors that are included and even considered highly important in conventional understandings of the media elite,
in particular media ownership and managerial leadership. In the six European countries under study, this group of elites first and foremost consists of
editorial elites, covering editors-in-chief, programme directors and section
heads in charge of domestic affairs and national politics, as well as in some
instances publishers, if they fulfil an active editorial function. Ranking lower
in the organizational hierarchy, *reporters*, in particularly (parliamentary) correspondents, qualify as specialized sub-elites of political communication due
to their crucial function in the political reporting of their media outlet, as well
as in its relationship to political elites.[6] Additionally, presenters and hosts of
the most important political broadcasting programmes are included.

While most media outlets conforming to this criterion will be national
media in terms of distribution and scope, regional media outlets additionally
play a significant role in opinion formation on national politics in all of the
included countries, save for the case of France.[7] The most relevant regional
media outlets in each country were generally selected based on their circulation, supplemented by country-specific criteria: in Sweden, where regional
newspapers tend to have a clear ideological position, newspapers were
selected based on ideological balance. In Denmark, only regional newspapers
with accreditation to the *presseloge* in parliament were included. The German sample additionally took frequency of inter-media citations, as well as
regional balance into consideration. In Austria, all regional newspapers with
daily circulation were included, as minor regional and local newspapers are
usually published weekly.

In contrast to the Northern and Central European newspaper countries,
regional broadcasters, in particular regional radio stations, form a significant
part of political reporting in Spain. Another characteristic of the Spanish
media landscape is the relatively low market share of public-service broadcasters, leading to the inclusion of a higher number of privately owned broadcasting stations. In the remaining countries, private broadcasters have only a

Table 4.3. Sample of Media Organizations

Sweden	Denmark	Germany	Austria	France	Spain
		Public Service Media: TV and Radio			
SVT, Sveriges Radio (SR)	DR, TV 2, DR Radio, TV 2 Radio	ARD, ZDF, Deutschlandfunk	ORF	France 2, i-télé Radio France	TV1, La 2 RNE 1
		Private Media: TV and Radio			
TV4	None	RTL, n-tv, N24	ATV, Pro7-Austria	TF 1, Canal+, LCI	9 TV. 8 radio stations[b]
		Private Media: Daily Newspapers (National and Selected Regional)			
Dagens Nyheter, Svenska Dagbladet, Dagens Industri, Göteborgs-Posten, Sydsvenska Dagbladet, Östgöta-Correspondenten, Nerikes Allehanda, Dala Demokraten (S), Nya Wermlandstidningen, Helsingborgs Dagbladet	Politiken, Berlingske Tidende, Information, Jyllands-Posten, Kristeligt Dagblad, Børsen, Fyens Stiftstidende, Nordjyske	Süddeutsche Zeitung, Frankfurter Allgemeine Zeitung, Frankfurter Rundschau, taz, Welt, Handelsblatt, FTD Tagesspiegel, Berliner Zeitung, Leipziger Volkszeitung, WAZ, Rheinische Post, Hannoversche Allgemeine	Die Presse, Der Standard, Kurier, Wirtschaftsblatt 13 regional newspapers[a]	Le Monde, Le Figaro, Libération, Les Echos, Le Parisien Ouest France	El País, El Mundo, El Periódico, La Vanguardia, ABC La Voz de Galicia, El Correo, La Razón, Avuí, Gara

(Continued)

Table 4.3 Continued

Sweden	Denmark	Germany	Austria	France	Spain
Private Media: Weeklies/Magazines and Tabloids/Free Sheets					
	Weekend Avisen, Søndagsavisen, Økonomisk Ugebrev, Kommunen, A4, Mandag morgen	Spiegel, Stern, Focus, Cicero, Zeit, Rheinischer Merkur	Falter, Die Furche, Die Ganze Woche, Format, News, Profil, Trend	L'Express, Le Nouvel Observateur, Le Point, Marianne, Paris Match	Interviú, Tiempo
Aftonbladet, Expressen Metro, City, Punkt	Ekstra Bladet, BT, Metro-Express, Urban, Nyhedsavisen, 24 Timer, Altinget	Bild	Neue Kronen Zeitung, Heute,		20 Minutos, Metro, Directo
News Agencies					
TT	Ritzau	dpa, AP	APA	AFP	EFE, Europa Press

aKleine Zeitung, Neue Kärntner Tageszeitung (SPÖ), Neues Volksblatt (ÖVP), Neue Vorarlberger Tageszeitung, Neue Zeitung für Tirol, Oberösterreichs Neue, Österreich, Salzburger Nachrichten, Salzburger Volkszeitung, Tiroler Tageszeitung, Vorarlberger Nachrichten, Wiener Zeitung. bAntena 3, Tele 5, Cuatro, Canal Sur, La Sexta, TV3, TeleMadrid, TVG, ETB Ser, Cope, Onda Cero, Catalunya Radio, Punto Radio, Sur Radio, Radio Euskadi, Radio Galega.

complementary role in political reporting. In the case of Denmark, private broadcasters virtually have no political role in the media landscape.

With respect to the political sector, members of the political communication elite are located more or less exclusively on the national level. Although modern politics are conducted at multiple levels of governance, elites on the national level of governance are still considered the crucial decision makers when it comes to political outcomes important to the society as a whole (Bürklin 1997, 16; Field and Higley 1980, 20; Keller 1963, 20). Correspondingly, the organizations included in the study comprise, first, the main bodies of government and administration, in particular the president's/prime minister's/chancellor's office, government ministries, as well as the governmental bodies dedicated to communication, information and press relations, where they exist. Second, high-ranking positions in parliament, as well as in all political parties, represented in parliament are included. To assure that included elites are primarily active on the national political level, members of the second chamber of parliament have not been included in Germany and France.

In the political sector, political communication elites are found among both established elected and specialized elites within political organizations (referred to as *decision makers* in the following) and the specialized sub-elites of political communication, constituted by various forms of *communication professionals* working within and for political organizations.

.Decision makers also take on a communicative role but do so from their position as (elected or appointed) decision makers in substantive politics. This group of elites includes high-ranking elected and non-elected officials in the executive and legislative sphere, as well as in political parties and the leading echelons of administration. Whereas specific elite positions (and corresponding titles) within the media sector are rather alike across the individual countries under study, this is not always the case for the political sector. Rather, political communication elite positions strongly reflect the particular setup of representative democracy, as well as the specific incorporation of communication-related positions into the political system in each country.

The group of communication professionals includes, first, high-ranking persons in charge of communication activities to the media and (however not exclusively) to the general public. In many (but not all) instances, these positions are called 'spokesperson', 'head of press office' or 'press secretary'. The group also includes high-ranking persons in charge of strategic planning and political manoeuvring in relation to media and public opinion, such as communication consultants and PR advisors, as well as positions that are informally referred to as 'spin doctors', who may also be hired externally (see also Tenscher 2003, 113).[8] Table 4.4 provides a detailed list of included political organizations and elite positions in each country.

Table 4.4. Sample of Elite Positions within Political Organizations

Sweden	Denmark	Germany	Austria	France	Spain
Government and Administration					
Regeringskansliet (Statsrådsberegningen; 12 Departamenter): Prime minister (P), ministers (P), secretaries of state (P), press secretaries (C), 'samordnare' (C), head of communication (C)	*Statsministeriet, Departamenter:* Prime minister (P), ministers (P), heads of department (A), special advisers (C), heads of press sections (C)	*Bundeskanzleramt, Bundesministerien, Presse- und Informationsamt (BPA):* Chancellor (P), ministers (P), parl. (P) and admin. secretaries of state (A), heads of pol. planning unit (P), spokespeople and deputies (C), heads of planning unit BPA (C)	*Bundeskanzleramt, Bundesministerien:* Chancellor (P), ministers (P), state secretaries (P), chief of staff (P), spokespeople of ministers and chancellor (C), press officers Bundespressedienst (C)	*Elysée, Hotel Matignon, Service d'Information du Gouvernement (SIG), Ministries:* President (P), prime minister (P), ministers (P), state secre-taries (P), policy (P) and communication (C) advisers in cabinets, heads of media-related planning units SIG (C)	*Presidencia del Gobierno, Ministerios:* Prime ministers (P), state secretaries and leading admin. staff, personal cabinet of prime minister (P), personalspokespeople and heads of communication units (C)
Legislative Bodies					
Riksdag: Speaker (P) and press secretary (C), PG leaders, press officers and campaign managers 'partikansliet' (C), chairs of parliamentary standing committees, deputies (P)	*Folketinget:* Speaker and deputies (P), PG leadership (presidents, vice presidents, secretaries, political spokespeople) (vice-) chairmen of standing committees	*Bundestag:* Head of parliament's press section (C), PG leaders (P), PG spokesperson + deputies (C), committee heads, MPs (P)	*Nationalrat & Bundesrat:* (Vice) presidents (P), spokespeople (C), head of parliament's press office (C), PG leaders + director (P), PG spokes-person, press secretaries (C), committee chairs (P)	*Sénat:* President (P) *Assemblée Nationale:* President of parliament and deputies (P), PG leaders and deputies, speakers of committees, MPs representing 'courants' (P)	*Congreso de Diputados & Senado:* President (P), 'portavoces' (P), PG leaders (P), president and spokespeople of policy committees (P)

Political Parties

SAP, MP, VP, Mod, KD, C, FP:	EL, SF, S, RV, V, C, DF, New Alliance:	CDU, CSU, SPD, FDP, Grüne, Linke:	ÖVP, SPÖ, FPÖ, Grüne, BZÖ:	UMP, PS, PCF, NC, Verts, Mouvement démocrate:	PSOE, PP, CiU, IU, UPyD and 18 smaller regional pol. parties:
Party leaders (P), executive members of party boards (P), secretary general (P), press secretaries (C), campaign managers, heads of strategic planning (C)y	(Vice-)President (P) secretary general (P),heads of press (C) communication and strategy advisers in 'secretariats' (C)	Party chairs (P), general secretary (P) executive director (P) spokespeople + deputies (C), external campaign consultants (C)	Party chairs (P), general secretary/ executive director (P), spokespeeople (C) external consultants (C)	Party executive boards (P) chief press officers of parties (porte-parole) (C)	President (P) (Vice-) general secretary (P)

Notes: PG = Parliamentary group; P = Politician/decision maker; C = Communicator; A = Administration; in cases, where individual elite actors hold multiple positions, their principal position is determined based on the following principles: (1) any government position overrules legislative and party-political positions; (2) within the party-political sphere, the highest ranking position is chosen (i.e. the position of a parliamentary group leader overrules being part of the party board while being a party chair overrules MP status); (3) communication experts that also hold a (rank-and-file) political position are classified as communicators.

COLLECTION OF SURVEY DATA AND FINAL SAMPLE

Actors included in the overall sample were asked to participate in a standardized survey containing items measuring the value, procedural and epistemological sources of elite cohesion and the guiding principles ideology,
publicity and pragmatism (see chapter 3 and appendix). The recruitment of
interview partners and conduction of interviews was guided by the principle
of functional equivalence, combined with pragmatic considerations about
elite approachability in each country. Correspondingly, the choice of interview mode (telephone, face-to-face, online survey or written questionnaire)
was adapted to the circumstances in each country, and in many instances,
potential respondents were offered different interview modes. The choice
of interview mode, however, had virtually no effect on the substance of the
answer, when controlling for sector and country (for more details on the fieldwork, see Maurer and Vähämaa 2014). Elites from the Nordic countries were
most willing to participate, whereas elites in France and Spain, as well as the
most high-ranking political elites, were least accessible. Item non-response
was generally very low, ranging from 2 to 4 per cent for epistemological
items and 5 to 10 per cent for procedural items (see appendix for a detailed
description of field periods, interview modes, number of respondents and
response rates in each country).

In all countries, surveyed media elites have long-lasting professional
careers, from in average sixteen years in Denmark to more than twenty-two
years in France (see appendix for details). Only a minority of media elites has
previously worked in the political sector, least so in the two Mediterranean
countries. With respect to political orientation, French and Spanish media
elites position themselves most clearly on the left of the political spectrum.
In Austria and Sweden, the leftist bias found in the South and to a lesser
degree in Denmark and Sweden, and sometimes assumed as a default condition in journalism more generally, is in turn more or less non-existent. For
Sweden, this can be interpreted as a direct result of the bi-partite elite structure, in which broadcasting elites are generally more aligned with the social-
democratic sphere and thus slightly more left-leaning, while newspaper elites
lean more towards the 'bourgeois' sphere (SOU 1990). Another noticeable
fact is the low percentage of women among media elites in Denmark (19 per
cent) and Germany (22 per cent), far lower than among the political elite (33
and 32 per cent, respectively). In Spain, the media elite is in turn far more
female (36 per cent) than the political elite (18 per cent).

Turning to the political elite, the average member in all of the included
countries still resembles the fifty-year-old male – though somewhat less
male in the North and somewhat younger in France. Large differences exist,
however, with respect to previous work experience. While professional

experience in journalism is characteristic of a quarter to a third of the political decision makers in the Nordic and Central European countries, such experience is largely unknown in France (3 per cent) and Spain (8 per cent).

Political communication professionals in the two Nordic countries are significantly younger than political decision makers and their peers abroad, suggesting a tendency to emphasize a fresh look on communication, in many cases based on a previous career in journalism, rather than a long-standing political career. Communication professionals of the two Nordic countries differ, however, when it comes to formal membership of a party as a direct result of the different administrative structures in Sweden and Denmark: Whereas the Danish administration – apart from the particular function of special advisor – is politically neutral, government communicators in charge of liaising with the media are politically recruited in Sweden (see also Falasca and Nord 2013). In the executive sphere, 72 per cent of Swedish but only 17 per cent of Danish communication professionals are members of a political party.

A similar contrast exists in the Central European group: Austria's communication professionals in government and administration are far more likely to be member of a political party than their German colleagues (44 versus 7 per cent). Similar to their peers in the North, the large majority of Central European communication professionals have some sort of professional background in journalism, but they are generally older and more experienced. Finally, the communication sub-elites in the Mediterranean countries do not set themselves apart from the decision-making elites in their demographic background. Noticeably, less than half (in France even less than a fifth) have a professional background in journalism. In France, communication professionals are neither ex-journalists nor party soldiers but presumably professionals recruited from a broader social science background (Sanders and Canel 2013). In Spain, the number of sub-elite positions in political communication is rather small to begin with and makes robust conclusions somewhat more difficult.

SUMMARY: STUDYING ELITE COHESION IN SIX EUROPEAN DEMOCRACIES

The overall goal of this chapter has been to translate the general model developed in chapter 3 into an operational framework for empirical analysis of the six countries in the ensuing chapters. The first part of the chapter has been devoted to a systematic mapping of context factors, enabling summary measures for the vertical and horizontal mobility of social structure as well as the level of autonomy and variety in the media system and the political system. Building on these measures, the general assumptions from chapter 3 linking context factors and elite cohesion can now be translated into specific expectations about the extent and pattern of both inter-sectoral and intra-sectoral elite cohesion for the six countries under study. This will be done in the following chapter.

The first order of business in the next chapter, however, is to explain the method for analysis of the attitudinal data collected from the sample of political communication elites just described. In order to measure the extent, source and principles of elite cohesion based on the various items included in the survey questionnaire, the empirical analysis rests on the calculation of dispersion and discriminance scores denoting, respectively, the degree of proximity and indistinction between elite actors. Together with the specific expectations about context factors, the discussion of dispersion and discriminance scores as the most basic method of data analysis sets the stage for the empirical analysis of cohesion on the inter-sectoral level (chapter 5) and intra-sectoral level (chapter 6).

The central aim of the ensuing chapters is to account for similarities in trends and patterns across countries that give way to more generalizable conclusions, while at the same time remaining sensitive to the particular interplay of elite relations and the systemic and historical context in each country. In this sense, the ensuing analytical chapters do not present a case-by-case analysis of elite cohesion in each of the six countries but analyse elite cohesion cross-nationally with regard to the analytical dimensions specified in the general model.

Chapter 5

Inter-Sectoral Cohesion in Political Communication

The basic line of argument in this study is that the level and form of elite cohesion are dependent upon the social structure, media system and political system attributes that constitute the framework for interaction between political communication elites in European democracies. In the most basic sense, the level and form of cohesion in political communication are a matter of the inter-sectoral cohesion between the two main sectoral elites involved in the creation and dissemination of political messages in modern democracies. Correspondingly, this chapter takes the first step in the empirical analysis of elite cohesion in political communication by mapping the attitudinal patterns that characterize political elites vis-à-vis media elites. Analysing the extent, prevalent patterns and dominant guiding principles of attitudinal consonance between media and political elites provides the first step towards an understanding of elite attitudes in political communication within and across the context of the six countries under study.

The analysis rests on the theoretically developed measures of dispersion (measuring the proximity of attitudes) and discriminance (measuring the indistinction of attitudes). Hence, the chapter begins with a brief operationalization of these two measures through so-called proximity scores. Following the expectations specified in the previous chapters, the first part of chapter analyses the level of attitudinal dispersion and discriminance for each of the three guiding principles, thereby shedding light on the overall extent of cohesion, as well as the relative weight of each principle in the countries under study. In the second part of the analysis, the individual guiding principles are then examined more closely in the various sources of attitudinal consonance. Examining the values, procedures and epistemologies underlying elite cohesion yields more detailed information about the patterns and stances of attitudinal consonance in the six countries under study.

MEASURES OF INTER-SECTORAL COHESION

The basic building block in the analysis of attitudinal consonance is the so-called *proximity score*, originally proposed by Dalton (1985) and widely applied as a measure of attitudinal congruence and issue proximity (see e.g. Dinas, Hartman and van Spanje 2016; Pettersson 2010). The proximity score indicates each respondent's (absolute) distance to the mean of a given reference group. A lower proximity score indicates low distance, and thus high proximity to the reference group. On the inter-sectoral level of analysis, the reference groups are the entire political communication elite, the media elite and the political elite. Based on these reference groups, three types of proximity scores have been calculated for the purposes of analysis in this chapter. These include the following:

- Prox (all): an individual respondent's distance to the general mean across both sectors
- Prox (inter): an individual respondent's distance to the mean of the other sector
- Prox (intra): an individual respondent's distance to the mean of own sector

Following the distinction introduced in chapter 3, these measures can be used to further calculate both the dispersion and the discriminance of attitudes within and between sectors.

When using the proximity scores to analyse *dispersion*, the mean value of prox (all), based on all respondents, can be seen as a direct measurement of the proximity of attitudes in a given elite population, indicating the level of dispersion for the entire elite population from both sectors. The lower the dispersion score, the lower the degree of dispersion, and thus the higher the proximity of attitudes between sectors. On a five-point scale, the dispersion scores have a maximum bandwidth of two scale points (0–2). By default, dispersion is defined as high, when respondents' mean distance to the general mean reaches at least half of the maximum distance, that is, if

Mean [prox (all)] > 1.0.   (5.1)

To account for transitional cases, a boundary zone from 0.9 to 1.1 is applied.

To further account for the fact that index building substantially reduces the degree of dispersion, corrective factors have been inserted for composite indices. This applies to the variable 'clash of interests' (difference index) as well as for composite indicators comprising all three items of a guiding principle (sum indices). To arrive at these corrective factors, a series of auxiliary indices was construed based on different attitudinal items applied in this study, as well as in the overarching project. These auxiliary indices were equal in structure (sum and difference indices), as well as in the number of included items (three in all cases) to the differences and sum indices used in this study. In a second step, dispersion scores were calculated for each individual test item, as well as for the test indices for all countries under study. The average divergence between the dispersion of an auxiliary index and the mean dispersion of all singular items, on which the auxiliary index was based, is taken as an approximation of the decrease in dispersion, that is, to result from index building vis-à-vis the use of singular indicators. For the difference index clash of interests, a corrective factor of 1.2 is consistently applied for all dispersion scores (Mean $[prox_{index}]*1.2=Disp_{corr}$). For the remaining sum indices, a corrective factor of 1.4 is applied (Mean $[prox_{index}]*1.4=Disp_{corr}$).

Proximity scores can also be applied as a measure of *discriminance*. Theoretically, attitudes of two sectoral elite groups can be defined as discriminant, when, on average, respondents' distance to the mean of the other sector exceeds the distance to the mean of their own sector, that is, prox (inter) > prox (intra). In practical application, discriminance is however only assumed once, on average, prox (inter) clearly exceeds prox (intra). To moreover account for differences in group size, discriminance between two sectors y and z is thus assumed, once

Mean [prox (inter$_y$) - prox (intra$_y$)] >0.1 and
Mean [prox (inter$_z$) - prox (intra$_z$)] >0.1.   (5.2)

As for the case of dispersion, a boundary zone is applied that ranges from 0.05 to 0.15. In the course of the analysis, the average of the discriminance scores for both sectors is interpreted as an overall discriminance score, indicating not only presence or absence but also the degree of discriminance.

INTER-SECTORAL COHESION FROM NORTH TO SOUTH

How likely are the political communication elites in the six countries under study to display high levels of inter-sectoral cohesion? Based on the expectations put forth in chapter 3, a fluid social structure is thought to decrease cohesion, while horizontal mobility should in turn increase inter-elite cohesion. Moreover, inter-elite cohesion can generally be expected to be high, when the media and political system are characterized by low degrees of (mutual) autonomy and high sectoral variety, in particular positional variety. Political autonomy from subjugation to or collusion with other third-party sectoral elites (interest groups, business, church, military, etc.) further increases the propensity of inter-elite cohesion between media and politics.

With respect to the patterns of cohesion, vertical mobility is expected to lead to similarity (B), horizontal mobility fosters mixing (C) or even consensus (D). A fluid social structure and low horizontal mobility, combined with high sectoral autonomy and low sectoral variety, will in turn make cohesion as separation (A) most likely. Turning to the political system and the media system, high positional variety and a lack of autonomy in the shape of collusion are assumed to result in indistinction and mixing (C), as opposed to similarity. Infringement of autonomy in the shape of subjugation, by contrast, is assumed to result in cohesion as similarity (B) or consensus (D).

Finally, the social structure and system conditions of a country have been assumed to make specific guiding principles dominant. For one, pragmatism has been argued to be particularly relevant for elite cohesion in countries with a fluid social structure and low horizontal mobility between elites. The principle of ideology has been associated with high positional variety in both sectors. Publicity has been linked to countries with a tradition of state intervention based on a thinking of social responsibility of societal sectors and a resulting commitment to a common good or the public interest. Given that the absolute extent of inter-elite cohesion presumably varies between countries, such effects should become visible in a relative accentuation of individual principles within each country. Similarities in the accentuation of guiding principles between countries must however not automatically mean that these countries display a common stance on a guiding principle. Rather, they signify that systemic conditions make an elite negotiation on this principle all the more immanent.

Taken together, general assumptions about the effect of context on inter-elite cohesion and the attributes of social structure, the media system and the political system outlined in the preceding chapter results in the following overall proposition: inter-elite cohesion can be assumed to increase from north to south, being low in the two Nordic countries, medium in the Central European and high in the Mediterranean countries.

Sweden displays a systemic context that most consistently suggests a low propensity for inter-elite cohesion (A) in political communication, based on the political autonomy of the media system, the de-concentration and contained polarization of the political system and a generally fluid social structure. However, a rather pronounced elite consensus is also part of a broader consensus orientation in society, which includes a strong commitment to state intervention in the name of public service. As a result of this tradition, cohesion among Swedish political communication elites is likely to rest on the principle of publicity, while the fluid social structure in Sweden suggests an additional focus on the principle of pragmatism. Overall, the Northern neighbour Denmark is assumed to display low levels of inter-elite cohesion (A) for similar reasons. However, Denmark also features partisan media audiences and a long-standing tradition of political polarization, which increases the propensity for inter-elite cohesion as mixing (C). Due to such polarization, cohesion in Denmark will rest more strongly on the principle of ideology than in Sweden, as well as on the principle of pragmatism.

The systemic context in Germany all in all suggests a medium propensity to inter-elite cohesion. Mass-orientation, de-centralization and a low degree of state intervention in the press sector are met by a clear adherence to a system of politics-in-broadcasting. Likewise, the political sector is characterized by a low degree of power concentration, but still far from a true multi-party system. Contained polarization and low partisanship in media audiences furthermore suggest that inter-elite cohesion will rest on similarity (B), rather than mixing. A relatively weak tradition for state intervention and partisanship suggest that cohesion will mostly rest on the principle of pragmatism. Overall, the social, medial and political context in Austria draws together a number of disparate elements, and attitudinal patterns are likely to reflect this. The propensity for inter-elite cohesion is likely to be higher than in Germany, especially due the weak autonomy of the media, as well as elements of corporatism and party-based clientelism in the political system. The relatively fluid social structure, however, does in turn lower the propensity for cohesion. As positional variety is rather contained in Austria, inter-elite cohesion should rest on similarity (B) and in some instances on consensus (D), rather than on mixing. As a result of its relatively open social structure, pragmatism can be expected to be the most defining principle of cohesion.

France, on the other hand, has a decisively higher propensity for inter-elite cohesion due to a closed social structure and the limits to media autonomy imposed by a high degree of state intervention, the model of politics-over-broadcasting, a rather elite-oriented quality press and limited journalistic professionalization. The autonomy of the political system is higher, although political polarization increases the propensity for inter-elite cohesion based on sectoral variety substantially, especially in terms of a potential non-discriminance of attitudes that may lead to cohesion as mixing (C) or in some instances as consensus (D). High degrees of polarization and a strong commitment to the common good also mean that cohesion in France is most likely driven by the principles of ideology and publicity. The propensity for inter-elite cohesion is even higher in Spain, due to an elite-oriented press, low degrees of journalistic professionalization and a weak system of public broadcasting prone to political instrumentalization. Lack of media autonomy is further reinforced by a strong bipartisanship in media audiences, as well as bipartisanship and front stage polarization in the political system, making Spain the most likely candidate to display cohesion as consensus (D), although decentralization of the political system and limited horizontal elite mobility (at least in regard to the media sector) may pull in other directions. Due to the high positional variety in the media sector, cohesion in Spain should be most firmly based on the principle of ideology.

Levels and Principles of Inter-Sectoral Cohesion: Overall Results

Figure 5.1 displays the dispersion and discriminance score for each of the three guiding principles in the six countries under study: ideology, publicity and pragmatism. The guiding principles are represented by a composite indicator that comprises the value, procedural and epistemological dimension of each principle. Countries are ordered according to their geographic position within Europe, from the northernmost (Sweden) to the southernmost (Spain), in order to give a visual indication of whether the assumed increase in attitudinal consonance along the three country groups from north to south can indeed be found. An increase of attitudinal consonance is equivalent to a decrease in dispersion or discriminance, which would suggest a downward sloping curve.

The assumed increase in attitudinal consonance can indeed be observed, albeit to varying degrees for the individual guiding principles. It appears most clearly for the principle of *ideology*, both for discriminance (rhombus/striped line) and for dispersion (rhombus/dotted line) scores. While there is

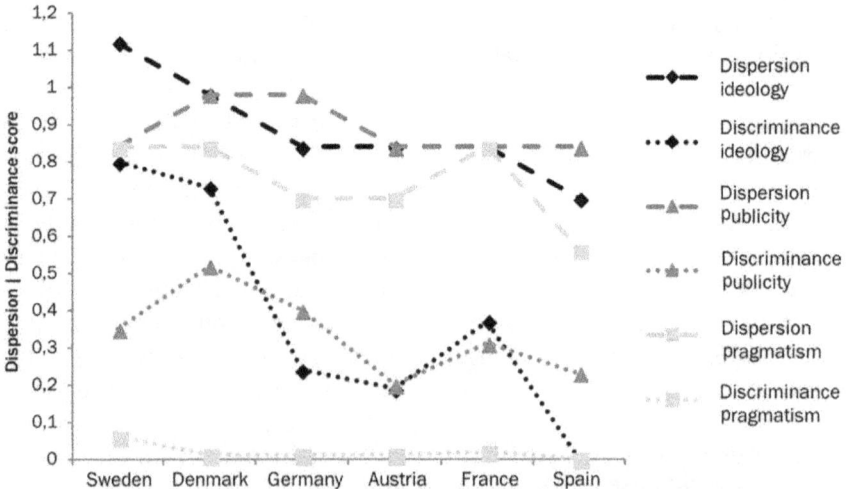

Figure 5.1. Inter-Sectoral Cohesion from North to South

Dispersion and discriminance scores by country and guiding principle; theoretical range of scale is 0 to 2 for dispersion scores, and −2 to 2 for discriminance scores. Cut-off points between high and low dispersion, resp. discriminance are defined as the theoretical middle of each scale, that is, 1 for dispersion and 0 for discriminance.

virtually complete absence of cohesion between media and political elites in Sweden when it comes to ideology, Danish media and political elites are already somewhat closer together, both with regard to the dispersion and discriminance of attitudes. In Germany and Austria, both dispersion and discriminance are as expected lower than in the two Nordic countries. France, however, resembles the Central European countries more closely than Spain, thus breaking with the assumed high level of inter-sectoral cohesion in the Mediterranean countries. Spanish elites are most consonant when it comes to ideology, in terms of both a low dispersion of attitudes and a virtual absence of attitudinal discriminance.

The *publicity* principle, for its part, appears more consistent across the different countries as the principle of ideology. Generally speaking, all countries are characterized by (in some cases weak) form of cohesion between media and political elites, as their dispersion scores are below or close to one. An increasing degree of consonance from north to south can, however, still be tentatively observed. Although differences in the basic dispersion scores are rather small (triangle/striped line), the degree of discriminance (triangle/dotted line) between the two sector groups nevertheless varies considerably across countries: the two sectoral elite groups can best be distinguished in Denmark, followed by Germany, Sweden and France, while the lowest levels of discriminance are found, as expected, in Spain, as well as in Austria.

Variation appears least pronounced in the case of *pragmatism*, that is, a guiding principle based on a more or less tacit agreement to largely mind each other's (sectoral) business, as well as an underlying understanding that – beyond all democratic and ideological considerations – everyone is in the end just doing his or her job.[1] Given the nature of such pragmatism, it may not be surprising that the level of contention, and thus the variation across countries, is rather limited. While discriminance is universally low (square/dotted line), a slight decrease in dispersion from north to south is nevertheless visible – once again with France as the main outlier (square/striped line).

Relative Importance of Guiding Principles

Figure 5.1 not only displays the changing level of attitudinal consonance from north to south but also shows the relative weight of each guiding principle within each country. Comparing the dispersion and discriminance of attitudes of a particular guiding principle vis-à-vis the other principles in this way gives a measure of the relative importance of the guiding principles in each country, irrespective of the absolute levels of dispersion and discriminance. In this respect, the results show that pragmatism is the principle yielding most cohesion in all countries in absolute terms.

This is even true for the French elites, for which cohesion was assumed to rest the least on pragmatism, due to its closed elite structure. However, France sets itself clearly apart from the remaining countries insofar as, at least in terms of dispersion, the principle of pragmatism is on par with both publicity and ideology. Sweden constitutes the only other case where pragmatism is matched by another guiding principle in a similar manner, albeit only by the principle of publicity in this case. The significant weight of publicity in both Sweden and France can be traced back to the strong traditions of state intervention for purposes of public interest characteristic of both countries. The relative strong focus on publicity as a guiding principle of cohesion in these two countries must however not be equated with a common stance on questions of openness versus secrecy, as the definition of 'public interest' and the 'common good' may well differ substantially between the French and the Swedish tradition.

Swedish elite cohesion has furthermore been expected to be least guided by ideology, which is supported by figure 5.1. In this respect, Sweden was expected to differ from neighbouring Denmark due to differences in the level of political polarization, according to which Danish elites should cohere stronger on ideology than Swedish elites. At the same time, pragmatism should also be an important principle of elite cohesion in Denmark. The empirical results corroborate this expectation: although consonance based on ideology is barely higher in Denmark than in Sweden in terms of discriminance, the relative level of attitudinal dispersion is indeed much lower, on par with publicity.

For Germany and Austria, pragmatism is as expected the dominant principle of cohesion. With regard to the remaining two principles, the weight of publicity in Austria is on par with ideology in terms of both dispersion and discriminance, and thus noticeably higher than in Germany. A likely explanation is the particular circumstances surrounding the level of state intervention in Austria: although not displaying the same level of public interest driven state intervention as Sweden and France, Austria has a strong tradition of direct press subsidies, resulting an ongoing negotiation of the public role of the media drawing substantial interest. As expected, the prevalence of ideology in Spain far exceeds any of the remaining countries. Although the degree of pragmatism is also an important element of elite relations in Spain, polarization and bi-partisanship make the negotiation of ideology a vital part of political communication.

In general, the comparison of dispersion and discriminance scores supports the expectation of a north to south axis and its underlying assumptions about the impact of contextual factors on the overall extent of attitudinal consonance across countries, as well as on the relative weight of specific guiding principles of elite cohesion within countries. However, the assumed increase of consonance from Northern to Southern Europe appears most pronounced for the guiding principle of ideology, whereas the guiding principles of publicity and pragmatism appear more subject to specific contextual conditions in individual countries. This latter observation provides a first indication of the different rationalities behind the cohesion of political communication elites in the six countries under study.

However, the analysis also conveys a rather general picture. The composite scores, on which the analysis is based, disregard the consistency, or lack thereof, of guiding principles. This means that differences between cohesion based on value, procedural and epistemological consonance are not taken into account. Attention to the individual sources of attitudinal consonance behind each principle yields further insight into the patterns of inter-sectoral cohesion across countries, which do not appear on the level of composite measures. Moreover, the more nuanced analysis of attitudinal sources reveals differences in stance towards various dimensions and hence the overall consistency of guiding principles. Indeed, as the following section will show, neither of the principles is accepted (or rejected) in a consistent manner across all sources of cohesion in any of the countries.

PRINCIPLES, PATTERNS AND STANCES OF INTER-SECTORAL ELITE COHESION

The following section analyses each of the attitudinal sources of the three guiding principles separately. Moving to a more disaggregated analysis in this way yields further insight into the extent of cohesion by concentrating on more specific patterns of attitudinal consonance based on various combinations of dispersion and discriminance of attitudes. As discussed in chapter 3, we can distinguish between four patterns of inter-sectoral cohesion: *separation* in cases where cohesion is entirely absent due to a combination of high dispersion and discriminance (Type A) and *consensus* where both dispersion and discriminance are low (D). The combination of high dispersion and low discriminance scores results in *cohesion as mixing* (C), while *cohesion as similarity* (B) denotes the case of low dispersion and high discriminance values.

Correspondingly, this part of the analysis presents data in a coordinate system representing these possible patterns of inter-sectoral cohesion for each of the guiding principles. In addition to the information displayed in the coordinate system, group means indicate the underlying stance, that is, whether cohesion is based on the common acceptance or rejection with regard to the particular sources of cohesion. In this way, the analysis additionally gives a deeper understanding of the underlying guiding principles of cohesion by focusing on the internal coherence of each principle in relation to the sources of cohesion, as well as the attitudinal stance associated with different principles and sources.

Ideology

In many ways, the guiding principle of ideology is the most fundamental one in the media-politics relationship in European democracies. 'When the newspaper began to emerge as a force in political life, [political advocacy] became its principal function in every [European] country' (Hallin and Mancini 2004, 26). The primacy of this function disappeared with the establishment of commercial media, opening up a wide spectrum of scenarios for the media-politics relationship, all of which revolve around the question of how media and political elites handle the question of neutrality and partisanship. If political alignment of the media can no longer be assumed as the normal condition, political communication elites are bound to negotiate a balance between advocacy and neutrality in political communication.

Ideology can, as is the case with all of the guiding principles, be linked to specific values and roles, procedural ideals and epistemologies. Thus operationalized, the guiding principle of ideology can be seen to express itself in the complementary roles committed to partisanship in political communication (editorial guide/gladiator), the procedural agreement on the relevance of political convictions for politicians and journalists in their encounters with each other, as well as the understanding that individual media outlets reflect political divisions (political parallelism).

Figure 5.2 juxtaposes the respective national dispersion and discriminance for all three sources of elite cohesion (values, procedures, epistemology). Each attitudinal item is displayed with a country label, as well as a distinct shape distinguishing the three sources of cohesion. Higher scores indicate higher levels of attitudinal dispersion or discriminance for each individual attitudinal item. The two axes intersect at the defined threshold between low and high dispersion, as well as low and high discriminance; the grey zone along the two axes marks corresponding boundary cases. Each point in the coordinate system can be directly interpreted as an expression of a particular pattern of inter-sectoral cohesion. Points in the upper-right corner indicate separation (A), in the upper-left corner, similarity (B), in the lower-right corner, mixing (C) and in the lower-left corner, consensus (D). Dispersion scores, discriminance scores, cohesion patterns and mean stances for all principles and sources are summarized in the appendix.

As can be seen, the gradual increase in inter-sectoral cohesion based on ideology from north to south is not the result of a uniform increase in value consonance (circles), procedural consonance (triangles) and epistemological

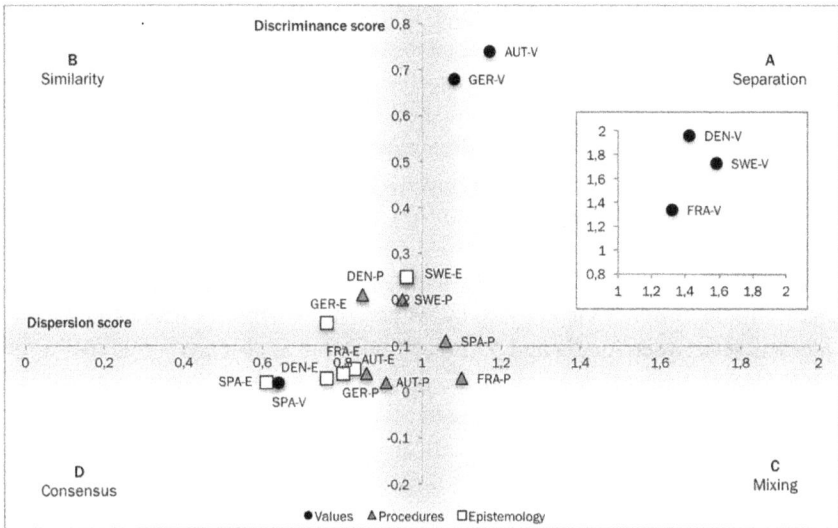

Figure 5.2. Ideology – Patterns and Sources of Cohesion
Dispersion and discriminance scores by country (SWE = Sweden, DEN = Denmark, GER = Germany, AUT = Austria, FRA = France, SPA = Spain) and sources of cohesion (V = Values, P = Procedures, E = Epistemology); theoretical range of scale is 0 to 2 for dispersion scores, and –2 to 2 for discriminance scores.

consonance (squares). Rather, the substantial lack of *value* consonance, indicated by high levels of attitudinal dispersion and discriminance (A), largely offsets the other sources of cohesion in all countries but Spain, where elites reach consensus also on the value dimension of ideology (D).

While the value consensus in Spain can be attributed to an accepting stance towards the role match between a politically active editorial guide and a gladiator-type politician, stances consequently diverge between media elites and political elites in the remaining countries, albeit to varying degree. Whereas the political role of gladiator is embraced by political elites in the Nordic countries, the role of editorial guide is outright rejected. Discrepancies in role adherence are, however, less drastic in the Central European countries, where media elites take an ambivalent stance on the role of editorial guide. Country groups can thus also be distinguished in the degree of absence of cohesion. Noticeably, France breaks decisively with the Mediterranean tradition of a common stance on partisan political communication roles, superseding even the Central European countries due to an outright rejection of the role of editorial guide by the French media elites.

Attitudinal consonance between media and political elites becomes somewhat higher when turning to the level of *procedural consonance*. However, it remains low in the case of the Nordic countries, placing them between absence of cohesion altogether and cohesion as similarity (A-B). In the remaining countries, cohesion based on the assessment of the procedural dimension of ideology results in non-discriminance or mixing (C): political and media elites cannot be distinguished based on the relevance of political convictions in their interaction with members from the other elite sector. It is, however, not the Mediterranean countries, as suggested by the initial assumption, but the Central European countries (C-D) that approach consensus in this matter.

This near-consensus in Germany and Austria is based on the shared stance that political convictions are largely, although not entirely irrelevant for the interaction between media and political elites, that is, a shared rejection of the procedural aspects of ideology. In the remaining countries, media elites rebuff the idea that political convictions matter for interaction even more than political elites do. Only the Spanish political communication elites assign some relevance to political convictions as a factor in interaction, but even here can media elites and political elites not find common ground on the matter.

Figure 5.2 finally reveals that the difference in cohesion levels between the two Nordic countries Sweden and Denmark stems exclusively from the *epistemological* aspects of ideology, that is, whether cohesion is based on a common understanding of the presence or absence of political alignment of media outlets (political parallelism). Whereas the dispersion and discriminance scores place Denmark within the pattern of cohesion as consensus (D), Swedish elites waver between complete separation and similarity (A-B). Indeed, political elites in both countries are rather similar in their stance by perceiving media outlets as somewhat politically positioned. When it comes to the media elite, however, only the Danish journalists and editors match the assessment of their political counterpart.

The state of consensus (D) found in Denmark is thus closer to the Mediterranean countries than to the fellow member of the Nordic group. In Spain and France, political communication elites unanimously judge the level of political parallelism in the media system to be substantial. As expected, sector differences are more pronounced in the Central European countries. While Austria's elites range somewhere between full cohesion and cohesion as similarity (B-D), Germany represents a clear case of cohesion of similarity (B): the overall dispersion of attitudes is rather low, but the two elite sectors are clearly discernible.

In sum, cohesion based on the principle of ideology is not consistent across the three sources of cohesion in any of the six countries. The variations in value, procedural and epistemological consonance display some important patterns. In all cases but the Swedish, political communication elites are consonant on at least one dimension of the principle of ideology. Consonance is most frequently reached on the epistemological dimension of ideology, not least due to the historical reminiscences of press-party parallelism. In this respect, Denmark, France and, to some extent, also Austria break away most decisively from the assumed state of cohesion of their country group. All three countries show a pattern of *externalized politicization*, meaning that the political leanings of the media are unanimously seen as a structural given but rejected on the level of roles at the same time.

In Denmark, consensus on the epistemological dimension may be interpreted as a sign of the ongoing polarization of the political sphere that has never really ceased to be relevant for Danish politics. Noticeably, Danish elites not only consent on the extent of political parallelism but also consent that such parallelism is alive and well, and not only a relic from the days of partisan newspapers. Even though they accept that political polarization does not spare the media sector, media elites keep their professional identity as neutral information gatherers and providers alive. France, for its part, is defined by a quite distinct journalistic self-understanding that may counterbalance polarization: media elites break away from the partisan consensus in refuting any partisanship in their professional self-understanding. In contrast to Denmark, the homogeneity of the French elite structure has a tempering effect on the procedural dimension. Here we find the pattern of cohesion as mixing (C) that was assumed to be characteristic for France in particular, and the Mediterranean model in general. The pattern can thus also be seen in Spain (A-C). Partisanship on the procedural level is a contentious issue, but one that cuts across sectoral lines.

Despite the influence of an Anglo-American form of objective and neutral political communication, it still appears easier for European political communication elites to consent on the acceptance than on the rejection of ideology as a principle guiding their interaction. The difficulty in maintaining cohesion based on the rejection of ideology becomes particularly obvious in the procedural dimension. In procedural terms, both political and media elites are relatively reluctant to accept ideological considerations as basis of interaction. With the exception of the Central European countries, however, journalists refute ideology as a procedural norm even more fervently than the political elites.

Publicity

Cohesion based on the publicity principle involves a common understanding of the democratic role of the media within society in general and the political sphere in particular. As in the case of ideology, the guiding principle of publicity goes to the core of the media-politics relationship: the principle of publicity can be said to give rise to a basic trade-off between transparency and secrecy that is still a matter of contention in political communication, just as the trade-off between ideological alignment and neutrality presents a persisting issue of contention in all modern democracies.

Looking at the sources of attitudinal consonance, the publicity principle is associated with the journalistic role of the watchdog with the political role of information provider on the level of values, with the legitimacy of journalistic disclosure on the level of procedures and the impact of the media on democracy on the level of epistemology.

The respective national dispersion and discriminance scores for these three sources of cohesion (values, procedures, epistemology) are juxtaposed in figure 5.3. Again, each point in the coordinate system can thus be directly interpreted as an expression of a particular pattern of inter-sectoral cohesion. Points in the upper-right corner indicate separation (A), in the upper-left corner similarity (B), in the lower-right corner mixing (C) and in the lower-left corner consensus (D). Dispersion scores, discriminance scores, cohesion patterns and mean stances for all principles and sources are summarized in the appendix.

As demonstrated by figure 5.3, all countries display patterns of consensus (D) or cohesion as similarity (B) when attitudes refer to values and epistemology, while procedural consonance is absent (A). In particular, Denmark,

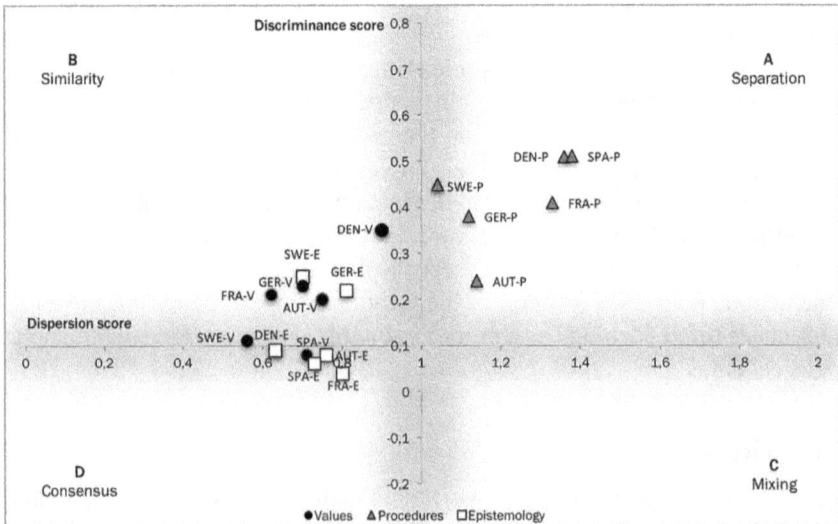

Figure 5.3. Publicity – Patterns and Sources of Cohesion

Dispersion and discriminance scores by country (SWE = Sweden, DEN = Denmark, GER = Germany, AUT = Austria, FRA = France, SPA = Spain) and sources of cohesion (V = Values, P = Procedures, E = Epistemology); theoretical range of scale is 0 to 2 for dispersion scores, and −2 to 2 for discriminance scores.

France and Spain display a strong separation of the two elite groups on procedural matters (triangles).

The high level of attitudinal separation on the procedural level stands in sharp opposition to the substantial level of cohesion based on *values* (circles). Indeed, the journalistic commitment to the role of a watchdog to government is so widespread that it can be considered a more or less universal self-perception of European political journalists (and indeed journalists across the globe [see Hanitzsch et al. 2011; Reese 2001]). As did the media role of a watchdog, the political information provider serving the public need for relevant information draws similar commitment from politicians in all of the included countries, suggesting a routine commitment to transparency and accountability on the political side (see also Håkansson and Mayerhöffer 2014). However, media elites embrace the idea of a watchdog to such an astonishing degree that they still fall short of being fully cohesive with the political elites, despite the fact that the latter group maintains strong support for their role of an information provider as well. Cohesion as consensus is approximated only in Spain and in Sweden (B-D), while Danish political elites most decisively diverge from their journalist colleagues (A-B).

As chapter 6 will show in more detail, a crucial factor in this result is the lack of internal consonance within the political sector, in particular between political decision makers and communication professionals, which is particularly pronounced in Denmark. Generally, political communication specialists and political decision makers do not embrace the role of an information provider to the same degree (see also data in appendix).[2] Put differently, the nature of their position gives communication professionals a soberer position towards the ambitious value commitment to publicity. Noticeably, this is not true for the Spanish communication professionals, presumably due to the lower differentiation into political decision making and political communication careers. If we preclude the group of communication professionals from the analysis, all countries indeed approach (B-D), with Sweden and Austria reaching consensus (D) on the role complementarity of political decision makers and media elites.

What seems almost common sense for political elites and media elites on the value level, however, does not translate to a mutual understanding on the *procedural* level. Although the shared role commitments may appear solid, agreement about the procedural norm of disclosure in the political sphere is much harder to attain. When it comes to judging the legitimacy of journalistic disclosure of confidential documents, elites from the media sector and the political sector clearly do not consent. Given that elites are strongly divided over the issue intra-sectorally (see chapter 6), the high degrees of discriminance are remarkable. Based on the degree of dispersion and discriminance alone, there are no national differences to be found in the procedural dimension: all countries display clear separation (A) on the issue (figure 5.3.). As shown in figure 5.4, however, some interesting results emerge if we look closer at the particular nature of this separation in terms of the actual degree of disagreement between the two sectors.

Indeed, the Mediterranean, Central European and Northern countries deal quite differently with the immanent struggle between transparency and secrecy in modern societies. Most strikingly, not even the watchdogs themselves perceive it as legitimate to publish confidential political information without permission in Germany and Austria. Roughly half of the journalists refute this in all or all but exceptional cases. Yet, even on this level, they do not reach common ground with the political elites, who are – in contrast to their more nuanced peers in the other countries – more or less unanimously rejecting the procedural aspect of publicity.

Media and political elites fall short of full cohesion on the level of *epistemological consonance* in all of the included countries (figure 5.3). High degrees of similarity approximating consensus do appear, however, in the two Southern countries, as well as Denmark and Austria. Yet, cohesion is only based on a shared acceptance of the structural dimension of publicity in Denmark and Spain. In France and Austria, media and political elites share a rather ambiguous evaluation of the media's contribution to democracy. In the latter case, the shared suspicion of how beneficial the media really are to democracy provides the structural basis for a scenario in which the commitment to political communication roles associated with transparency stands in sharp contrast to the negation of the procedural norm of disclosure. Germany and Sweden, finally, represent clear cases of cohesion as similarity (B), in which acceptance within the media sector exceeds the more reluctant stance of the political sector elites.

Looking *across* all three attitudinal dimensions, the level of internal inconsistency on the principle of publicity shows that the struggle between transparency and secrecy challenges elite relations in all countries under study. In contrast to the principle of ideology, however, the lines of conflict are less clear-cut and not country-specific. Apart from the near-global commitment to watchdog journalism and transparency in the value dimension, two patterns can be tentatively observed. For one, cohesion between media and political elites primarily rests on epistemological consonance in Denmark, Austria and France. However, the north/south axis is by no means completely irrelevant for the principle of publicity. The three country pairs largely follow this axis is judged by the procedural stance on publicity, albeit in terms of how substantial the level of disagreement is rather than the overall level of cohesion (figure 5.4).

In general, the Nordic media elites seem to have resolved the struggle between transparency and secrecy through a journalistic position in clear

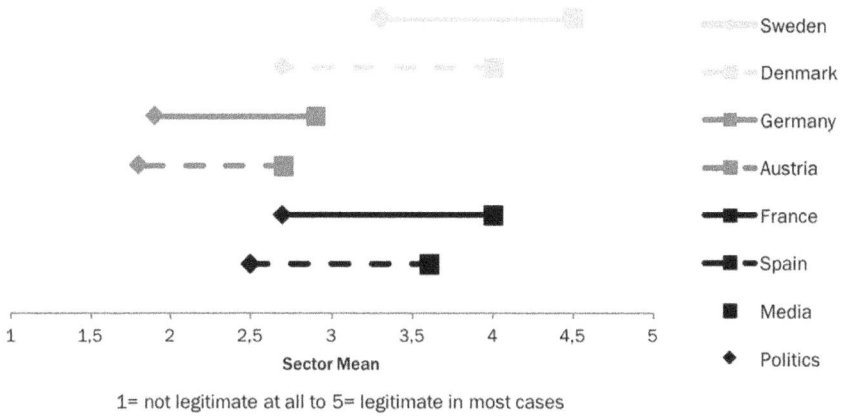

Figure 5.4. Legitimacy of Disclosure (Sector Means by Country)

favour of disclosure, which inevitably leads to built-in conflicts with the political elites, displaying the transition from former party press days to a modern checks-and-balances relationship between media and politics. The Mediterranean countries, for their part, lack a long-standing tradition of investigative journalism (Hallin and Mancini 2004) but are accustomed to higher degrees of polarization and contention in politics and political communication. The case of Spain, in particular, shows that cohesion based on ideology and publicity are not mutually exclusive: 'In the Spanish case, investigative reporting . . . [is] more closely tied to party politics in the sense that media . . . [reveals] scandals about their partisan enemies' (Hallin and Mancini 2004, 124).

Finally, Germany and Austria display a particularly striking discrepancy between value commitment and procedural stances. A tentative explanation is provided by the fact that the political communication context in Germany and Austria in many ways takes a middle position between the Nordic and the Southern models (see chapter 4). While these contextual conditions often result in what could be called tempered attitudinal patterns among its political communication elites, the same Central European middle-way appears to be most conflicted in the struggle between transparency and secrecy. While models of quasi-institutionalized indiscretion (e.g. 'speaking terms' and 'background circles') are of course in place in all political communication environments, it appears that this model has come under particular pressure in the German-speaking countries, leaving media elites largely undecided, whether and when the established arrangements of (in)confidentiality may be bypassed.

Pragmatism

In addition to the principles of ideology and publicity, the media-politics relationship can be guided by the recognition of the instrumental needs of both sectors, resulting in a give-and-take relationship where publicity can be exchanged for information. Cohesion based on such instrumental recognition of the different interests that drive the two political communication elites can be said to entail a guiding principle of pragmatism, based on which the two sides may choose to act both cooperative and antagonistic towards each other. Being part of a business-like relationship is by no means alien to political communication elites in modern democracies.

Given the nature of pragmatism, the complementary roles constituting the value source of cohesion are somewhat different from the case of ideology and publicity. In the case of pragmatism, the roles are rather self-referential and focused on the fundamental interests of either sector: journalists seek to maximize the reach of their published goods, while politicians transfer their basic political ambition to the public arena by striving to influence political decisions via the media. On the procedural level, the principle of pragmatism is measured as the degree to which conflicts between politicians and journalists are seen to derive from an inevitable clash of interests. Finally, in terms of epistemological consonance, the principle of pragmatism is associated with recognition of the commercial pressures that drive the media and hence produce a fundamentally different logic than the logic found on the political side of the table. The overall distribution of dispersion and discriminance scores across the three sources of cohesion (values, procedures, epistemology) is displayed by figure 5.5. As for the previous sections on ideology and publicity, each point in the coordinate system can be directly interpreted as an expression of a particular pattern of inter-sectoral cohesion. Points in the upper-right corner indicate separation (A), in the upper-left corner similarity (B), in the lower-right corner mixing (C) and in the lower-left corner consensus (D). As many of the individual country scores are clustered closely together, figure 5.5 displays all scores in the overall coordinate system, as well as in an enlarged section. Dispersion scores, discriminance scores, cohesion patterns and mean stances for all principles and sources are summarized in the appendix.

In general, the results display a clear gravitation towards full cohesion, or consensus (D), for all countries. However, differences between the source of cohesion and countries can still be discerned. The tendency towards consensus is most noticeable for epistemological consonance (squares). For value and even more procedural consonance, both the dispersion and the discriminance of attitudes become more pronounced. Cohesion is somewhat less pronounced in Germany and Sweden, where the two sectors are still discernible

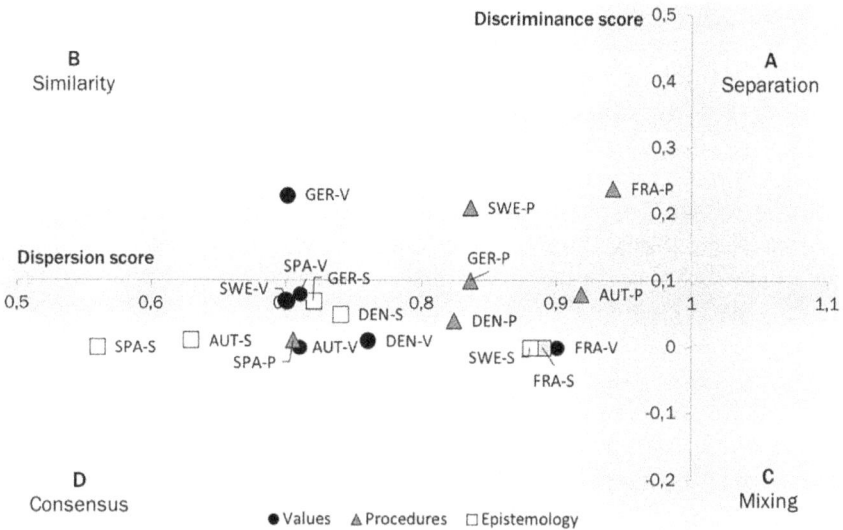

Figure 5.5. Pragmatism – Patterns and Sources of Cohesion
Dispersion and discriminance scores by country (SWE = Sweden, DEN = Denmark, GER = Germany, AUT = Austria, FRA = France, SPA = Spain) and sources of cohesion (V = Values, P = Procedures, E = Epistemology); theoretical range of scale is 0 to 2 for dispersion scores, and –2 to 2 for discriminance scores. Axes are shortened for reasons of visualization.

to some degree. France, on the other hand, shows signs of cohesion based on non-discriminance (C), as attitudes are overall quite dispersed. Thus, as has been seen already in the previous section, the principle of pragmatism predominantly sets apart countries *within* the same country group.

With regard to *values* as a source of cohesion, the self-referential roles of the journalistic mass communicator and the strategic political communicator find widespread support within both sectors in all countries. The purpose of reaching the largest audience possible and using the media for purely instrumental purposes as a politician are widely accepted and thus form the backbone of the overall convergence towards cohesion as consensus (D). As seen in figure 5.5, this widespread acceptance is somewhat less pervasive in Sweden (B-D), Germany (B-D) and France (C-D).

Turning to the *procedural level*, cohesion between the two sectors can still be observed in the case of Denmark, Germany and Spain, albeit based on an ambiguous rather than an accepting stance. In the remaining countries, media elites assume a more affirmative stance towards the notion that conflicts derive from an inevitable clash of interests than their political counterparts. These different procedural approaches to pragmatism can also be seen in the significance media and political elites assign to a structurally given clash of interests as a reason for conflict between media and political elites, relative to four other potential reasons (incorrectness of information given/rendered, unfairness, disrespect and non-compliance with agreements,[3] see also Pfetsch et al. 2014).

In Spain and Denmark, diverging interests rank equally high among media and political elites as the reason for conflicts with members from the other sector (as the second and first most important reason, respectively). In Germany and Austria, political elites rate incorrect information in the media as a more likely cause of conflict than a structural clash of interests, thus slightly diverging from the stance of the journalistic elites in this respect, who perceive a structural clash of interests as the most decisive reason for conflict. More fundamental divergence is found in France and Sweden: French media elites name diverging professional interests as the main reason for conflict, while politicians on average assess this as the least important of all. Although operating on a lower level of perceived conflict overall, a similar discrepancy appears for the Swedish elites (see also Pfetsch et al. 2014).

Media and political elites are competitors in the public arena, but they are not competing for the same end. Thus, their attempts to fulfil their sectoral goals may be beneficial to members of the other elite group in one instance and detrimental in another. The real competition awaits them in their home sector. In 'epistemological' terms, this state of affairs can be said to come to fore only with the development of commercial media organizations and a degree of market orientation, which influences media reporting as well as political attempts to influence political decision making via communication. As shown in figure 5.5, all countries approach or reach full cohesion when judging the influence of commercial restraints on media reporting. Differences appear rather minimal and, moreover, deviate from country groupings along the north/south axis.

Spanish and Austrian elites are fully consonant in their perception of the commercial orientation in media reporting (D), while German elite attitudes set themselves slightly apart with a faint distinction between the two sectors (B-D). The two Nordic countries and France, on the other hand, are characterized by cohesion as mixing, bordering on consensus (C-D). In other words, political communication elites in the latter three countries are divided over the issue of commercial influences on media reporting, but not along sectoral lines. The sectoral stances show that the Nordic countries also part ways with the other countries in another respect: in contrast to the remaining countries, cohesion in Denmark and Sweden is based on the rejection or at least hesitation to regard commercial restraints on media reporting as a structural condition of political communication. This struggle with the commercial nature of media takes place across sectoral lines, leading to this particular form of cohesion.

In general, the results with regard to attitudinal patterns of pragmatism *across* the different sources of cohesion are rather mixed in relation to the expectations advanced in chapter 4. For Spain and Germany, the results are largely as expected: the former is once again the country with the most consistent and pervasive cohesion between media and political elites, the latter a good example of cohesion as similarity. However, the German elites approach consensus more strongly than originally assumed. This is even more pronounced in Austria. In contrast to the three remaining countries, dispersion of attitudes is clearly contained in the Central European countries, underlining the assumption that they will resort to cohesion as mixing only in exceptional cases (C). Cohesion based on low discriminance rather than low dispersion of attitudes is – as expected – the domain of the socially homogeneous and horizontally mobile French elites operating in a systemic environment characterized by political polarization and an ongoing fundamental reassessment of the role of political journalism.

The fact that both Nordic countries are more cohesive than expected, as well as more polarized (cohesion as mixing) with regard to epistemological consonance is puzzling at first. It does, however, correspond to the previous finding for the principle of ideology, which showed countries with a lower degree of positional variety (in that case Germany and Austria) to display some features of cohesion as mixing as well. In contrast to the Mediterranean countries, however, cohesion as mixing only occurs here in connection with a negative stance on the principle in question. Given that instances of consonance based on the rejection of or reluctance towards a guiding principle are rather few, this allows for a tentative conclusion: cohesion as mixing is not only characteristic of countries with high positional variety in the political communication environment but more generally also for cohesion based on the rejection of a particular guiding principle.

SUMMARY: COHESION BETWEEN MEDIA AND POLITICAL ELITES

The analysis of the levels of inter-elite attitudinal consonance has shown that the extent of cohesion between media and political elites does indeed vary substantially across European countries. For one, levels of cohesion between media and political elites increase from north to south, roughly setting apart the Northern European, Central European and Mediterranean countries in terms of cohesion among political communication elites. Yet, these country groups are not characterized by a uniform or specific type of elite cohesion but rather share characteristic features in the congruence, discriminance and substance of their attitudinal patterns. These characteristics are further

characterized by substantial national idiosyncrasies in line with each country's particular systemic context discussed in the previous chapter.

As expected, a great deal of these national particularities can be traced back
to differences in adherence to the three guiding principles at the heart of elite
interaction in political communication: ideology, publicity and pragmatism.
Depending on the particular constellation of contextual conditions in each
country, elite cohesion rests on these three principles to a varying degree.
As a result of a strong tradition of state intervention in the media system, the
principle of publicity is relatively significant in Sweden and France, as well
as in Austria. Ideology, on the other hand, is a particularly important principle
of cohesion in Spain. While pragmatism is an important guiding principle of
elite cohesion in political communication in all countries, it is particularly
crucial in relation to the other principles in the Central European countries,
as well as Denmark.

With regard to the expected patterns of cohesion, the more general observation of increasing consonance from north to south is subject to an important
amendment: one of the two countries belonging to the three hypothesized
groups constitute a textbook example of the patterns associated with that
group (Sweden, Germany, Spain), whereas the other country in the three
pairs (Denmark, Austria, France) deviates from this default pattern. The most
likely explanation for this rather systematic distinction of cohesion patterns
within each of the three country pairs is that the latter three countries are in a
particularly transitional period within political communication. As chapter 4
has shown, the nature of the media-politics relationship in each of these three
countries is being challenged and redefined – not least in the face of growing
polarization and populism in the political sphere.

Sweden is the most consistent example of a country with limited cohesion in the political communication elite. The majority of cases qualify as
separation (A) or cohesion as similarity (B). However, even in the case
of Sweden, we find notable exceptions, in particular, with regard to the
principle of pragmatism. The level of cohesion in Denmark is also rather
low. In contrast to Sweden, however, the Danish case oscillates between
separation (A) and consensus (D), indicating an underlying polarization
of political communication. Germany is the prime example of a country
with a moderate level of cohesion based on similarity (B). While Austria
shares the emphasis on cohesion as similarity with its German neighbour,
the overall picture includes other patterns. This is also the case in France,
which is nevertheless characterized by a relatively high degree of emphasis
on cohesion as mixing (C). Finally, Spain represents a good example of
a country mostly characterized by cohesion as consensus (D) within the
political communication elite.

Cross-National Similarities

Albeit on different levels, there are substantial cross-national similarities in the extent and form of cohesion between the different sources of attitudinal consonance. Cohesion based on epistemological consonance appears most frequently, in particular, in connection with a low dispersion of attitudes, that is, cohesion as consensus (D) or similarity (B). Value consonance is also rather pronounced. The case of ideology shows that the match of two theoretically complementary roles may, however, also result in complete separation (A). Finally, cohesion as procedural consonance clearly proves the most elusive form of cohesion. At the same time, the overall difficulty in reaching shared procedural norms, also within sectors, leads to a relative high amount of cases of cohesion as mixing (C).

Although the (presumably) varying level of contention about individual attitudinal items must of course be taken into account here, prominent outlier cases for all guiding principles demonstrate that the degree of contention is not a structural feature engrained in the attitudinal item itself. Whether individual items appear contentious or not is in many ways already part of the belief system. Complete absence of cohesion between the two sectors in all countries appears in only one case, that is, the legitimacy of disclosure (indicating procedural consonance based on publicity). At the same time, the contentious nature of disclosure differs again from country to country, ranging from 'we can't agree whether it is never or pretty much never ok' to 'we can't agree whether it is always or almost always ok'. Again, the contentiousness of a given attitudinal item is clearly not cast in stone, in particular, seen in comparative perspective.

The lack of a consistent type of cohesion on any of the guiding principles, that is, a consistent stance towards one principle across all sources of cohesion, constitutes another important cross-national result. In the case of ideology, for example, elites may reject partisan communication roles, while still perceiving political parallelism as a prevalent structural condition. Elites from different sectors may also separate fundamentally on the value dimension of ideology while being fully coherent on the procedural dimension and structural conditions of ideology. One methodological reason behind this is certainly that the guiding principles (for good reasons) have been deduced theoretically, rather than empirically, thus presupposing a relationship between singular attitudes that may or may not be given in the actual elite belief systems.

With the political communication environment being subject to continuous transitions, the belief system of the political elites and media elites may be subject to changes at different speeds. As the results have shown, this may well lead to situations in which one dimension outpaces the other. Or, put differently, a situation in which elites adopt a new value stance while still adhering to established procedural norms or epistemologies. This is also reflected in the fact that instances of consonance based on the rejection of a guiding principle are very few. This is not to say that the two sides may not share the rejection of a certain aspect of interaction within political communication. However, they still diverge in their disagreement to such a degree that cohesion is rarely achieved, and, if it is achieved, it takes the shape of mixing rather than similarity.

The Impact of Social Structure: Alternative Explanations

The attitudinal patterns of media and political elites in each of the country under study have been explained as a result of (1) general assumptions about the nature of elite attitudes and principles of cohesion, (2) country groups from north to south and (3) specific contextual conditions in each country. Of the different factors thought to impact on the levels of inter-elite cohesion, the assumed impact of social fluidity and mobility on elite cohesion has appeared the most questionable. Most prominently, this can be seen in the case of France, where levels of cohesion have appeared much lower than originally expected.

A second look at the results reveals that it is in fact the country with the relatively more closed social structure within each country pair (Sweden, Germany and France, respectively) that displays lower overall levels of cohesion between media and political elites. This clearly opposes the original assumption that functional elites with a shared social background will be more cohesive; that is, that conformity in the elite structure brings about attitudinal ties. One possible explanation would be that the specific nature of elite relations between media and political actors makes it a particular case that deviates from the normal assumptions about elite relations. As discussed in chapter 2, some elite theorists (e.g. Hartmann 2007b) debate the elite status of high-ranking journalists entirely, while many others point to the specific role of media elites as counter-elites (e.g. Etzioni-Halevy 1993).

If one regards media elites as being *outside* of established elite circles, elite homogeneity would indeed lower the propensity for elite cohesion in political communication, so the argument goes, as it creates a more distinct dividing line between established political elites and media non-elites or counter-elites. However, the analysis of the different social contexts in chapter 5 has shown that, judged by their demographic background, media elites are generally on par with their political peers and in some cases, namely in France and Sweden, well integrated into class-based elite circles. Even if one considers the general social set-up (such as the permeability of the class structure) and, in particular, the social status of high-ranking media actors, the overall extent of inter-elite cohesion in political communication is comparatively low, and definitely lower as these social factors suggest.

Further cause connection between increased elite heterogeneity and decreasing cohesion can be found in the work of Suzanne Keller. Keller argues that the increasing complexity and differentiation of the elite structure as a whole, as well as a lack of 'ties of kinship and social class' (Keller 1963, 147), among elites renders cohesion among them more difficult, both across and within sectors. Keller's conclusion is based on an observation that reads somewhat pessimistic at first:

> To the various social ills that have periodically afflicted the social order a new one has been added: the problem of social cohesion among strategic elites no longer united by ties of blood, social status, and wealth, but by functional interdependence. How to preserve and maintain their unity without stifling their diversity is a serious, and as yet unresolved, problem. (Keller 1963, 149)

Put differently: Keller assumes that social ties bring about cohesion. Thus, as social ties vanish, 'new sources for a unity of outlook' (Keller 1963, 147) among elites are needed to re-establish elite cohesion, which is seen as a requirement for social order and stability. Yet, more than fifty years after Keller's observations, modern democracies are still alive and well in spite of the alleged problem. Consequently, the question may have to be put differently: if new sources for cohesion become all the more crucial as traditional elite ties vanish, it may be precisely shared attitudes and common belief systems that constitute the new source for cohesion among functionally differentiated elites. In this line of argument, attitudinal ties come to replace traditional ties. Thus, a homogeneous political communication elite may not require consonance in attitudes to guarantee functional elite relations.

If attitudinal ties replace social ties, inter-elite cohesion in France would be lower than the attributes of the media system and political system suggests, and higher in Austria and Denmark, where political and media elites decisively break away from the established elite circles. Indeed, this alternative assumption fits the presented data. Within each of the country pairs, cohesion is higher in those countries in which media elites have a comparatively lower social background. In Denmark and Austria, this is the expression of the less exclusive nature of the political communication elite. In otherwise relatively classist Spain, media elites are (while still largely of a middle- or upper-middle-class background) not an established part of traditional elite circles. In contrast, socially homogeneous political communication elites may in fact sustain a higher level of attitudinal discrepancy. Although this alternative explanation is tentative, it merits further consideration in future research.

Chapter 6

Intra-Sectoral Cohesion of Media and Political Elites

The previous chapter has yielded two overall results. On the one hand, attitudinal patterns of European political communication elites reflect general characteristics of the systemic environment, in which elite relations in political communication are embedded. On the other hand, elite cohesion is also subject to national idiosyncrasies. While the state and transformation of social structure, the political system and the media system may display certain general trends seen from the outside, the impact on the belief system of elites is particularly contingent on the different systemic conditions in each country. In order to further explore elite cohesion and its link to the contextual conditions within and across countries, the following chapter looks at the extent and patterns of cohesion *within* the political and the media elite. This analysis of cross-national patterns of intra-sectoral cohesion will proceed in two main steps.

First, the level of intra-sectoral attitudinal congruence will be analysed for the two sectors vis-à-vis each other, in order to test comparative assumptions about the expected absolute and relative level of intra-sectoral congruence, as well as the relative weight of congruence based on individual guiding principles. Analysing intra-sectoral levels of attitudinal congruence against each other furthermore contributes to a deeper understanding of the cohesion patterns on the inter-sectoral level described in the previous chapter. By directly comparing the presence as well as absence of intra-sectoral agreement on the different attitudinal items, it will be revealed whether a potential lack of cohesion on the inter-sectoral level is due to the explicit opposition of stances in each sector, or whether such lack of inter-sectoral cohesion is rather founded in intra-sectoral incongruence in one or both sectors in question.

The second part of the analysis concerns the emergent *patterns* of intra-sectoral cohesion in each sector, based on the degree of order and consistency of attitudes within each sector. Such patterns indicate differences in intra-sectoral differentiation, assumed to match the level of sectoral autonomy and variety. The analysis of intra-sectoral patterns of cohesion, moreover, provides insight into the question of role specialization, as well as the hierarchical organization of the sector in elites and sub-elites, which is particularly decisive for relation between political decision makers and political communication professionals in the political sector.

MEASURES OF INTRA-SECTORAL COHESION

As discussed previously in relation to the inter-sectoral part of the analysis, intra-sectoral congruence, order and consistency are calculated based on proximity scores. Three specific proximity scores that follow are central to the analysis of attitudinal patterns on the intra-sectoral level:

- Prox (intra): an individual respondent's distance to the mean of own sector
- Prox (sub): an individual respondent's distance to the mean of own sectoral subgroup
- Prox (intersub): an individual respondent's distance to the mean of the other sectoral subgroup.

Prox (intra) serves as the baseline measure of *intra-sectoral congruence*, that is, the proximity of attitudes of elites within the same sector. In contrast to chapter 5, where prox (intra) served to calculate levels of discriminance on the inter-sectoral level, the mean of prox (intra) now indicates the level of dispersion on the sectoral level, and thus intra-sectoral congruence. In line with the thresholds defined for the inter-sectoral level, intra-sectoral congruence is assumed when dispersion ranges below the specified boundary zone that ranges from 0.9 to 1.1 (see 'Measures of Inter-Sectoral Cohesion' section in chapter 5):

$$\text{Mean [prox (intra)]} < 0.9. \tag{6.1}$$

In addition to this *absolute* measure of intra-sectoral congruence, a *relative* measure of intra-sectoral congruence is calculated as the degree of intra-sectoral congruence that ranges clearly below the inter-sectoral level of dispersion. This is assumed to be the case when the difference in the respective mean proximity scores exceeds 0.2:

$$\text{Mean [prox (all)]} - \text{Mean [prox (intra)]} > 0.2. \tag{6.2}$$

The introduction of prox (sub), secondly, put in relation to the overall level of sectoral congruence (prox (intra)), yields a measure of *intra-sectoral order*.

Attitudes in sector y are defined as *ordered* if the level of dispersion within each subgroup 1y and 2y is the same or lower than dispersion on the superior level. In practical terms, this is assumed to be the case if

Mean [prox (intra$_y$)] – Mean [prox (sub$_{1y}$)] ≤ 0.1 and
Mean [prox (intra$_y$)] – Mean prox (sub$_{2y}$)] ≤ 0.1. $\hspace{2cm}$ (6.3)

Additionally, ordered patterns require the levels of dispersion of each subgroup to be in balance to each other, that is, decrease evenly in comparison to the superior level. This is assumed to be the case when the difference in the respective mean proximity scores does not exceed 0.2.

| Mean [prox (sub$_{1y}$)] – Mean [prox (sub$_{2y}$)] | ≤ 0.2. $\hspace{2cm}$ (6.4)

Prox (intersub), finally, provides a measure of *intra-sectoral (in)consistency*. For intra-sectoral patterns of differentiation, *inconsistency* of attitudinal patterns corresponds to the definition of discriminance on the inter-sectoral level applied between sub-sectoral groupings (see chapter 5). Inconsistency between the attitudes of two subgroups y and z is assumed, if, on average, respondents' distance to the mean of the other sectoral subgroup (prox (intersub)) clearly exceeds the respondents' distance to the mean of their own sectoral subgroup (prox (sub)):

Mean [prox (intersub$_y$) – (prox (sub$_y$)] > 0.05 and
Mean [prox (intersub$_z$) – (prox (sub$_z$)] > 0.05. $\hspace{2cm}$ (6.5)

As was the case for dispersion, the boundary value of 0.05 follows the lower end of the boundary zone applied on the inter-sectoral level.

ATTITUDINAL CONGRUENCE ON THE SECTORAL LEVEL

Given the book's dual perspective on two elites bound together in the construction and dissemination of political messages, the overall balance of cohesion between the two sectoral elites emerges as a key issue for the state of political communication in the included countries. The level of intra-sectoral cohesion within each sector, in absolute terms and relative to the degrees of dispersion on the inter-sectoral level, is assumed to be affected by the degree of autonomy and variety in the political and media system. As discussed in chapter 4, the six countries under study set themselves apart quite significantly in terms of the degree of sectoral autonomy and variety. These differences can thus be expected to be reflected in the degree of intra-sectoral cohesion among media elites and political elites in each of the countries.

Media autonomy and journalistic professionalization suggest a relative high propensity for intra-sectoral cohesion among media elites in Sweden and Denmark. Within the political sector, Sweden and Denmark both stand out in terms of high rational-legal authority and bureaucratic autonomy, although combined with a long-standing tradition of corporatist interest mediation. Moreover, Denmark and, albeit to a lesser extent, Sweden have time undergone substantial public-sector reforms: involvement of stakeholders, network governance, openness in administrative recruitment and adherence to NPM principles make the political sector less closed around bureaucratic principles and thus less prone to intra-sectoral cohesion. In both sectors, the propensity for intra-sectoral cohesion is diminished by the degree of sectoral variety. All in all, intra-sectoral cohesion is therefore likely to be higher among media elites than among political elites in Denmark and Sweden.

In Germany, journalistic professionalism is counterbalanced by a lower degree of political insulation, as well as a high degree of regional decentralization, and thus institutional variety in the media sector, suggesting a medium propensity for intra-sectoral cohesion in the media sector. Weak journalistic professionalism and lack of political insulation suggest even lower intra-sectoral cohesion in the Austrian media sector. With regard to the political sector, Germany and Austria are defined by the persistence of traditional rational-legal authority, as well as established bureaucratic and party-political career paths. Politicization within the administrative branch further leads to a certain level of closure within the German political elite, whereas Austria's system of party patronage lowers the autonomy of the political sector to some degree. The propensity for intra-sectoral cohesion in the political sector can all in all be described as rather high in Germany and medium in Austria, which means that political elites in both countries are more prone to be internally cohesive than media elites.

The potential for subjugation of the media and the lack of a common professional creed do not provide fertile grounds for intra-sectoral cohesion in the media sectors of France and Spain. In both countries, the limited institutional variety, attributed to regional centralization in France and concentration in the media market in Spain, is countered by the presence of positional variety. All in all, propensity for intra-sectoral cohesion in the media sector therefore remains rather low. In spite of the formal corps structure in the political sector of both countries and a strong tradition of rational-legal authority in France, high positional variety reduces the possibility of overarching cohesion among political elites in France, as do regional disparities in Spain. Furthermore, the Spanish elite settlement that is associated with the transformation to democracy has always been of a general character and never resulted in sectoral professionalization, nor managed to permanently overcome bipartisan tendencies. Consequently, propensity for intra-sectoral cohesion in the political sector is rather low in both France and Spain, and thus expected to match the level of intra-sectoral cohesion in the media sector.

Table 6.1 shows how the media and political sector in each country relate to each other in terms of the internal congruence of its elites (see also appendix for detailed congruence scores). For each country and sector, the table displays the number of attitudes (the maximum number of attitudes is nine) that meet the requirements of absolute and relative intra-sectoral congruence specified earlier in the text, providing an overall indication of the internal congruence within the media sector and the political sector in each country. Moreover, table 6.1 indicates the sum of differences between the proximity scores of the media and the political sector, based on all individual attitudinal statements. This provides a comprehensive measure for the overall difference in congruence between the media sector and the political sector in each country.

As assumed, congruence in absolute terms is highest in the autonomous media sectors of Sweden, Denmark and Germany as well as in the political sector in Germany. Intra-sectoral congruence does occur in the political sectors of the Nordic countries and the German media sector, albeit lower than in their counterpart sector both in absolute and in relative terms. As expected, intra-sectoral congruence is relatively low in the Austrian media sector, well behind the German media sector and the political sectors of both countries. France, however, does not conform to overall assumptions: although the congruence of the media elite is indeed towards the lower end, the political sector elites are more congruent than expected, indicating that autonomy outweighs variety in this case. Expectations are not met for Spain, where both sectors appear highly congruent in absolute terms. However, this result must be seen in conjunction with inter-sectoral cohesion: in only one instance is the sectoral congruence in Spain actually higher than on the inter-sectoral level.

Table 6.1. Cohesion in the Media Sector versus Political Sector

	SWE	*DEN*	*GER*	*AUT*	*FRA*	*SPA*
Number of attitudes with high congruence (absolute | relative to inter-sectoral level)						
Media sector	7 | 4	7 | 4	7 | 1	4 | 1	3 | 2	7 | 1
Political sector	5 | 2	5 | 1	8 | 2	6 | 1	6 | 2	7 | 0
Sum of differences between prox (intra$_{media}$) and prox (intra$_{politics}$) – all attitudes						
Media versus politics	−.6	−.6	+.6	+1.3	−.1	−.2

Note: Based on in total nine attitudinal statements; high congruence is assumed for prox (intra) < .9

More generally, this reflects the particular situation in Spain where we are dealing with a highly consensual political communication elite. Interpreted together, the absolute and relative level of intra-sectoral congruence fit the expectations rather well.

Differences along the north/south axis become even clearer when looking at the level of cohesion within the political sector vis-à-vis the media sector: In Sweden and Denmark, the media sector is, as expected, more congruent than the political sector. Even though both sectors in these countries are characterized by bureaucratic formalization and professionalization, it remains clear that congruence in the political sectors is pulled in the other direction by the sectoral variety of the Nordic political sectors, as well as the limitations on sectoral autonomy imposed by established corporatist structures and presumably also the more recent introduction of NPM principles. The opposite is true for Germany and Austria. Despite federalism, decision making is more centralized, and political careers within parties and institutions largely remain the result of 'climbing the greasy pole', which results in a more uniform professional socialization in the political sector. As a result, political elites are internally more congruent than their counterparts in the media sector. In Spain and France, finally, none of the two sectoral elite groups is substantially more cohesive than the other. Noticeably, the higher level of absolute congruence in the French political sector that contracted expectations is now qualified by the more affirmative result that the overall level of congruence for the French political sector and media sector is indeed rather balanced.

The results displayed in table 6.1 do not take the guiding principles of consonance into account (for a full discussion of this issue, see Mayerhöffer 2015). It is worth noting, however, that European media elites by no means cohere on the same principles. In Germany, Austria and Spain, the intra-sectoral cohesion of both the media elite and the political elite is most pronounced for the principle of pragmatism. In both Sweden and France, the principle of pragmatism once again stands out as the key principle for the political elite, while the media elite in both countries is most coherent on the principle of publicity. Denmark, in turn, stands out as the only country where intra-sectoral congruence is most pronounced for the principle of ideology. Indeed, this is the case for the media elite as well as the political elite in Denmark.

Denmark, moreover, produced the only instance where the stances of the media sector and the political sector directly contradict each other: media elites reject the role of an editorial guide, while political elites in Denmark accept the role of a gladiator for party politics. This is at the same time the only instance where an absence of cohesion on the *inter-sectoral* level is explained by contradicting sectoral stances. In most other cases, inter-sectoral cohesion as separation appears in situations where one or even both elite sectors lack a congruent stance on the issue in the first place, rather than being the result of two clashing belief systems. Conflicting stances are somewhat more frequent where an ambiguous stance in one sector is met by clear acceptance in the other sector.

In addition to the overall levels and dominant principles, the internal congruence of the media elite and the political elite may differ in the relative importance of values, procedures and epistemology as sources of attitudinal consonance. As was the case on the inter-sectoral level, procedural congruence emerges as the most difficult form of cohesion to achieve on the intrasectoral level: only Swedish media elites consistently build their intra-sectoral cohesion on procedural congruence, while it appears the least prominent source of cohesion in all remaining countries and sectors. The prominence of the two remaining sources of cohesion, however, varies between countries and guiding principles. Given that the overall likelihood to achieve cohesion is not stable across different sources of cohesion, the intra-sectoral relevance of cohesion based on the different sources of cohesion is thus better analysed in relative terms.

Based on the proposed model of elite cohesion, the relative importance of the three sources of cohesion can be assumed to vary across countries and sectors in relation to degrees of sectoral autonomy and variety. Procedural congruence, for its part, has been linked to (high) degrees of autonomy, in particular through sectoral professionalism; value congruence has been linked to (low) positional variety and epistemological congruence to (low) institutional variety. Based on the degrees of sectoral autonomy, procedural congruence should be most strongly pronounced in the autonomous media sectors of Sweden and Denmark and in the political sector in Germany, and particularly weakly pronounced in the media sectors of Austria, France and Spain.

Figure 6.1 displays the relative weight of value and epistemological congruence in each sector and country, measures against the level of procedural congruence. Negative average dispersion scores, plotted above the *x*-axis, indicate that the level of value or epistemological congruence in a given sector is higher than procedural congruence. Indeed, procedural congruence carries the lowest relative weight in the two Mediterranean media sectors, where sectoral professionalism is generally least developed among the countries under study. In the comparatively autonomous and professionalized French political sector, the relative importance of procedural congruence is furthermore somewhat higher than in the media sector.

Although sectoral autonomy and professionalism are also rather low in the Austrian media sector, the relative weight of procedural congruence is not as low as assumed. This is, however, due to the overall weakness of intrasectoral cohesion in the Austrian media sector, rather than an indication of strong procedural congruence. In absolute terms, procedural congruence or

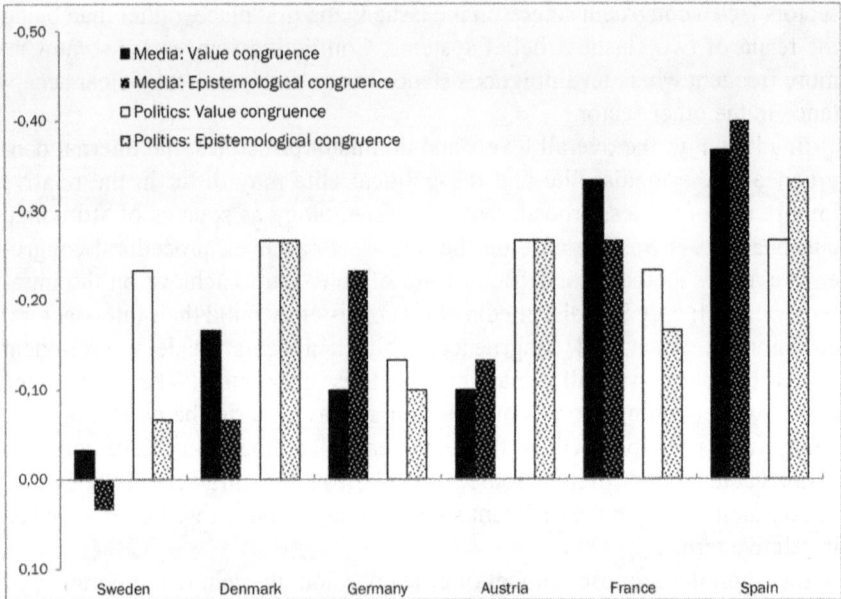

Figure 6.1. Relative Weight of Sources of Cohesion by Country and Sector

Baseline: average procedural congruence by country and sector; negative values indicate that the sector is more congruent on this dimension than on the procedural one and vice versa (e.g. dispersion scores of German media elites on the value dimension are in average .1 lower than on the procedural dimension).

rather incongruence in the Austrian media sector is on par with the corresponding sectors in France and Spain (see appendix for detailed congruence scores). Procedural congruence is in turn most substantial for the political sector in Germany, as well as for the media sectors in the Nordic countries. These three sectors stand out among the countries under study thanks to a particular well-established degree of sectoral professionalism.

Moreover, sectors are expected to differ in the relative importance of *values* and *epistemology* as sources of congruence, based on their institutional and positional variety. In the Mediterranean countries, in which positional variety outweighs institutional variety, epistemological congruence is expected to be comparatively high. Epistemological congruence indeed supersedes the degree of value congruence in both sectors in Spain, although not to a very high degree. Epistemological congruence is, however, relatively weak in France. At least for the case of the media sector, this unexpectedly high level of value congruence in France can be traced back to the practically universal embracement of the watchdog role. Despite the low average score of dispersion displayed in figure 6.1, the watchdog indeed is the only role model French media elites have a congruent internal stance on.

For the Nordic and Central European countries, the assumed relation between value and epistemological congruence can most clearly be observed in the political sectors. As can be seen in figure 6.1, the political sectors in Austria and Denmark, for which levels of institutional and positional variety are balanced, are equally coherent on values and epistemology. In Sweden and Germany, where institutional variety supersedes positional variety, value congruence is dominant. A similar correspondence between sectoral variety, value and epistemological congruence, however, cannot be observed for the media sectors of the countries in question. Rather, value congruence surpasses epistemological congruence in the Nordic countries, while the opposite is true for the central European media sectors.

A particularly noticeable result is that the German media elites are quite incongruent on the value dimension, relatively speaking, despite the fact that institutional variety clearly outweighs positional variety in the German media landscape. This incongruence is the expression of a profound role specialization between public and private media, as well as between print and broadcasting elites that is particularly characteristic for the German media elite (see also 6.3). In sum, the results are somewhat mixed when it comes to the relation between attributes of the media system/political system and the relative importance of the different sources of attitudinal consonance. Systemic attributes work best to account for internal congruence in the political sector, as well as for the extent of procedural congruence.

PATTERNS OF INTRA-SECTORAL COHESION

Variations in sectoral autonomy and variety are, finally, assumed to result in specific patterns of intra-sectoral cohesion. Based on the degree of order and consistency of attitudes, four patterns of intra-sectoral cohesion have been distinguished: *sedimentation* occurs when the stance of the entire sector is the basis for equally or increasingly firm cohesion within the subgroups of the sector, also referred to as an ordered and consistent pattern. Sedimentation can thus be seen as a baseline pattern of intra-sectoral cohesion. *Segmentation* describes a pattern of ordered but inconsistent (i.e. discriminant) patterns on the intra-sectoral level, while *concentration* refers to disordered but consistent patterns. *Fragmentation*, finally, results from disordered and inconsistent attitudinal patterns, that is, a scenario where the various subgroupings display distinct levels of congruence, as well as distinct attitudinal stances.

The empirical analysis of such intra-sectoral patterns depends, first of all, on vertical and horizontal distinctions between different sub-sectoral groups. For the purposes of this analysis, vertical distinctions between subgroups in the media sector include (1) public and private media organizations and

(2) broadcasting and print outlets. The key horizontal distinction in the media separates (3) editorial elites from reporters as specialized sub-elites. In the political sector, the following subgroups have been distinguished as the basis for the analysis of intra-sectoral patterns: (1) Executive or governmental elites vis-a-vis party-political elites constitutes the first level of horizontal differentiation, with (2) a left/right-split serving as a second level of differentiation within the party-political elite. Hierarchically organized subgroups identified by horizontal distinction include political decision makers vis-à-vis the sub-elite of communication professionals.

In terms of general effects of the systemic context on the patterns of intra-sectoral cohesion, it has been suggested that higher degrees of autonomy foster ordered attitudinal patterns, that is, levels of dispersion that decrease steadily with every sectoral sub-division. Consistency in attitudinal patterns, that is, attitudinal stances that do not diverge substantially between sectoral subgroups, has in turn been linked to low positional and institutional variety within a given sector. Based on the level of sectoral autonomy and variety present in the media and political sectors in the six countries under study, different dominant patterns of intra-sectoral cohesion can be expected for each of them.

Taking the specific set-up in each of the countries and sectors into consideration, we can assume the autonomous media sectors in Sweden and Denmark to be largely ordered, that is, show patterns of segmentation or sedimentation. In Sweden, where the media sector is characterized both by moderate positional and by institutional variety, consistency in attitudes and thus attitudinal sedimentation will be more pronounced than in Denmark. The relatively pronounced variety in the political sectors in the Nordic countries is in turn to result in inconsistent patterns, that is, patterns of segmentation and fragmentation.

Both the media and political sector in Germany are characterized by autonomy and relatively high degrees of institutional variety and can thus be expected to be predominantly segmented in their attitudinal patterns. By contrast, both the Austrian media and political sector are characterized by relatively low sectoral variety, which suggests consistent patterns of cohesion. Due to the differences in sectoral autonomy, consistent patterns will more likely take the form of sedimentation (consistency + order) in the Austrian political sector, and of concentration (consistency + disorder) in the less autonomous Austrian media sector.

A lack of autonomy combined with high levels of positional variety suggests both disorder and inconsistency and thus fragmented attitudinal patterns in the French media sector. Attitudinal differentiation in the French political sector can in turn be expected to be somewhat more ordered, and thus be characterized by both segmentation and fragmentation. Finally, a lack of sectoral autonomy paired with low levels of sectoral variety can be expected to produce largely concentrated attitudinal patterns in the Spanish political sector. As a result of the high level of positional variety, the Spanish media sector is in turn likely to show signs of both concentration (disorder + consistency) and fragmentation (disorder + inconsistency).

Figure 6.2 displays the patterns of intra-sectoral cohesion in the media sector and political sector for each of the nine attitudinal statements included in the study (corresponding to the three sources and three guiding principles of cohesion). In order to determine a clear pattern of intra-sectoral cohesion based on the horizontal and vertical subdivisions outlined earlier in the text, attitudinal differentiation is interpreted as *segmented*, if all subdivisions yield an ordered, but at least one of the subdivisions yields an inconsistent pattern; as *concentrated*, if all subdivisions yield a consistent, but at least one of the subdivisions yields a disordered pattern; as *fragmented*, if at least one of the subdivisions, though not necessarily the same one, yields an inconsistent and a disordered pattern; and as *sedimented*, if elites display a thoroughly ordered and consistent attitudinal pattern on all levels of sub-differentiation. Put differently: if only one of the three possible sub-divisions in each sector is characterized by disordered and/or inconsistent patterns on a given attitudinal statement, the attitude in question will be recorded as disordered and/or inconsistent.

In general, assumptions about the impact of media system characteristics on the attitudinal patters of media elites hold up well for the degree of sectoral autonomy, while results are somewhat more mixed for the degree of sectoral variety. Figure 6.2 shows that ordered attitudinal patterns (sedimentation or segmentation) indeed dominate in the countries with high media autonomy, that is, Sweden, Denmark and Germany. The moderate level of autonomy and low variety found in the Austrian media sector result in a somewhat blurred mix of attitudinal patterns marked by a high level of sedimentation. France and Spain, finally, as expected display the lowest degree of ordered attitudinal patterns.

Moreover, instances of inconsistency in attitudinal patterns (segmentation and fragmentation) appear most frequent in those countries that are either characterized by high institutional *or* positional variety: Denmark, Germany, France and Spain. Especially the substantial segmentation of attitudes in Denmark and Germany stands out. For Germany, in particular, this points to a higher degree of inconsistency in attitudes than the sectoral variety suggests. Here, it seems that the profound institutional variety in the German media sector is formative for the attitudinal patterns of its media elites, compensating for the more limited positional variety in the German media sector.

Noticeably, the attitudinal patterns of the Swedish media elite are even more sedimented than the moderate degree of sectoral variety suggests. Indeed, not a single attitude is characterized by segmentation. Given that

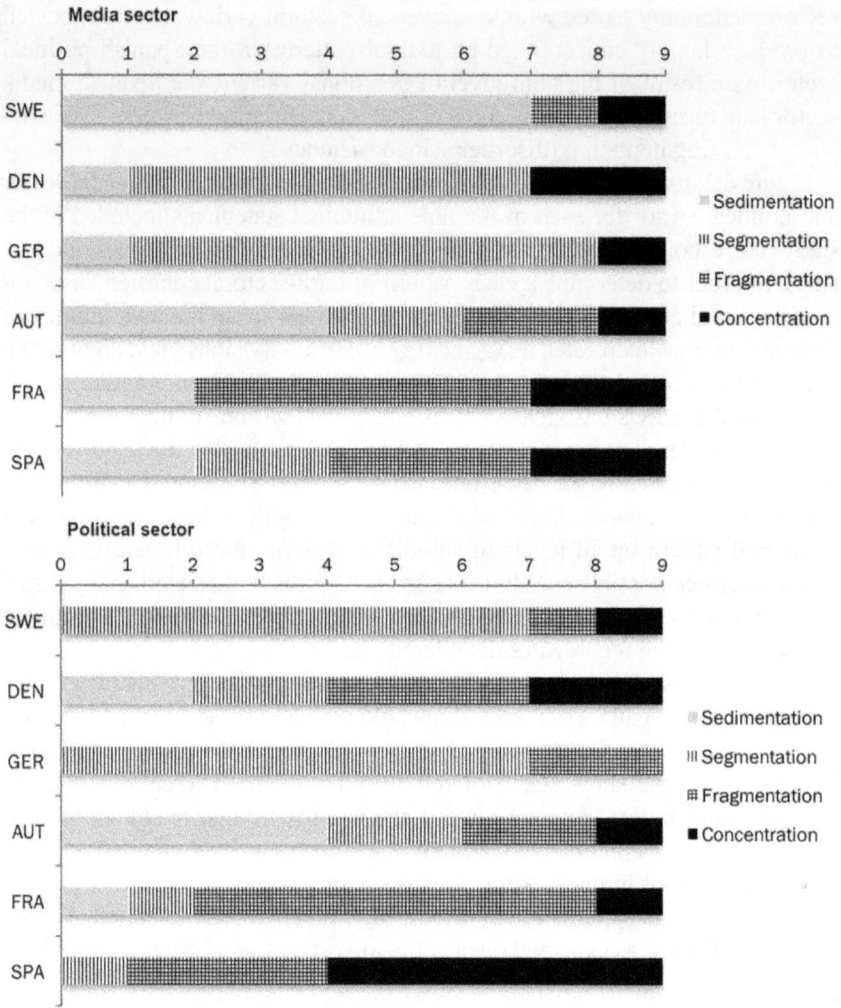

Figure 6.2. Patterns of Intra-Sectoral Cohesion in the Media and Political Sector

Distribution of patterns of sectoral sub-differentiation across nine attitudinal statements, based on sub-sectoral divisions in the media sector between public broadcasting elites, private broadcasting elites, print sector elites, as well as between editorial elites and reporters (sub-elites); in the political sector between executive and party-political elites, and herein elites to the left and right of the political middle, as well as between decision makers and communication professionals (sub-elites).

the Swedish media sector is subject to significant market concentration, the sedimented Swedish media sector could point to the conclusion that concentration in the media market weighs stronger for the degree of sectoral variety and thus attitudinal consistency than originally assumed. This conclusion is, however, not backed by the results for the remaining countries. While Austria – where market concentration is equally substantial – is indeed equally characterized by substantial sedimentation of attitudes, this is clearly not the case in Spain, which displays the third highest degree of media market concentration. The sedimentation of attitudes in the Swedish media system must thus primarily be seen as an expression of a particular consensus-based culture among Swedish journalists rather than a more general consequence of market concentration that would be immediately transferable to other cases.

Turning to the political sector, patterns of intra-sectoral cohesion do not quite fit the expectations in the two Nordic countries. In contrast to the highly sedimented Swedish media sector, the Swedish political sector is character-ized by a pervasive segmentation of attitudes, which corresponds well with its higher levels of sectoral variety. At the same time, the high degree of segmentation also indicates an unexpectedly high level of order in the Swed-ish political sector, despite the limitations in its sectoral autonomy. The Dan-ish patterns appear very mixed, displaying all four possible patterns almost evenly. This signifies a substantial degree of remaining consistency that is in contrast to the high level of variety in the Danish political sector.

The assumed relationship between sectoral autonomy and variety and pat-terns of intra-sectoral cohesion do in turn hold up rather well for the Central European countries. Both countries display largely ordered attitudinal pat-terns, as suggested by the comparatively high levels of sectoral autonomy. The German political sector is, as expected, characterized by substantial segmentation of attitudes, whereas the mixed Austrian patterns suggest a retreat to the baseline sedimentation of attitudes, in which neither of the vari-ous sub-differentiations dominates. In line with the high levels of positional variety in the political sector, attitudinal patterns appear largely inconsistent in France. Despite the substantial degree of sectoral autonomy, this incon-sistency appears however almost exclusively as fragmentation, rather than segmentation. Finally, Spanish political elites are, as expected, particularly characterized by patterns of concentration, although significant inconsistency in attitudes remains. In sum, the assumed link between contextual conditions and patterns of intra-sectoral cohesion is only partially corroborated. This is not least due to the fact that patterns of intra-sectoral cohesion appear more varied than assumed. With the exception of the German political sector, all sectors display a mix of ordered and disordered, as well as of consistent and inconsistent, attitudes. Most clearly supported is the link between sectoral autonomy and ordered attitudinal patterns, which – with the prominent excep-tion of the French political sector – can be traced in all sectors under study.

ROLE SPECIALIZATION

The patterns of intra-sectoral cohesion can, moreover, be linked to the ques-tion of intra-sectoral specialization. So far, segmentation and fragmentation have been discussed merely as a counterpoint to sedimentation and concentration for purposes of overall cross-national comparison. However, the two inconsistent patterns of intra-sectoral cohesion can also be interpreted as an indication of specialization and a division of labour between different sub-sectoral groups, whereas consistent patterns of intra-sectoral cohesion rather suggest an absence of specialization. Thus understood, segmentation suggests a rather clear-cut internal division of labour, whereas fragmentation can be interpreted as a form of incomplete or deficient specialization.

If inconsistency in attitudinal patterns can indeed be seen not merely as divergence but also as a sign of sectoral specialization, the extent of value congruence vis-à-vis procedural and epistemological congruence should reflect this. More specifically, the distribution of labour should be reflected directly in a specification and separation of roles on the value dimension of cohesion, whereas sectoral specialization can be assumed to be least pronounced on the epistemological dimension. Specialization does not require, and may in fact even be obstructed by, diverging interpretations of structural conditions and constraints of the common environment.

Consequently, the level of inconsistency is expected to be higher on the value dimension as a consequence of role specialization within a sector. Whereas the lack of procedural and epistemological consonance is a potential source of instability among a sectoral elite group, role specialization may also be the result of a more or less conscious division of labour among sectoral subgroups, in particular in the case of segmentation. For similar reasons, inconsistency is generally expected to be lower on the horizontal dimension of sectoral differentiation. In general, specialization is instrumental to the functional separation of subgroups on the same level, whereas the hierarchical principle of differentiation underlying the separation of sectoral elites and sub-elites is less conducive to specialization. This argument holds both for the media and the political sector. However, the group of communication professionals identified as the primary sub-elite in the political sector is a rather particular one characterized not only by hierarchical subordination but also by a distinct professional identity. Hence, the analysis will go into more detail with this group after the overall results for the media sector and the political sector have been presented.

Role Specialization in the Media Sector

For the six media sectors under study, the degree of attitudinal inconsistency (segmentation or fragmentation) is indeed slightly less pronounced in the procedural and epistemological dimension than in the value dimension. With the notable exception of the Danish media sector, instances of inconsistency on the value dimension are as frequent as or more frequent than for the other two in all countries. The most pronounced cross-national pattern of segmentation is found in the case of the *editorial guide* (ideology). With the exception of Denmark, the role of editorial guide seems to divide suggest a division of labour between media subgroups throughout Europe, in particular along the dividing line between broadcasting media and the print media elites (see appendix for a detailed overview of levels of congruence and stances for individual subgroups). Noticeably, private broadcasting elites reject the role of editorial guide almost as strongly as their peers in the public service media. Moreover, broadcasting elites are not only more averse to the role of the editorial guide, but also internally more congruent on the matter than print media elites. Hence, the role of editorial guide is specific to print media, that is, the backbone of the party-political and ideological press, including the specific journalistic genres of commentary and opinion-pieces that has survived the formal decline of the party press. In Spain, however, where the evolution of a print press market has not followed this pattern, segmentation rather occurs between the more elite-oriented print and public broadcasting media elites on the one side, and the mass-oriented private broadcasting elites on the other side, who adhere to the role of editorial guide to an even stronger degree.

By contrast, role specialization in relation to the *watchdog* role (publicity) is much less pronounced, occurring only in Germany (where role adherence is lowest for private broadcasters) and Spain (where public broadcasting elites are somewhat more reluctant). Once again, this emphasizes that the watchdog role has become an almost universal value base for media elites in Europe. Role specialization is again more prevalent in the case of the *mass communicator* (pragmatism). Curiously, however, commitment is particularly strong where it is not immediately suggested by the organizational logic of the news outlet in question: in the public-service media in the central European countries, as well as in the print media with exclusive readership in the South.

As expected, inconsistency in attitudes is lower and, indeed, virtually absent when looking at the hierarchical division between editors and journalists. The attitudinal patterns of editors and reporters are largely sedimented in all countries for values as well as on the procedural and epistemological level. However, Denmark constitutes a noteworthy exception: here, specialization between the different media sub-sectors is completely lacking, whereas the horizontal division between editors and reporters constitutes the most important line of sub-sectoral differentiation. A tentative explanation for this hierarchical subdivision of elites is the particular status of the Danish reporter elites, who are located within parliament premises rather than within their outlet's editorial offices – and consequently appear to have developed a somewhat distinct take on the structural constraints of their work.

A more general observation is that role specialization appears to be the driving force in the creation of consistently differentiated belief systems.

Where role segmentation can be observed, segmentation in the procedural and epistemological dimension is likely to follow, although with some remaining instances of fragmentation. If we reverse the relation, fragmentation in the value dimension does not produce a similar effect on other dimensions. Indeed, consistent patterns can be found in at least one of the other two dimensions in all cases of role fragmentation. Fragmentation, which can be considered a more incomplete and volatile type of role specialization, does not produce the pervasive differentiation of belief systems found in the case of role segmentation. Such pervasive differentiation of belief systems thus seems to be premised on a transition from role fragmentation to an ordered and thus more stable state of role specialization as segmentation.

Role Specialization in the Political Sector

As in the media system, segmentation or fragmentation based on values is indeed the dominant form of vertical sub-differentiation within the political sector compared to procedures and epistemology (as stated, the hierarchical distinction between the political elite and the sub-elite of communication professionals will be dealt with separately). Looking at the distinction between the executive and party-political elites, instances of segmentation or fragmentation are at least as frequent as or more frequent on the value dimension than on the other two dimensions in all countries. However, the magnitude of specialization follows a north/south axis insofar as political elites in Sweden, Denmark, and Germany display more role differentiation than elites in Austria, France and Spain. The case of Austria notwithstanding, this result fits the logic of systems with strong political parties and an executive that largely abstains from acting in an openly party-political manner (i.e. in the Nordic and German-speaking countries).

As opposed to the media system, however, role orientation does not result in a clear division of labour with sub-sectoral groups dividing roles among themselves. More specifically, party-political elites support all of the included roles to a higher degree than the executive elites in all countries. The vote- and office-seeking behaviour normally associated with political parties thus seems to express itself clearly in an embrace of all available communication roles to a degree that is not found in the executive elite. Within each sub-sectoral group, the priority given to the individual communication roles may however vary substantially.

In contrast to their peers in the party-political sector, Nordic executive elites identify most strongly with the role of a *gladiator*, that is, the media and publicity-related role that is most clearly party-political. Austrian executive elites, by contrast, stand out with a particularly congruent and firm commitment to the role of *strategic communicator*, a finding that appears puzzling at first, given the weak strategic orientation of Austrian government communication in structural terms. It does, however, correspond rather well with the Austrian tradition of grand coalitions: under these conditions, the strategic communicator in the executive branch communicates via the mass media about government plans that at least formally have bipartisan support, rather than partisan political programmes, propositions and bills. Mediterranean executive elites, finally, most strongly adhere to the role of *information provider*.

The inherently party-political role of gladiator, not surprisingly, finds strong support among the party-political elites. This is the case for all countries but France, where party-political elites overwhelmingly identify with the publicity-driven role of information provider. Noticeably, Danish party-political elites identify particularly strongly with the role of strategic communicator, corresponding to the observation that *spin* as a defining element in Danish politics pertains to not only the executive but also the party-political domain.

Whereas role specialization between executive and party-political elites is substantial, the two groups are almost entirely consistent in their attitudes when it comes to the procedural and epistemological dimension of elite cohesion. This is, however, not the case *within* the party-political sphere itself. A clear pattern emerges that places role specialization within the institutional division of powers within the political system, whereas procedural and epistemological stances predominantly vary according to the position of elites within the party-political spectrum.

As such, party-political elites left of the political middle are internally more congruent in the South, whereas the opposite is true for the Central European and Nordic countries. This finding is independent of the current governmental majority but can be seen to reflect a more long-standing fragmentation of parliamentary blocs. The parliamentary left in Northern and Central Europe in particular unites both the 'old' and 'new left', that is, traditional socialist parties, ecological parties, catch-all social democrats and social-liberal parties, which contributes to substantial discrepancies in attitudinal stances. The differences in congruence between elites to the left and right of the political spectrum vary, furthermore, between the distinct guiding principles, in particular for the three countries with the largest differences, Denmark, France and Spain. In all three countries, elites left of the political middle are more congruent on the principle of ideology, while elites to the right are particularly congruent on pragmatism. For the principle of publicity, elites to the right are more congruent in Denmark, and elites to the left in the Mediterranean countries.

A Case of Its Own: Communication Professionals as Sub-Elites in the Political Sector

Theoretically as well as empirically, the hierarchical division between decision-making elites and the sub-elite of communication professionals is more profound than the hierarchical division between reporters and editors in the media. Whereas editors and reporters are both regarded by themselves and others as journalists, political communication professionals are clearly not politicians in a similar sense. In terms of cohesion, a number of assertions can be made against this background.

The first assumption refers to the question, in which way the attitudinal patterns of communication professionals diverge from those of the political decision makers. Due to the fact that political communication professionals have been asked to state their idea about the political communication roles of politicians, rather than their own role, inconsistency in role orientation between the two subgroups must be interpreted differently. Segmented or fragmented patterns of cohesion on the value dimension are not a sign of role specialization but of a discrepancy and a potential source of miscommunication between general elites and specialized sub-elites. Consequently, consistency or at best weak segmentation based on values can be expected for the horizontal division of elites in the political sector.

Second, the question arises whether communication professionals are a more cohesive group than political decision makers. Being a group of specialized elites in the field of political communication, communication professionals can be expected to be more internally cohesive than political decision makers. This issue has direct bearings on professionalization of political communication. As a general trend, professionalization involves loss of sectoral autonomy alongside increased sectoral variety, which should lead to a more fragmented pattern of intra-sectoral cohesion in the political system. Professionalized political communication involves the emergence of specialized elite group that challenges existing routines with outside expertise and viewpoints, making divergences in belief systems and fragmentation a more likely scenario than consistent attitudinal patterns between decision makers and communication professionals.

Empirically, however, the group of communication professionals is not more cohesive than political decision makers in any of the countries under study. The internal dispersion within the group of communication professionals is largely on par with the dispersion levels among the political decision makers in all countries and across sources of consonance. The presumably professional outlook on the conditions under which political communication takes place, in other words, seems not to offset the fact that the group of political communication professionals is in itself very heterogeneous, comprising individuals with diverse educational and professional backgrounds, as well as current positions (ranging from bureaucrats to special advisors to outside consultants). Due to the fact that communication professionals do not present a particularly cohesive sub-elite, there is only limited evidence of fragmented patterns of intra-sectoral cohesion, that is, a situation, in which attitudinal patterns of communication professionals are substantially different *and* internally more congruent than those of decision makers.

By contrast, the sub-elite of political communication professional does set itself apart from political decision makers in the sources and principles of cohesion. Attitudinal patterns are characterized by substantial inconsistency between decision making and communication elites in all countries but Austria. This is particularly true for the value dimension, pointing to a substantial inconsistency in how political decision makers and communication professionals view politicians' role as *media personae,* and consequently to a potential source of misunderstanding between both sides. In general, however, differences in attitudinal stances are not drastic and political communication professionals generally remain closer to the attitudinal stances of political-decision makers than to those of media elites.[1]

While these general observations apply to all countries, it is possible to discern national profiles of the political communication sub-elites. In the Nordic countries, communication professionals are characterized by relative independence from the political decision makers, as illustrated by particularly substantial discrepancies on the value dimension. The publicity-related role of information provider, in particular, produced remarkable differences between the two groups in that communication professionals assign only moderate importance to a role largely embraced by political decision makers. By contrast, Swedish communicators are far more committed to the procedural and epistemological aspects of publicity than political decision makers, which may explain why they are not quite as convinced that the associated role of information provider has high priority for politicians.

German communication professionals may be best described as negotiators, as it is predominantly procedural segmentation that distinguishes them as sub-elites: German decision makers highlight the importance of ideological convictions, whereas the group of communication professionals more strongly adheres to the procedural norms associated with publicity and pragmatism. Austrian communication professionals are largely incorporated into the belief system of political decision makers, as indicated by a profound sedimentation of attitudes. In France and Spain, finally, elite communication professionals are predominantly found in various forms of advisory and cabinet positions. Much more than in the remaining countries, these sub-elites are (also) politicians or constitute potential recruits for political positions. This ambiguous role does not, however, result in congruence with the attitudinal patterns of decision makers but rather in a highly unsystematic pattern of cohesion for both countries.

Among the countries under study, attitudinal patterns of French communication professionals display the clearest indication of their status as strategists, in particular on the value dimension: Rather than reaffirming the decision makers role commitment in a somewhat more contained fashion, they not only are internally more congruent, but also reorganize the decision makers' self-understanding in political communication: the citizen-oriented information provider loses importance in relation to the partisan gladiator and the strategic communicator role. This stands in sharp contrast to Spain, where the attitudinal differentiation of communication professionals is rather spurious and draws a diffuse picture.

Overall, these results suggest that professionalization of political communication alone does not account for the role and function of the new communication sub-elite in the political sector. Rather, the attitudinal patterns of communication suggest that the position of communication professionals in the political system is the result of sectoral differentiation rather than a direct result of professionalization per se. In this respect, the division into decision-making and communicating elites in the political sector largely confirms the expectations regarding differences in intra-sectoral patterns of cohesion between the countries under study.

The independent communication professionals in the North work within a context of high institutional variety and sectoral autonomy, albeit the latter is tempered by openness towards societal actors and third parties. The German negotiators are located in a political sector with somewhat less variety and a particular high level of sectoral autonomy based on relative closure to outside interests – which thus facilitates the systematic differentiation of procedural standards. Austria's incorporated communication professionals are in line with the baseline sedimentation that was expected to result from ambiguous levels of sectoral autonomy and variety. The level of inconsistency between decision makers and communicators is, however, higher in the two Mediterranean countries than institutional variety in the political sector suggests. Moreover, patterns of sub-differentiation are generally so unsystematic that clear-cut relationships are difficult to establish. Focusing on the value dimension alone, patterns of concentration and sedimentation in the Spanish case do however reflect its lower institutional variety. Other than a relative high degree of disorder, no systematic relationship can be found in France. In the French case, the country-specific environment of a semi-presidential system, multiple, but weak, parties and the resulting strategic streak in political communication takes the upper hand in relation to general assumptions on sectoral autonomy and variety.

SUMMARY: INTRA-SECTORAL COHESION

The intra-sectoral analysis of elite cohesion has shed light on the complex interplay between the specific structural set-up of the political and media system and the attitudinal patterns of its elites. Beyond any country-specific outcomes and national circumstances, the presented results confirm that sectoral autonomy and variety are highly relevant for the consolidation and differentiation of sectoral stances on political communication. *Sectoral autonomy* has been assumed to result in (1) a higher propensity for intra-sectoral cohesion, (3) ordered patterns of sectoral differentiation and (3) a relative high weight of procedural consonance within the sector. *Sectoral variety* has been assumed to lead to (4) a lower propensity for intra-sectoral cohesion and (5) inconsistent patterns of sectoral differentiation. *Institutional variety* has moreover been associated with (6) a relative low weight of epistemological consonance within a sector, while *positional variety* has been assumed to lead to (7) a relative low weight of value consonance within a sector. Across all countries, (8) the level of inconsistency was expected to be highest on the value dimension as a result of role specialization within sectors.

The overall propensity of intra-sectoral cohesion is best understood in terms of a relative comparison with the level of inter-sectoral cohesion. Taking this into account, sector-specific levels of autonomy and variety indeed explain the empirical results for the countries under study quite well. In the Nordic countries, the more autonomous media systems display a higher level of elite consonance than the rather diverse and open political systems, while the opposite is true for the Central-European countries. For the Mediterranean countries, finally, none of the sectors is substantially more cohesive than the other. The more disaggregated results on the level of guiding principles do not fundamentally challenge this finding, but each display distinct constellations of attitudinal congruence and stance of the political sector vis-à-vis the media sector. Second, more autonomous systems display more ordered attitudinal patterns, which can either lead to segmentation or sedimentation of sectoral attitudes. Although patterns of attitudinal disorder are found in all sectors under study, they are far more frequent in the less autonomous sectors. Prime examples in this respect are the Mediterranean media sectors. The assumed link between low sectoral variety and consistency in sectoral patterns, however, is only partly supported.

Third, inconsistency of attitudes indeed becomes particularly prevalent on the value dimension, as suggested by the assumption of a role specialization within sectors. Role specialization is least pronounced in the Nordic media sectors, as well as in the Mediterranean political sectors. In line with an assumed decrease in ordered patterns of differentiation from north to south, role specialization is instead partly replaced by value sedimentation in the North and value concentration in the South. Fourth, inconsistency of attitudes is, as assumed, less pronounced on the horizontal level of differentiation in the media sector. Distinct attitudinal patterns between the editorial top-elites and the sub-elite of reporters only occur for the Danish media sector and are virtually absent in all other countries. The hierarchical distinction between the decision-making top-elites and the sub-elite of communication professionals in the political sector is in turn a more decisive one. Albeit not drastically, communication professionals frequently diverge from the attitudinal stances of decision-making elites but do not represent a particularly cohesive sub-group in themselves.

Finally, the results show that the relative weight of individual dimensions of attitudinal consonance (value, procedural, epistemological) varies between countries. Again, the level of sectoral autonomy is best suited to explain these differences. Sectoral autonomy and professionalism lead to a relatively higher emphasis on procedural consonance, the fact that procedural congruence in absolute terms is generally hardest to achieve notwithstanding. The effect of institutional and positional variety on the relative weight of epistemological and value consonance, respectively, can only be partly confirmed. While a link between low institutional variety and an emphasis on epistemological consonance, as well as between low positional variety and an emphasis on value consonance, can be accounted for in the political sectors under study, this link does not consistently appear for the media sectors.

Chapter 7

Elite Cohesion as an
Explanatory Factor

So far, the analysis has examined the attitudinal patterns along and across the sectoral boundaries between the two elites involved in the construction and communication of political messages. This chapter takes a somewhat different approach by examining cohesion as an explanatory factor in itself. This approach involves two steps. First, the relative importance of inter-sectoral elite cohesion between media and political elites is further probed and tested by comparing it to other significant social and political cleavages. Second, the analysis examines potential effects of inter-sectoral consonance on interaction patterns of individual elites.

The first step in the analysis extends the preceding analysis by comparing the functional separation of elites with other factors that may separate elites and thus serve as alternative frameworks for cohesion between distinct groups of elites. Such factors may, for example, refer to gender, as well as religious, racial or regional cleavages. For political communication in European democracies, however, ideological cleavages and generational splits appear as the most likely factors to have an influence on elite formation and cohesion. Probing whether the differentiation into sectors is superseded by other forms of differentiation thus provides a test of whether the analysis of elite cohesion based on the assumption of sectoral elites is the most imminent one in European democracies. While not presenting an independent variable as such, elite attitudes here serve to assess the degree of functional differentiation among political communication elites.

The second step in the analysis focuses on the effects of elite cohesion for elite interaction, thus putting cohesion in the place of the independent variable in the analysis. As discussed in chapter 3, a central assumption of the theoretical model applied in the study is that elite cohesion has consequences for political communication specifically and the public sphere more generally. Although it is not within the scope of this study to determine these consequences empirically on the country level, it is nevertheless possible to conclude the analysis by approaching the question on the level of individual elites.

FUNCTIONAL, IDEOLOGICAL AND GENERATIONAL SEPARATION

So far, cohesion has been analysed based on an assumption of functional separation between the media sector and political sector. In the European democracies under study, this assumption is potentially challenged by alternative factors of group separation including, first and foremost, that of ideological cleavages. Ideological cleavages, in particular along the political left-right-axis, plausibly still play a crucial part in political communication in all of the countries under study, given the historical experience with press-party linkages that may still give rise to revised forms of political parallelism. The question is, then, whether left-right orientation still may challenge or even overrule the functional orientation involved in the separation of media or political sector elites. Correspondingly, a (binary) cross-sectoral measure of left-right orientation among elites is introduced to the analysis.

For political elites, this measure of left-right orientation is based not on individual ideological self-positioning but on personal party membership or work affiliation with a particular party. Ideological position is thus an organizational characteristic that follows from the position of the elite member. By this criterion, attribution of ideological position is not applicable in a number of cases where the required information is not available. For the media elites, by contrast, left-right positioning cannot be inferred from organizational affiliation. Instead, the political orientation of media elites is operationalized as the self-positioning of the respondents on a seven-point left-right scale (Mair 2007).[1] To arrive at a binary measure, values below the country median are coded as 'left-leaning', values above the median as 'right-leaning'. Media elites placing themselves on the median are not assigned to either side.[2]

Second, generational differences may play a role. In the course of the last decades, the political communication environment has seen substantial transformation in all European countries, which can be seen to potentially introduce a generational gap between classical forms of political communication and what has been called the 'third age of communication', including, inter alia, campaign professionalization, permanent campaigning and the increased importance of online communication (Blumler and Kavanagh 1999). Moreover, generational shifts may be sparked by events such as the German reunification and subsequent relocation of the German capital from

Bonn to Berlin (see Maurer and Mayerhöffer 2009) and not least the end of the Franco regime and reinstallation of democracy in Spain.

Correspondingly, two generational splits are introduced in the analysis to account for two potential generational gaps. Whereas the transformations associated with the third age of communication suggest a distinct set of attitudes of younger political communication elites (below the age of forty), the mentioned breaks in national history are presumably related to a distinct set of attitudes of older generations (above the age of fifty) that have (at least partly) been socialized under different systemic conditions.

Whereas the previous measures of discriminance and dispersion have been applied to individual items or consistent group of items, overall group separation must be tested for a number of variables that are theoretically unrelated. Correspondingly, the analysis is based on the measure of *Wilk's Lambda*, which is central to *discriminant analysis*. In contrast to the analysis of discriminance based on relative proximity scores in the preceding chapters, discriminant analysis based on Wilk's Lambda probes the relative strength of different distinctions (in this case group distinctions) as separators of otherwise-unrelated items (in this case attitudes).

However, the attitudes investigated here do not fulfil criterions such as normal distribution and the absence of multi-collinearity that are required for multivariate analyses of group separation, based on discriminance functions. Under these conditions, Roose (2012) proposes an 'index of cultural similarity' based on Wilk's Lambda of a pair-wise discriminant analysis. In this approach to group separation, individual attitudes are not weighted equally. Rather, discriminant analysis assigns more weight to those attitudes that serve best to distinguish (in this case) two groups. These attitudes are not necessarily identical between countries. Put differently: the analysis yields information about the separability of groups based on a catalogue of attitudes, irrespective of the internal structure of these attitudes. When comparing group separability between countries, it does not require the same attitudes to be accountable for separation.

This measure will be referred to in somewhat more formal terms as a *separability measure* in the following, in order to emphasize the focus on the separability of groups. A separability score of zero indicates complete separation, that is, the full absence of any attitudinal overlap between members of the different groups in question. A score of one in turn means that attitudinal stances do not yield the slightest indication of group membership (complete indistinction). For the five-point-scale items used here, complete separation is mostly a theoretical scenario, as the range of attitudinal expression is by forehand so reduced that some overlap will even remain for items with very low consonance.

Based on the outlined approach, figure 7.1 compares the respective *separability scores* (Wilk's Lambda) for each of the three group distinctions (sector, left-right, age), country by country. Country scores for the sectoral distinction are displayed as circles, scores for the left-right split as triangles and scores for the generational splits as squares.

As displayed in figure 7.1, the sectoral split is clearly the best available separator of elite attitudes in all countries, when compared with ideology and generation. The sectoral distinction (displayed in circles) overrules ideological and generational group distinctions in all countries under study. However, significant country differences can also be observed. The Wilk's Lambda for the two Nordic countries, 0.23 and 0.33 for Denmark and Sweden, respectively, indicate a very high degree of separation between media and political sector elites, compared to 0.71 for Spain, indicating weak separability between attitudes based on the sectoral split. As such, the results for the sectoral split based on Wilk's Lambda support the findings about the extent of inter-sectoral cohesion based on proximity scores very well (see chapter 6): separation is highest in the Nordic countries, while Spanish elites are by far the most indistinct, whereas Germany and Austria take up a middle position between separation and indistinction. The outlier position of France previously identified is also confirmed with a Wilk's Lambda score of 0.37, which indicates a rather clear separation of attitudes between the two sectoral elite groups and places France between the Nordic and the central European group.

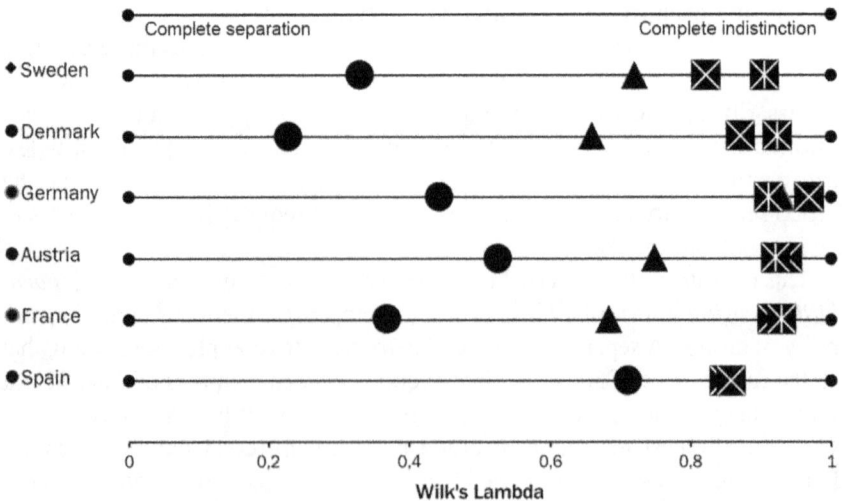

Figure 7.1 Separability Scores (Wilk's Lambda) – Sector versus Ideology and Generation
Data points indicate the Wilk's Lambda for a pairwise discriminant analysis between two subgroups of all political communication elites within a country; circle: sector split; triangle: left-right split; simple cross: age split – 'youngsters' (< forty years); starred cross: age split – 'oldies' (> fifty years)

Political communication elites in the six countries are in this sense first and foremost functional elites in the true sense of the word. The split into functionally differentiated sectors clearly outweighs the left-right distinction and generational differences. The generational split, for its part, appears largely irrelevant. However, some noticeable patterns can be seen. In the Nordic countries, the younger elite generation (below forty years) can be singled out to some extent based on their attitudinal patterns. Moreover, both generational splits separate Spanish political communication elites equally well (or rather not well) as the ideological distinction. For Denmark and Spain, this split can directly be linked back to the changing nature of the guiding principle of publicity. While the younger elite generation in Denmark (age less than forty years) consistently has a more reluctant stance on the principle of publicity, the opposite development can be seen in Spain, where the generation fifty and above is more hesitant towards the acceptance of publicity as a guiding principle.

The ideological left-right split, however, is by no means irrelevant for the attitudinal separation of elites. In absolute terms, the discriminatory power of left-right positioning is considerable in the two Nordic countries, as well as in Austria and France, whereas it is virtually absent in Germany. Although left-right positioning barely provides enough ground for separation of elites in Spain, the difference to the separability score for the sectoral split is also the lowest here. Put differently: elite cohesion approaches consensus in Spain to such a degree that none of the grouping variables reveals any systematic separation.

In all countries but Germany, the traditional left-right cleavage has not yet ceased to be relevant. In France, it is rooted in political polarization; in Austria, on a deeply engrained *Proporz* culture in political life; in the Nordic countries, it is based on the historical experience of an elaborate system of press-party-parallelism and in particular in Denmark, the result of an ongoing re-politicization of political communication. Indeed, when calculating *separability scores* only based on the procedural and epistemological sources of cohesion, the left-right separation (Wilk's Lambda 0.66) even supersedes the sectoral split (Wilk's Lambda 0.73) in Denmark. The attitudinal left-right split is furthermore consistent in substance across all countries. In all countries, right-leaning media and political elites rate both the legitimacy of disclosure and the commercial orientation in political news making substantially higher than their left-leaning counterparts. The latter, by contrast, adhere more strongly to the complementary role set of editorial guide and gladiator.

Moreover, the relative weight of inter-sectoral separation vis-à-vis ideological separation varies substantially between the three guiding principles. Ideology, in particular, emerges as an even more decisive separator between sectors when contrasted with the alternative scenario of a left-right split. In all countries but Spain, ideology is a matter of stark opposition of the two sectors, in large parts due to the profound cross-sectoral mismatch between the (rejected) role of editorial guide and the (embraced) role of party gladiator in the public sphere. In Spain, the principle of publicity separates sectors most clearly. In all countries, pragmatism is least suited to separate sectoral elites based on their attitudinal stances.

In the cases of Spain and Denmark, sectoral separation based on pragmatism is indeed so weak that it is superseded by the left-right split. Whereas this result is mostly the continuation of the generally weak sector separation in Spain, it underlines once again the substantial degree of politicization present in the Danish political communication environment that exists alongside a strong media and political sector. In contrast to the polarized countries in the South, such cross-sectoral alignment is based on an equal standing of political and media elites, rather than a more subordinate role of media alignment that mirrors and follows polarization in the political sphere. Although the discriminatory power of the left-right split is still rather modest for the case of pragmatism in Denmark (Wilk's Lambda 0.75), combined with the fact that a large share of the Danish media elites does not place themselves clearly on either side of the political left-right scale and thus do not enter this part of the analysis, this result remains remarkable.

ELITE COHESION AND ELITE INTERACTION

Whereas the first part of the chapter has probed and tested attitudinal separation against other forms of group distinctions, the second part of the analysis turns to the question of effect. Indeed, this latter part fundamentally reverses the causal relationship underlying the analysis in chapters 5 and 6 and looks at the effects *of* elite cohesion rather than the impact of contextual conditions *on* elite cohesion. As discussed in chapter 3, the theoretical model includes the assumption that elite cohesion has important effects on the construction and communication of political messages and the overall function of the public sphere. Although it is beyond the scope of the book to test outcomes on elite interaction, political news, messages and decisions, it is possible to analyse some effects on attitudes and behaviour of elites themselves. Although more explorative in nature, such an analysis can nevertheless provide a deeper understanding of the effects of elite cohesion.

This analysis builds on the proximity scores calculated for the individual position of each elite actor. So far, the proximity scores have been used to determine degrees of attitudinal dispersion and discriminance for a given group of elites. Rather than being a stepping-stone towards information about attitudinal discrepancies between sectors or groups, as has been case in the preceding chapters, individual proximity scores can also be used to conduct further analysis based on the position of each individual actor within a larger group of elites, both within his or her own reference group and in relation to other elite (sub-)groups.

In principle, this can be analysed on all levels of sub-differentiation applied in previous analysis. In the following, however, the analysis will be restricted to the inter-sectoral perspective, and in particular to the question of how close the attitudes of an elite actor are to the opposing elite group, which indicates a potential function as a *bridge* between elite groups. The lower the individual prox(inter) score, the more can the individual elite actor be assumed to qualify as a bridge.

This numerical expression of the attitudinal position of each elite actor can then be linked to perceptions, as well as to self-reported behaviour. Drawing connections between attitudinal position and perceptions in this way obviously runs the risk of becoming tautological if attitudes based on the interaction between media and political elites are linked to another set of attitudes and perceptions on the same matter. In such a scenario, it becomes difficult to determine what belongs to the belief system of elites and what qualifies as its consequences. To avoid this, the study analyses the attitudinal positions of elite members in relation to indicators that are clearly set apart from the applied cohesion indicators in that they refer to self-reported behavioural patterns of elite interaction, specifically the individual relationship of elite members with elites from the other sector (see also Schwab Cammarano and Díez Medrano 2014):

Frequency of personal contact: (a) *formal-professional* (initiated by political elites to outline their political views); (b) *informal-professional* (at receptions and other social events); (c) *informal* (over lunch, dinner, etc.) (1 = never, 2 = a few times a year or less, 3 = several times a month, 4 = several times a week, 5 = once a day or more);

Friendship: Number of members of other elite sector one would describe as friends;

Harmony: 'As how harmonious or contentious would you describe your relationship with politicians [journalists]?' (1 = very contentious to 5 = very harmonious).

The main underlying assumption is that elite actors who take up an attitudinal position as bridges in one sector have a closer relationship with elites from the opposing sector. This connection should be particularly pronounced for more informal forms of interaction. Thus, a high prox(inter) score on the individual level should be inversely related to frequency and quality of intersectoral interaction. Furthermore, this connection is likely to differ between the respective guiding principle of cohesion on which an elite actor serves as a bridge. Consequently, the analysis is conducted both for the overall prox(inter) score and for each of the guiding principles (prox(inter$_{ideology}$), prox(inter$_{publicity}$), prox(inter$_{pragmatism}$)).

In order to test how individual prox(inter) scores are related to self-reported frequency and quality of inter-sectoral elite interaction, a series of linear regression analyses has been conducted. Given that the consequences for individual elites, rather than country-level consequences, are in the foreground, the analysis diverges from previous ones in that it is based on the entire population of sampled elites across countries. Countries and sectors differ, however, in the overall assessment of frequency and quality of interaction. Consequently, they are introduced as dummy variables into the regression model. Regression analyses are conducted block wise. The first block assumes an effect on frequency and quality of interaction for country and sector of origin, as well as a number of variables that have been central in previous parts of the book:

Generational differences are entered as age (in years; see 'Functional, Ideological and Generational Separation' section in chapter 7), as well as professional experience within the sector (in years), as an explanatory factor.

Left-right differences are entered as a three-point measure that distinguishes left-leaning elites and right-leaning elites, as well as elites that cannot be identified by a clear left or right stance, whether such middle position is explicitly stated or implicitly inferred notwithstanding (rather than excluding these from this part of the analysis altogether, see 'Functional, Ideological and Generational Separation' section in chapter 7).

Elite hierarchy is included as a binary variable following the (cross-sectoral) distinction between elites and sub-elites (see chapter 6).

A measure of *horizontal mobility* is provided by a binary variable specifying previous work experience in the opposite sector.

Prox(inter) scores are added in the second block of the analysis, once as an overall measure that comprises all analysed attitudinal items as well as separately for each guiding principle. Dependent variables include the frequency of professional-formal, professional-informal and informal personal contact, as well as the self-reported number of friends among members of the other sector and the perceived degree of harmony in their interaction with actors from the opposite sector (see earlier). Results are presented in table 7.1.

Results for the base model (1) show that country and sector of origin are substantial factors in explaining the frequency and quality of (self-reported) elite interaction.[3] Political sector elites consistently report a more frequent and harmonious relationship than media elites (for a more detailed analysis, see Pfetsch et al. 2014). By the same token, younger elites, as well as those with a longer work experience, report more frequent personal contact with elites from the opposite sector on all levels of formality. Age and experience are, however, less decisive for how harmonious these interactions are

Table 7.1. Frequency and Quality of Interaction (OLS Regression)

Model	variable	Standardized coefficients (beta)				
		Frequency of personal contact				
		(a) Professional formal	(b) Professional informal	(c) **Informal**	(d) **# of friends**	(e) **Harmony**
(1)	(Constant)	(−33.058)	(−25.241)	(−24.347)	(10.440)	(5.426)
	Denmark	**.083**	−.039	−.052	.001	−.050
	Germany	**.125**	**.251**	**.358**	**.183**	**−.197**
	Austria	.039	.031	**.221**	**.180**	**−.131**
	France	.002	−.012	−.040		.051
	Spain	**.114**	**.418**	**.431**	.058	−.028
	Sector (0 = media)	**.201**	**.236**	**.179**	**.296**	**.379**
	Age (years)	**−.160**	**−.153**	**−.153**	.009	.017
	Years of prof. experience	**.140**	**.150**	**.161**	**.120**	.016
	Horizontal mobility (0 = none)	**.125**	**.106**	.060	**.234**	.062
	Hierarchy (0 = sub-elite)	**−.095**	−.027	.009	**−.098**	**−.083**
	Left-right	.010	**.053**	**.056**	.038	**.082**
	Adjusted R Square	.077	.239	.263	.203	.218
(2a)	Prox(inter)	−.029	**−.073**	**−.105**	−.039	**−.117**
	Adjusted R Square	.077	.243	.272	.204	.229
	Increase in R Square	.000	+.004	+.009	+.001	+.011
(2b)	Prox(inter_ ideology)	−.038	**−.083**	**−.092**	−.014	−.054
	Prox(inter_ publicity)	−.013	−.042	**−.078**	**−.072**	−049
	Prox(inter_ pragmatism)	.006	.011	.009	.031	**−.076**
	Adjusted R Square	.076	.245	.274	.206	.228
	Increase in R Square	−.001	+.006	+.011	+.003	+.010

Note: Country names indicate dummy variables, for which Sweden serves as a baseline; significance levels technically do not apply to full samples. For reasons of readability, they are marked in bold to indicate the relative importance of coefficients. Data for self-reported number of friends are not available for France.

perceived. A consistent relationship between the frequency and quality of interaction can also be observed for elites with previous work-experience in the other sector (horizontal mobility). Both the frequency of interaction and the quality of the relationship are rated higher, in particular with regard to friendships across sectoral lines.

A less consistent pattern emerges for the distinction between elites and sub-elites. In both sectors, specialized sub-elites (i.e. political communication professionals and political reporters) are, by virtue of their position, in charge of liaising with elites from the other sector. Consequently, they have more frequent professional personal contact (a), as well as more friends among members of the other elite sector (d) and rate the inter-sectoral relationship between elites as more harmonious (e). Noticeably, however, the specialized sub-elites no longer display any differences to political decision makers and editors when it comes to more informal elite encounters such as personal contact at social events (b) and at more private settings (e.g. meetings over lunch, c). Here, the top elites get into the game.

Finally, left-leaning elites report significantly fewer professional informal (b) and informal (c) inter-sectoral encounters and generally perceive the mutual interaction as less harmonious (e). At the same time, left-right orientation does not affect professional contacts (a), as well as friendship (d) as the most intimate form of interaction. In particular, the latter result implies that left-leaning elites do not generally hesitate to self-report more informal interaction with elites from the opposite sector. A tentative interpretation is that the differences in informal contact rather result from the fact that most countries under study have had a centre-right government at the time of data collection.

The impact of attitudinal proximity to elites from the other sector becomes evident in models (2a) and (2b) in table 7.1. The most general measure of attitudinal proximity, prox(inter), is consistently negatively related to all indicators of reported interaction. Bearing in mind that a lower proximity score signifies less distance, this indicates that those elites who can be regarded as general bridges between sectors indeed maintain more frequent interactions and view these interactions as more harmonious. The described relation is, however, insignificant for the number of friends (d), as well as for the frequency of formal professional interaction (a).

This is corroborated for the prox(inter) scores relating to individual guiding principles (model 2b). None of the three scores has a significant effect on the frequency of formal professional contact (a). This is in line with the assumption that the effect of individual attitudinal proximity to the opposite sector is least pronounced for more formal and professional forms of interaction. Political and media elites need to uphold this form of interaction attitudinal divergences and lack of cohesion notwithstanding. Furthermore, elites that are closer to the opposite sector in attitudinal terms may not have to resort to formal-professional forms of contact to the same degree but can fall back on more informal ways of interaction.

As assumed, it is not only the overall level of proximity that is of relevance here, but rather the guiding principle on which this proximity is founded. Elites who are close to the stance of the opposite sector in terms of the role of ideology report significantly more informal contacts, both in a more professional (b) and in more private setting (c). Private interaction, that is, meeting members of the opposite sector for lunch or dinner (c), or even calling one or more of them friends (d) is in turn a matter of how close an elite actor is to the other sector's overall stance on the principle of publicity, that is, questions of transparency versus secrecy. Given that the private setting is particularly prone for potential violations of publicity norms, it helps to be on the same page attitudinally speaking to enter this form of interaction. Pragmatism, finally, is less of a matter for frequency, formality and informality of interaction. A similar stance on pragmatism is however significantly related to the perceived harmony of the interaction (e). If elites are well aware of whether other sectoral elites view inter-sectoral relations as a matter of business rather than in an idealist way, and share this sentiment, they are consequently less likely to perceive this relationship as conflict ridden.

Overall, individual proximity to the attitudinal stances of the opposite sector prove to have a clear effect on the frequency and quality of interaction between media and political elites. While much of the differences in self-reported patterns of interaction are naturally founded in an elite's structural position in elite interaction (sector, hierarchy, experience, mobility, etc.), the influence of inter-elite cohesion is not negligible. Overall proximity of an elite actor to the opposite sector in attitudinal terms increases the frequency and quality of in particular more informal modes of interaction, while ideology, publicity and pragmatism as guiding principles of cohesion are clearly associated with particular aspects of interaction between media and political elites.

Given that elite attitudes and behaviour are in large parts interrelated, the outlined effects of individual attitudinal proximity and elite interaction might be questioned by claiming a reverse effect. In this view, attitudinal proximity between different sectoral elites would be a consequence of elite contact rather than the other way around. Such an objection is by no means trivial, given that the model in chapter 3 has specified elite composition and communication as a factor that translates systemic conditions into elite attitudes. In contrast to the more general attitudes that make up elite cohesion, the applied interaction variables are however of a more short-term character, asking for the current state of personal contact and harmony between the two sides. The impact of inter-elite contact in the formation of elite belief systems notwithstanding, attitudes can in this case thus safely be assumed to precede reported behaviour.

SUMMARY: THE SIGNIFICANCE OF SECTORAL BELIEF SYSTEMS

In order to supplement the preceding analysis of inter- and intra-sectoral cohesion under varying systemic conditions, this chapter has approached elite cohesion rather as an explanatory factor. First, the chapter has tested the strength of the sectoral line of demarcation compared to other cleavages and lines of separation of social and political significance. Second, the chapter has tested whether attitudinal consonance has an effect on the behaviour of political communication elites. Taken together, the results have confirmed the significance of the sectoral belief systems of political elites and media elites.

The first part of the analysis has proven that the sectoral line of demarcation between media elites and political elites is a valid starting point for an analysis of elite cohesion. Even when compared with other significant cleavages such as ideological and generational differences, sectoral belief systems stand out as the most pronounced group divider. In this sense, political communication elites are first and foremost sectoral elites in all countries under study: we are dealing with a political communication elite composed of political elites on one side and media elites on the other, rather than young versus old or left versus right, the particular case of Denmark notwithstanding.

The second part of the analysis has linked elite cohesion to the behaviour of the political communication elite. More specifically, the distance between the attitudes of an individual elite member to the attitudes of the opposite sector has proven to have significant effects on the level and quality of interaction with members of the other elite group. While, as chapter 3 has argued in detail, elite belief systems have important consequences for political news, messages, decisions and opinions, the second part of this chapter has approached this issue empirically and found evidence that elite cohesion *does* matter in the realm of behaviour and individual elite interaction.

Chapter 8

Conclusion

The book has taken a first step towards filling the lacuna currently surrounding the existence and importance of the political communication elite. It is now time to summarize the results, insights and new questions yielded by this endeavour. In order to do so, this concluding chapter proceeds in three steps. Firstly, the main theoretical, methodological and empirical contributions of the book are briefly presented and discussed. Secondly, the chapter looks further into some of the more surprising results, new puzzles and queries produced throughout the book, giving rise to a number of reflections on the proposed framework and guidelines for future studies of the political communication elite. Finally, the consequences of elite cohesion in political communication are revisited in a discussion of the possible effects on stability, plurality and civility.

PUTTING A NEW ELITE ON THE MAP

The political communication elite is not just another elite among others in any straightforward sense. Due to the particular position of the political communication elite at the intersection of media and politics and a shared structural dependence on the political public, the book has combined and developed existing research traditions. In this respect, the book has sought not merely to identify a new elite but also to some degree a new field of study requiring a distinct theoretical framework as well as certain methodological innovations. Correspondingly, it is necessary to briefly restate the theoretical and methodological contributions of the book before the main empirical results are recapitulated.

Theoretically, the book has sought to advance the cross-disciplinary integration of political communication studies and elite research. Indeed, the relation between these two traditions is the missing link in existing research. Whereas political communication research has provided us with convincing arguments about the increasing importance of media and communication under the conditions of mediatized politics and democracy, it has – with few exceptions – lacked a firm grasp of the continuing importance of elites in political communication processes. Elite research, in turn, provides us with the tools and insights of such an approach but lacks an understanding of the particular dynamics of political communication, the role of media and mediatization in a wider sense.

Building on this premise, the book has sought to develop a more systematic and comprehensive understanding of actor relations in political communication through the introduction of an elite-oriented approach to the analysis of the media-politics relationship. A key issue here is the need to understand high-ranking journalists and editors as strategic elites in current society. To date, neither political communication studies nor elite research has sufficiently come to terms with the role of journalistic actors as elites in their own right. On this point, the identification of a political communication elite that consists of persons within political organizations *and* media organizations also provides a definitive argument in favour of considering high-ranking journalists and editors elites. As political communication elites they are in a position to affect political outcomes regularly and substantially through their influence on the public debate over political issues.

Moreover, the book has argued for a focus on elite attitudes or belief systems as a crucial entry point to a better understanding of the political communication elite. This approach builds on the established concept and question of elite cohesion, albeit with some important corrections. As the book has demonstrated, cohesion cannot be understood in terms of an all-out consensus or a simple question of absence or presence of agreement, if one is to grasp the complexity of relations that characterize an elite working within and across the sectoral boundaries of media and politics. Indeed, it matters greatly whether cohesion is based on role definitions, on specific codes of conduct or simply on perceptions of the common environment (sources of cohesion), which overall logics of interaction elites find important (guiding principles of cohesion), and not least whether elites are bound together by accepting these principles, or rather by agreeing on that these principles do not matter for their relationship (stance of cohesion).

This amendment to the traditional question of elite cohesion, furthermore, has required a degree of methodological innovation. Hence, the book has pointed to the problems associated with simple measures of cohesion that focus on consensus, agreement and unanimity too one-sidedly in empirical studies of elite attitudes. To overcome these limitations, the book has developed analytical concepts and measures to empirically assess the interplay of political and media elites as a matter of attitudinal consonance. A key proposition here is that cohesion among modern, functionally differentiated, elites is a matter of not only proximity of attitudes but also indistinction between attitudes, which occurs if individual elite groups and factions cannot be distinguished based on their attitudes. The combination of proximity and indistinction has, in turn, been used to distinguish between distinct patterns of cohesion on the inter-sectoral as well as the intra-sectoral level of cohesion.

Additionally, the book has sought to further the use of comparative methodology in the chosen field of study. The comparative approach is already well established in political communication research and elite research. Building on these traditions, the book has proposed a comprehensive framework enabling a more systematic study of the relation between contextual factors and elite cohesion. The application of this framework, moreover, has led to a combination of, on the one hand, extensive data on social structure, the media system and the political system in the six countries under study and, on the other hand, a unique set of attitudinal data on the political elites and media elites in these countries.

Empirically, the comparative approach has then been systematically applied to analyse the belief systems of political communication elites in six European democracies, thus advancing the extensive discussion of the interplay between media and political actors beyond the more or less anecdotal evidence available about the countries under study (and many other countries worldwide). One main proposition of the book has been that features of the social structure, media system and political system are decisive in determining the extent and patterns of inter-sectoral cohesion as well as intra-sectoral cohesion between and within the media elite and the political elite. On the most general level, this proposition has motivated the expectation that cohesion between media and political elites should roughly vary along a north/south axis, dividing the Nordic, German-speaking and Mediterranean country pairs. The empirical analysis of attitudinal consonance among elites in the six countries under study has shown that this is indeed the case – albeit with a number of qualifications.

The extent of inter-sectoral cohesion increases from Northern to Southern Europe, roughly following a decrease in sectoral autonomy as well as social fluidity along the same axis. Levels of cohesion in France, however, have proven to be lower than expected, challenging assumptions about the relationship between social mobility and elite cohesion in particular. Furthermore, low sectoral variety, which is least pronounced in the German-speaking countries, does indeed lead to patterns of cohesion that are based on similarity rather than indistinction. For the guiding principles of cohesion, where assumptions no longer quite follow the north/south-axis, context also proved capable of explaining observed differences: ideology is a particularly decisive factor for elites in Spain and Denmark, publicity for elites in France and Sweden and pragmatism for elites in Austria and Germany.

Sector-specific levels of autonomy and variety furthermore explain the relative balance of cohesion within the media sector and the political sector in each country. In the Nordic countries, the more autonomous media systems display a higher level of elite consonance than the rather diverse and open political systems, while the opposite is true for the Central European countries. For the Mediterranean countries, finally, none of the sectors is substantially more cohesive than the other. More autonomous sectors (e.g. the media sectors in the North and the German political sector) also display more ordered attitudinal patterns, that is, patterns of cohesion in which individual subgroups of elites are equally congruent and put higher emphasis on cohesion based on procedural consonance, that is, consonance on the rules of the game. Sectoral variety, however, proved to have somewhat more inconclusive effects on the extent and level of intra-sectoral cohesion. Finally, the intra-sectoral inconsistency of attitudes between individual subgroups was linked to the question of (role) specialization and division of labour within sectors.

The final part of the analysis involved a change of strategy, approaching elite cohesion rather as an explanatory factor. First, the relative importance of the sectoral split between media elites and political elites was tested against ideological cleavages and generational differences. Despite the large differences in the extent and patterns of inter-elite cohesion, elites in all countries under study proved to be first and foremost functional and sectoral elites in the true sense of the word: no other factor of group separation (e.g. ideology and age) was all out better suited to explain differences in attitudinal patterns. At the same time, the degree of attitudinal consonance based on ideological ties could only be completely discarded in Germany, whereas it still proved relevant in Denmark and Spain. Second, the last part of the analysis looked at the consequences of elite cohesion on patterns of interaction among individual elite members. Results based on the individual attitudinal positions of elites in relation to their own sector as well as the opposing sector showed that the individual proximity to the opposite sector's attitudinal stances increased the likelihood of informal contact across sectors and contributed to a more amicable relationship between elites.

MODIFICATIONS AND PROSPECTS FOR FUTURE RESEARCH

Even with the geographical and cultural proximity of European nation-states, elites diverge in important ways. As shown in the preceding sections, these variations can to a large extent be explained by differences in social structure, the media system and the political system along the north/south axis. As such, the comparative approach has proven able to detect generalizable patterns of the influence in the relation between context and elite cohesion, thus moving beyond established truths and conclusions about elites in general, and political communication elites in particular, which are all too often based on single-case studies and anecdotal accounts of the relations between media and political actors. However, not all expectations about the mechanisms determining the level and nature of cohesion among political communication elites have been supported, suggesting a need to look into certain national and historical particularities, alternative explanations and new lines of inquiry.

Given the number of cases and overall design, a certain level of balance between the pursuit of universal mechanisms of attitude formation and complementary observations of national specifics is clearly built into the study, that is, a balance between more or less global differences and the unique constellations of systemic and cultural features in each individual country. The trade-offs involved in large-N studies vis-à-vis comparative case studies are well known. One advantage of the latter, however, is that attention to national particularities can help to shed light on more complex and fine-grained linkages between the systemic environment and elite cohesion in cases where general assumptions have had to be refuted in ways that suggest that they have not been sufficiently accounted for in the overall model.

The most important conclusion to be drawn from such considerations is that each country pair along the north/south axis can be divided into a textbook representative of the group and a more transitional group member. On the one hand, we have three textbook countries displaying levels and patterns of cohesion in accordance with previous expectations: Sweden is the most consistent case of weak cohesion in the political communication elite, as expected for the Nordic countries. Germany is the prime example of a country with a moderate level of cohesion based on similarity. Spain represents the Mediterranean group of countries, where media and political elites were expected to come closest to cohesion as consensus.

Denmark, Austria and France, on the other hand, display a number of deviations and contradictions, although combined with characteristics associated more directly with their country group. This result has been interpreted as a sign of elevated pressure, upheaval in processes of political communication and a transitional state of affairs in all three countries. The nature of this transition is, however, particular to each country. The key trend in Denmark is a re-politicization of political communication. Austria, for its parts, is seeking a new model to replace established *Proporz* principles, while the results for France can be seen as a result of an ongoing transition from more idealist models in political communication and political journalism to a more distant and adversarial relationship.

The key outlier emerging from this pattern is France, which in many ways resembles the fellow transitional case of Denmark to a larger degree than its southern neighbour Spain. Although the discussion of context factors has already shown that France is not an archetypical representative of the Southern European tradition, these results remain puzzling. In the course of the analysis, a number of explanations have been discussed that give rise to a refinement and further testing of the developed model and its main assumptions. First, the low degree of inter-elite cohesion in France has questioned the assumption that traditional elite ties, as engrained in the social structure and social mobility, naturally coincide with attitudinal elite ties. While this should not lead to hasty conclusions on the role of social structure for modern day elites, it certainly suggests further research on how traditional, class-based assumptions on elite composition and cohesion can be transferred to elite relations in overall more fluid and mobile societies.

A second issue concerns the lack of a clear link between sectoral variety and patterns of attitudinal differentiation. Generally, the findings have suggested that more attention should be paid to how institutional and positional variety each contribute to the segmentation and fragmentation of intra-sectoral belief systems, as well as to the specific interplay of both types of sectoral variety in shaping elite attitudes.

In a broader sense, such deviations and modifications suggest a need to solidify the proposed model through application of the developed framework to other countries. This would include, first and foremost, broadening the pool of countries beyond Europe but within the sphere of democratic rule. In a second step, however, defect democracies or authoritarian regimes will of course provide further insight into the relation between national context and elite cohesion. However, an application of the proposed model to non-democratic cases will clearly involve careful attention to the specific systemic factors, which may not all apply once we move outside the realm of established democracies. In other words, whereas the general model and overall distinction between social structure, media system and political system presented in chapter 3 should be sufficiently general to merit consideration also in the non-democratic context, the specific attributes highlighted and discussed in chapter 4 will have to be adapted accordingly once moving beyond the analysis of European democracies.

Whereas such cross-sectional considerations are a natural extension of the conducted study and the comparative approach in a wider sense, the question of development over time is less straightforward. While the book is not in the position to advance firm longitudinal claims, it does provide some indications of relevant lines of inquiry. The first of these is directly related to the identification of the group of transitional countries. In a wider sense, such transition adds a temporal dimension to the relation between attitudinal patterns and systemic and structural conditions. On one level, this dimension has to do with changes in the systemic environment and the speed with which elite attitudes can be expected to react to such changes, that is, the inertia of belief systems in relation to systemic transitions. At a deeper level, a longitudinal approach draws attention to potential feedback relations between attitudinal patterns and the systemic environment, and thus to elite attitudes as a precursor to systemic changes.

In both cases, however, temporal dynamics suggest themselves as possible explanations for the gaps and inconsistencies between structural conditions and elite attitudes found in cross-sectoral observations. The existing body of literature on the various transitions political communication has been undergoing in different countries can be of help to make sense of some of the results. The end of the party press in the Scandinavian countries or the changing nature of French journalism may thus be interpreted in a way that suggests that the Swedish editorial guides and the French idealists are a remnant of previously dominant belief systems.

Second, longitudinal reflections can also be linked to the disorder and volatility of intra-sectoral cohesion. Disordered belief systems appear in cases where, in the same sector, one or more (formally defined) groups of elites with a high degree of internal congruence face other group(s) of elites that are in high internal disagreement on the same matter, clearly challenging the internal balance of elites. None of the observed sectors is entirely free of such elements of disorder and volatility. The analysis of role specialization in particular has pointed to the special role of attitudinal disorder in the formation of elite belief systems: role fragmentation was observed in otherwise largely consistent belief systems, whereas role segmentation was accompanied by a more fundamental differentiation of belief systems also on the procedural and epistemological dimension. This can be interpreted in two ways.

One scenario suggests that role fragmentation indicates that more pervasive sectoral changes and alterations are in their infancy: one subgroup begins to question an existing consistent understanding of elites' role in political communication, manifested in an increasing level of incongruence within this group. Role fragmentation would then precede a more thorough segmentation of attitudes. Adopting a more or less cyclical perspective on changes, a related, yet alternative, interpretation puts role fragmentation at the end of the cycle: preceding full sedimentation, role fragmentation can also be seen as a relic from earlier, now largely discarded belief systems. Elites share a consistent stance on the procedural and epistemological foundations of political communication but have not equally translated these into a consistent interpretation of roles. The two interpretations of role fragmentation are not in contradiction but rather express the crucial role of role fragmentation in changing elite belief systems.

More generally, such reflections raise the question of the stability and consistency of observed levels and patterns of elite cohesion over time. Longitudinal observations of elite cohesion in political communication will thus help to shed light on the formation of elite belief systems and their relation to the systemic environment in which they are embedded. As always, longitudinal studies seem most wanting where cross-sectional observations have been the priority. While the empirical extraction and confirmation of principles of cohesion from the attitudes of elites themselves has merits in its own right, it also fails to uncover the decisive ruptures and inconsistencies in elite belief systems that may be crucial in explaining the very consequences of elite attitudes.

A final, yet vital, consideration for future research concerns the relation between elite attitudes and mass beliefs. The distinction between elite and mass beliefs may have served to single out the former for empirical study already in the introduction to this book, but it also indicates a continued relevance of elite-mass (in)congruence for political communication and politics in a wider sense. Even in times where the division between a communicating elite and an audience at the receiving end is more and more questioned, the focus on elites within established institutions of the media and political sector vis-à-vis popular mass attitudes is still a vital focal point for future studies of political communication. Even if digital democracy and new forms of governance is seen to question the elite-mass divide, it remains as pertinent as ever.

CONSEQUENCES OF ELITE COHESION IN EUROPEAN DEMOCRACIES

The spectre of a single and unified power elite in control of society has haunted elite research since its origin. In popular debate and imagery, this all-powerful elite often takes the shape of secret clubs, networks and outright conspiracies. Indeed, it is exactly this image of an elite conspiracy that has been invoked by populist movements in their claims to represent the voice of the people. However, the empirical analysis provides no evidence that such an elite exists in the sphere of political communication. The extent and patterns of elite cohesion do not resemble a closed or ideologically unified elite exercising control of the public sphere. Inter-sectoral cohesion does not overrule sectoral borders in any of the six countries, even in countries with strong politicization tendencies such as Denmark. Sectoral differences, moreover, generally win out if put to the test against ideological or generational differences across all of the countries under study.

However, the question of consequences remains. Although we can dispense with the idea of an internally cohesive and ideologically united political communication elite, the extent and patterns of attitudinal consonance can nevertheless be assumed to have an impact on politics and society. In other words, are media elites and political elites too close or too far apart, judged by their consequences for political news, messages, decisions, public opinion and, in the last instance, current democracy? To be clear, this question extends beyond the parameters of the empirical analysis, which has not been designed to test consequences of elite cohesion in and of itself. The overall model advanced by the book does, however, provide an analytical framework for some concluding reflections on the issue.

First and foremost, the results have some bearing on the question of *stability*. As discussed in the introduction, some would hold that elite cohesion should preferably flourish up to a level just short of complete ideological unification in order to ensure the overall stability of democracy. Less radical arguments for elite cohesion, however, tend rather to take a more open approach to the question of how much cohesion between different elite actors and groups is necessary in order to ensure stability without infringing on sectoral autonomy and underlying divisions of power. Even if sectoral autonomy has not been fundamentally questioned by the results, the distinction between the three textbook countries (Sweden, Germany and Spain) and the three transitional countries (Denmark, Austria and France) does correspond largely to a distinction between countries with largely (though by no means entirely) coherent patterns of consonance that suggest a high degree of stability vis-à-vis three countries with more incoherent patterns that suggest a higher degree of instability.

It may seem counter-intuitive at first to expect stability to follow from elite belief systems in Sweden and Germany, given that degrees of inter-elite cohesion are relatively low in both countries. Indeed, Spain would have to be seen as the country where elite cohesion is most strongly associated with stability if inter-sectoral consensus was the sole criterion. However, stability also requires ordered attitudes on the sectoral level, which is true for Sweden and Germany, but only partially present in Spain. Stability in the Spanish case is thus more a matter of inter-sectoral subjugation and sectoral concentration of attitudes. Moreover, Swedish elites display a comparatively high level of inter-sectoral and intra-sectoral procedural consonance, which indicates a high potential for stability in interaction between media and political elites, even if the partially unsettled stances to partisan communication roles does indicate a certain level of instability.

By contrast, the three transitional countries Denmark, Austria and France display rather incoherent levels and patterns within and between sources and principles of consonance. This is exemplified by the principle of ideology, which is accepted as an epistemological given, but either contested or, in the case of France, even rejected for the two remaining sources of attitudinal consonance. If stances and levels of consonance contradict each other within guiding principles, the potential for ruptures in elite relations increases.

In a wider sense, and with some added hindsight since the time of data collection, it is of course rather noticeable that the group of transitional countries can all be considered front runners in the emergence of right-wing populism that has become such a pronounced trend in European democracies. France, Austria and Denmark have all seen a rather early emergence of populist parties and in the case of Denmark and Austria a subsequent degree of integration and even normalization of these parties in parliamentary politics. Sweden and Germany, by contrast, saw the emergence of populist parties later and largely resist integration and normalization in parliamentary politics. Spain represents a somewhat particular case here, once again due to the relatively recent historical experience with right-wing autocratic rule. It has, however, seen the emergence of a strong left-wing populist party in recent times.

This observation raises the question of the extent to which the transitional dynamic in this group of countries is in fact related to the rise of populism. In an empirical sense, this would suggest that these countries were in some sense 'ahead of the curve' at the time of the study, leading to the expectation that attitudinal patterns in Sweden and Germany will move closer to the transnational group, or have perhaps already done so. In a more normative sense, the issue at stake is whether more incoherence and instability in political communication are a necessary response to the populist challenge. This issue is clearly dependent on the deeper question of whether integration and normalization in parliamentary politics and public debate, as opposed to a strategy of rejection and silencing traditionally associated with the Swedish and German response to the populist challenge, is viewed as desirable in the first place. In other words, more incoherence and instability in elite cohesion may be a necessary part of a democratically viable reconfiguration in response to populism.

Second, cohesion in the political communication elite can be seen as a question of *plurality*. Whereas the questions of stability, and some extent the question of civility, are normatively ambiguous and subject to the opposing arguments for and against elite cohesion, plurality is routinely considered a core democratic value in political communication emphasizing the need to have all relevant viewpoints are publicly communicated and debated. Assuming that public/mass opinion is shaped by available information and viewpoints in the public sphere furthermore suggests that citizens' political attitudes are largely elite-driven and hence that patterns of attitudinal consonance in the political communication elite can be linked to mass attitude formation.

According to one line of argument, elite cohesion should be considered fundamentally detrimental to plurality insofar as it invokes the image of a more or less tacit elite consensus on a retreat from public debate whenever critical information has to be exchanged or potentially controversial decisions have to be made. Conversely, such a retreat is put forth as a fundamental necessity by the more radical proponents of the case for elite cohesion, that is, as a premise for political and democratic stability. Setting aside the more radical arguments from the outer ends of the normative spectrum, however, the different levels and patterns of cohesion can be seen to impact on the plurality of messages and news in a more nuanced way. Indeed, the study gives rise to the observation that all belief systems are structured in a way that presents potential impediments to plurality. For each country, we can thus identify critical points in the belief systems of the political communication elite that deserve particular attention as potential barriers to plurality in political communication, even if we accept the premise of elite-driven attitude formation.

On a general level, plurality can be assured in two ways: through the mutual commitment of elites to plurality or through the existence of distance and conflict, which guarantees plurality by the mere fact that elites do not agree on specific issues of debate, nor on particular forms and styles of communication. Against this background, Sweden and France stand out as the countries most conducive to plurality based on both parameters. In both countries, communication elites have been seen to rely to a relatively high degree on the principle of publicity so essential to plurality in political communication and, moreover, display a rather pronounced level of distance and conflict between media elites and political elites. Additionally, intra-sectoral cohesion is also segmented and fragmented in France. There are, nevertheless, some critical points even in these two countries. For one, the pivotal status of publicity versus secrecy in the elite negotiations and compromises of the two countries also makes the commitment to publicity potentially volatile and subject to reversal if elite notions of how best to achieve the common good change.

Moreover, the highly consistent media sector in Sweden presents a high risk for limiting the plurality in news making. By contrast, plurality in communication largely benefits from very clear patterns of role specialization in both the media sector and the political sector in Germany and Austria. In this way, the systematic (self-)assigning of different communicative roles and tasks to different factions of media elites and political elites may foster plurality in a way more akin to cooperation than conflict. The prime impediment to plurality is thus located on the inter-sectoral rather than the intra-sectoral level. Here, cohesion based on the similarity of sectoral belief systems, as well as the weak role of publicity as a guiding principle of cohesion, makes the relationship between media and political elites a bit too cosy.

Such 'cosiness', in turn, is clearly not the prime impediment to plurality in Spain and Denmark, despite the substantial overall inter-elite consensus in Spain, and the marked epistemological consensus in Denmark. Rather, both countries have also been seen to be most prone to an ideological split between left-leaning and right-leaning elites that may supplement or in the final instance even cover over the sectoral division between media elites and political elites. The resulting ideological struggle in political communication may at first glance evoke an image of plurality but is in fact detrimental to the plurality of issues and voices as it limits the public debate to the prevailing issues at stake on the ideological battleground.

A political communication elite defined by ideological struggle, finally, points to the question of *civility* as the third major consequence of elite cohesion. Civility in political communication is generally seen to be under attack from political campaign logics such as smear techniques, partisan journalism and not least populist movements that show explicit disregard for established norms of debate. As a consequence, incivility finds a potential breeding ground in elite belief systems characterized by polarization and a strong acceptance of the principle of ideology. At the same time, the principle of ideology alone cannot account for incivility in itself. In order for a political communication elite defined by its ideological orientations to end in an ideological struggle characterized by incivility, other factors must come into play.

As outlined in chapter 3, incivility can be linked to a number of factors discussed throughout the book. For one, elite cohesion based on a strong acceptance of the principle of pragmatism suggests an instrumental approach to political communication that provides fertile ground for incivility. Moreover, blurring or mixing of sectoral belief systems may indicate formation of cross-sectoral alliances that overrule established agreements on civility between the two sectors. Finally, incivility may be driven by intra-sectoral fragmentation of attitudes. Taking these together, the dissolution of established professional creeds in conjunction with an overall pragmatic and interest-driven take on political communication provides the breeding ground for ideology-driven incivility.

Even though this study is in no position to empirically conclude on the extent and patterns of cohesion of the U.S.-American political communication elite, the discussed scenarios do point to a number of aspects that could very well be characteristic of this elite and thus a potential explanation for the surge of incivility in the past years, which is culminating rather than being caused by the arrival of Trump in American politics (Berry and Sobieraj 2014; Herbst 2010). Of course, none of the European countries under study display trends on par with the U.S. experience in this respect. However, it is still worth considering some critical points and potential red flags, even if deep and pervasive incivility in political communication is not immanent. In this respect, some countries do seem more prone to incivility than others.

In Spain, inter-sectoral cohesion is firmly rooted in ideology and pragmatism, laying the groundwork for potential incivility, which is only countered by a somewhat more idealistic stance on the procedural aspects of pragmatism. Moreover, sectoral fragmentation, as well as the fundamental lack of sectoral boundaries in attitudinal terms, indicates that media elites and political elites are lacking the kind of professional creed that can be assumed to dampen incivility. The risk of incivility in France, more so than in Spain, is caused by the ongoing transition from more ideologically driven to a more neutral form of political communication, as well as a wavering between more pragmatic and idealist approaches to political communication that cuts across sectoral lines. Instances of cohesion as mixing and a high degree of sectoral fragmentation amend the picture of a belief system characterized by a high degree of uncertainty and transformation, providing an entry point for incivility as a feature of political communication. While the Mediterranean countries thus provide the most fertile ground for incivility in political communication, there is also some signals that put Denmark in the risk of increasing incivility in public debate, first and foremost the fact that a left-right-split within the political communication elite is, while not in full bloom, a realistic scenario based on the observed attitudinal patterns.

When raising questions of the stability, plurality and civility of the public debate and the overall political process, elite belief systems are naturally just one part of the puzzle. It is however exactly this piece of the puzzle that this book can contribute – both in theoretical and in empirical fashion. Thinking of high-ranking political and media actors as elites inherently points to the fundamental question of a balance between stability and autonomy raised by elite theory. As discussed, this overall question carries over to questions of plurality and civility more akin to political communication elites as such: How can an elite of political communication not only hinder but also safeguard plurality? How is a high level of civility maybe also a way for established communication elites to protect the status quo of political communication and their position within it?

It is precisely because of questions like these that the study very explicitly refrains from passing normative judgement on the observed patterns of elite cohesion. What the study though does not refrain from is from passing judgement on our way of conceptualizing the role of individual attitudes and perceptions, as well as of more complex belief systems in understanding the status and role of elites in modern societies and the consequences that follow from it. Our understanding of elite attitudes is in dire need of more nuanced conceptions and measures – especially in times where an abundance of network data seemingly provides us with an easy way out in understanding elite relations in political communication and beyond. Studying the complexity of attitudes is not an easy task, but attitudinal measures cannot be simplified in order to produce seemingly straightforward answers.

Appendix

Table A.1. Cohesion Indicators by Guiding Principles and Sources

Ideology	
	Combined indicator guide_glad
	Editorial guide (Media): 'When covering politics, how important is it for you to voice particular views on political developments?' (1 = not important at all to 5 = very important)
	Gladiator (Politics): 'When communicating through (mass) media, how important is it for you to promote your party's political position?' (1 = not important at all to 5= very important)/communicators: 'Politicians communicate through (mass) media to promote their party's political position'. (1 = strongly disagree to 5 = strongly agree)
	Convictions: 'How strongly do the political convictions of journalists/politicians affect your professional interaction with them?' (1 = not strongly at all to 5 = very strongly)
	Parallelism: 'When thinking about the media landscape in your country, would you say that individual media reflect particular political positions?' (1 = strongly disagree to 5= strongly agree)

Publicity	
	Combined indicator watch_info
	Watchdog (Media): 'When covering politics, how important is it for you to investigate political claims and serve as a watchdog to political elites?' (1 = not important at all to 5= very important)
	Information provider (Politics): 'When communicating through (mass) media, how important is it for you to provide citizens with information they need to make informed decisions about politics?' (1 = not important at all to 5= very important/communicators: 'Politicians communicate through (mass) media to provide citizens with information they need to make informed decisions about politics'. (1 = strongly disagree to 5 = strongly agree)
	Disclosure: How legitimate is it for journalists to publish confidential political information without approval?' (1 = never legitimate to 5 = legitimate in most cases)
	Democracy: 'How would you rate the media's impact on how democracy functions in this country?' (1 = very negative to 5 = very positive)

(Continued)

Table A.1.   Continued

Pragmatism

Combined indicator mass_infl

Mass communicator: 'When covering politics, how important is it for you to produce content of interest to a large audience? (1 = not important at all to 5 = very important)

Strategic communicator: 'When communicating through (mass) media, how important is it for you to influence political decision-making?' (1 = not important at all to 5 = very important) /communicators: Politicians communicate through (mass) media to influence political decision making (1= strongly disagree to 5 = strongly agree)

Difference indicator

Clash of interests: Conflicts associated with diverging professional interests versus social reasons (1 = primarily structural reasons); *calculated as:*

Interests: 'How frequently does conflict occur as the result of the diverging professional interests of journalists and politicians?' *minus average of*

Fairness: 'How often does conflict arise because politicians treat journalists unfairly (M)/journalists treat politicians unfairly (P)?' *and*

Respect: 'And how frequently are conflicts because politicians lack respect for journalists (M)/journalists lack respect for politicians (P)?' (1 = very infrequent to 5 = very frequent)

Commercial orientation: Generally speaking, how strong do you think is the impact of commercial restraints (like profit orientation, audience ratings) on the media coverage in your country? (1 = not strong at all to 5 = very strong)

Note: All indicators are original or re-coded five-point Likert scales, for which 1 represents strong disagreement and 5 represents strong agreement to each attitudinal indicator; for all guiding principles, the value dimension is understood as the *complementarity* of distinct and sector-specific political communication roles; for political sector elites, communication professionals ('communicators') were not asked for their own role perception but to state their idea about politicians' political communication roles. The procedural and epistemological dimensions are operationalized by *corresponding* attitudes, that is, identical statements for both sectoral elite groups; identical items, obtained by back-translation of the English master questionnaire, were used in all countries under study; internal consistency (Cronbach's α) for ideology .42, for publicity .38, for pragmatism .12.

Table A.2. Number of Contacted Persons, Respondents, Response Rates, Field Period and Interview Modes

	Sweden			Denmark			Germany			Austria			France			Spain		
	(c)	(r)	%	(c)	(r)	%	(c)	(r)	%	(c)	(r)	%	(c)	(r)	%	(c)	(r)	%
Media Elites	272	161	60	125	86	69	342	187	55	422	154	37	393	100	25	300	91	30
Print	137	85	62	73	47	64	182	93	51	179	76	43	222	61	27	129	31	24
TV	84	51	61	29	21	72	135	74	55	135	41	30	127	17	13	76	33	43
Radio	42	24	57	7	4	57	17	14	82	97	31	32	29	9	31	76	20	26
News Agency	9	1	11	16	14	88	8	6	75	11	6	55	29	13	45	19	7	37
Political Elites	223	118	53	102	46	45	411	105	26	205	77	31	682	60	9	238	57	24
Executive	58	14	24	34	6	18	60	16	27	41	10	24	100	42	42	92	20	18
Parliament	127	82	58	58	34	59	313	69	22	73	27	30	582	18	3	67	22	33
Parties	38	22	65	10	6	60	38	20	53	91	26	29	10	6	60	79	15	19
C.professionals	89	61	69	88	59	67	122	68	56	124	55	44	189	42	22	59	16	27
Executive	34	26	77	51	32	63	63	30	48	54	17	31	144	34	24	38	9	24
Party/Parliament	39	25	64	32	24	75	29	20	69	30	17	57	45	8	18	8	3	38
External	16	10	63	5	3	60	30	18	60	40	21	53	-	-	-	13	4	31
Field Period	April–November 2008			April 2008–January 2009			April 2008–March 2009			April–June 2008			November 2009–March 2010			April–July 2008		
Interview Mode	CATI/Online			CATI/Mail/Online			CATI/Mail/Face-to-Face/Online			CATI/Mail/Face-to-Face			CATI/Online			CATI/Mail		

(c) = contacted; (r) = responded; % = response rate; CATI = computer-assisted telephone interview; group categories apply to the schematic used in the overall project and thus slightly diverge from the division in sub-sectors and hierarchies specified here; response rates were unaffected by interview mode, with the exception of a slight increase in non-response in the case of online participation; interviews were conducted by participants of the project 'Political Communication Cultures in Western Europe', as well as by Gesis ZUMA (GER) and TNS Sofres (FRA). Item non-response was generally very low, ranging from 2 to 4 per cent for epistemological items and 5 to 10 per cent for procedural items; interview mode had virtually no effect on the substance of the answer, when controlling for sector and country; for more details on the fieldwork, see Maurer and Vähämaa 2014.

Table A.3. Demographic and Professional Background of Surveyed Media and Political Elites

	Sweden	Denmark	Germany	Austria	France	Spain
	Media Elites					
Share of women (%)	42	19	22	34	26	36
Average age (years)	46.2	43.4	46.4	44.0	47.5	43.7
Average work experience (years)	20.7	16.0	21.4	19.3	22.4	20.4
Work experience in political sector (%)	17	14	10	13	3	8
Left-right self-positioning (mean; 1 left – 7 right)	3.8	3.6	3.6	3.9	3.3	3.0
	Political Elites					
Share of women (%)	41	33	32	28	28[a]	18
Average age (years)	44.9	41.8	49.2	46.5	43.4	51.6
Decision makers	*49.3*	*48.4*	*52.5*	*48.1*	*44.4*	*51.1*
Communication professionals	*36.3*	*36.9*	*44.5*	*44.2*	*41.2*	*53.4*
Work experience in journalism (%)	38	48	43	52	11	15
Decision makers	*27*	*24*	*27*	*33*	*3*	*8*
Communication professionals	*59*	*59*	*66*	*78*	*21*	*40*
Average work experience (years)	15.1	11.8	12.6	14.3	12.7	18.1
Decision makers	*19.0*	*17.2*	*13.3*	*13.5*	*12.6*	*19.1*
Communication professionals	*7.1*	*7.3*	*11.5*	*15.3*	*12.8*	*13.9*
Party membership of comm. professionals (%)	76	40	33[b]	55	28	n/a
. . . in the executive	*72*	*17[c]*	*7[b]*	*44*	*17*	*n/a*

[a]16% in group of decision makers, 43% in group of communication professionals; [b]numbers may be underreported ('no' answers and non-responses together); [c]split between special advisors (40%) and ministerial spokespeople (11%)

Table A.4. Inter-Sectoral Cohesion: Patterns, Dispersion Scores, Discriminance Scores and Means (Media Elites [M]/Political Elites [PI])

		Sweden	Denmark	Germany	Austria	France	Spain
Ideology							
Editorial guide/ Gladiator	Pattern	A	A	A-B	A	A	D
	Dispersion	1.6	1.4	1.1	1.2	1.3	.6
	Discriminance	1.73	1.96	.68	.74	1.34	.02
	Mean M/P	1.9/4.4	1.5/4.0	2.7/4.1	2.6/4.1	1.7/3.8	4.1/4.3
Political Convictions	Pattern	A-B	A-B	C-D	C-D	C-D	B-C
	Dispersion	.9	1.0	.9	.9	1.1	1.1
	Discriminance	.21	.20	.04	.02	.03	.11
	Mean M/P	1.6/2.3	1.7/2.4	2.0/2.3	2.0/2.2	2.1/2.5	2.5/3.0
Political Parallelism	Pattern	A-B	D	B	D	D	D
	Dispersion	1.0	.8	.8	.8	.8	.6
	Discriminance	.25	.03	.15	.05	.04	.02
	Mean M/P	2.6/3.4	3.5/3.7	3.0/3.6	3.3/3.7	3.5/3.7	4.4/4.3
Publicity							
Watchdog/ Information Provider *(italics: without communication professionals)*	Pattern	B-D *B-D*	A-B *B-D*	B *B-D*	B *D*	B *B-D*	B-D *B-D*
	Dispersion	.6 *.5*	.9 *.8*	.7 *.7*	.8 *.6*	.6 *.5*	.7 *.5*
	Discriminance	.11 *.02*	.35 *.06*	.23 *.13*	.20 *.04*	.21 *.08*	.08 *.08*
	Mean M/P	4.8/4.4 *4.8/4.7*	4.5/3.6 *4.5/4.3*	4.5/3.9 *4.5/4.1*	4.6/3.9 *4.6/4.4*	4.8/4.3 *4.8/4.6*	4.6/4.2 *4.8/4.6*
Disclosure	Pattern	A-B	A	A-B	A-B	A	A
	Dispersion	1.0	1.4	1.1	1.1	1.3	1.4
	Discriminance	.45	.51	.38	.24	.41	.35
	Mean M/P	4.5/3.3	4.0/2.7	2.9/1.9	2.7/1.8	4.0/2.7	3.6/2.5
Democracy	Pattern	B	B-D	B	B-D	B-D	B-D
	Dispersion	.7	.6	.8	.8	.8	.7
	Discriminance	.25	.09	.22	.08	.11	.06
	Mean M/P	4.1/3.4	4.0/3.5	3.7/3.0	3.3/2.9	3.6/3.1	3.8/3.4

(Continued)

Table A.4. Continued

		Sweden	Denmark	Germany	Austria	France	Spain
Mass/Strategic Communicator	Pattern	B-D	D	B-D	D	C-D	D
	Dispersion	.7	.8	.7	.7	.9	.7
	Discriminance	.07	.01	.05	.00	.00	.03
	Mean M/P	4.4/4.0	3.9/4.0	4.1/3.7	4.0/3.9	3.8/3.7	4.2/4.0
Clash of Interests	Pattern	B	D	B-D	B-C	A-B	D
	Dispersion	.8	.8	.8	.9	.9	.7
	Discriminance	.21	.04	.10	.08	.24	.01
	Mean M/P	3.6/3.0	3.5/3.2	3.6/3.2	3.7/3.2	3.6/3.0	3.3/3.4
Commercial Orientation	Pattern	C-D	C-D	B-D	D	C-D	D
	Dispersion	9	1.0	.7	.6	.9	.6
	Discriminance	.00	.01	.07	.01	.00	.00
	Mean M/P	2.8/2.9	3.3/3.5	3.5/4.0	3.8/4.0	3.6/3.7	4.0/4.1

Pragmatism

Table A.5. Intra-Sectoral Cohesion – Internal Congruence and Role Specialization (Proximity Scores, Group Means and Patterns)

	Sweden	Denmark	Germany	Austria	France	Spain
	Internal Congruence: Media Sector versus Political Sector (Mean Prox (intra)) [Mean (intra)]					
Editorial Guide/ Gladiator	1.2 [1.9] / 0.6 [4.4]	0.7 [1.5] / 0.6 [4.0]	1.0 [2.7] / 0.6 [4.1]	1.2 [2.6] / 0.6 [4.1]	0.9 [1.7] / 0.8 [3.8]	0.6 [4.1] / 0.6 [4.3]
Political Convictions	0.8 [1.6] / 0.9 [2.3]	0.7 [1.7] / 1.1 [2.4]	0.8 [2.0] / 0.9 [2.3]	0.9 [2.0] / 0.9 [2.2]	1.1 [2.1] / 1.1 [2.5]	1.1 [2.5] / 0.9 [3.0]
Political Parallelism	1.0 [2.6] / 0.9 [3.4]	0.8 [3.5] / 0.7 [3.7]	0.6 [3.0] / 0.8 [3.6]	0.9 [3.3] / 0.7 [3.7]	0.8 [3.5] / 0.8 [3.7]	0.6 [4.4] / 0.6 [4.3]
Watchdog/Info. Provider	0.3 [4.8] / 0.7 [4.4]	0.6 [4.5] / 1.0 [3.6]	0.6 [4.5] / 0.7 [3.9]	0.6 [4.6] / 0.8 [3.9]	0.4 [4.8] / 0.7 [4.3]	0.6 [4.6] / 0.8 [4.2]
Disclosure	0.6 [4.5] / 1.2 [3.3]	1.1 [4.0] / 1.1 [2.7]	1.1 [2.9] / 0.8 [1.9]	1.2 [2.7] / 0.9 [1.8]	1.1 [4.0] / 1.2 [2.7]	1.2 [3.6] / 1.3 [2.5]
Democracy	0.5 [4.1] / 0.7 [3.4]	0.5 [4.0] / 0.7 [3.5]	0.7 [3.7] / 0.7 [3.0]	0.9 [3.3] / 0.7 [2.9]	0.7 [3.6] / 0.8 [3.1]	0.6 [3.8] / 0.8 [3.4]
Mass/Strat. Communicator	0.6 [4.4] / 0.7 [4.0]	0.8 [3.9] / 0.7 [4.0]	0.8 [4.1] / 0.7 [3.7]	0.8 [4.0] / 0.6 [3.9]	0.9 [3.8] / 0.8 [3.7]	0.7 [4.2] / 0.7 [4.0]
Clash of Interests	0.8 [3.6] / 0.6 [3.0]	0.8 [3.5] / 0.8 [3.2]	0.8 [3.6] / 0.7 [3.2]	0.8 [3.7] / 0.9 [3.2]	0.9 [3.6] / 0.7 [3.0]	0.7 [3.3] / 0.7 [3.4]
Commercial Orientation	0.8 [2.8] / 0.9 [2.9]	1.1 [3.3] / 0.9 [3.5]	0.7 [3.5] / 0.6 [4.0]	0.7 [3.8] / 0.6 [4.0]	0.9 [3.6] / 0.9 [3.7]	0.6 [4.0] / 0.5 [4.1]
	Role Specialization on the Sub-Sectoral Level (Mean Prox (sub)) [Mean (sub)])					
	Media Sector: Editors vs. Reporters					
Editorial Guide	1.1 [1.8] / 1.2 [2.0]	*0.9 [1.7] / 0.5 [1.3]*	1.0 [2.9] / 1.0 [2.6]	1.2 [2.6] / 1.1 [2.6]	0.9 [1.8] / 0.9 [1.8]	0.6 [4.1] / 0.7 [4.1]
Watchdog	0.2 [4.9] / 0.4 [4.8]	0.5 [4.6] / 0.7 [4.5]	0.5 [4.6] / 0.6 [4.5]	0.6 [4.5] / 0.5 [4.6]	*0.2 [4.9] / 0.5 [4.7]*	0.6 [4.5] / 0.5 [4.7]
Mass Communicator	0.6 [4.5] / 0.6 [4.4]	**0.7 [4.2] / 0.9 [3.7]**	0.7 [4.2] / 0.8 [3.9]	0.8 [4.1] / 0.8 [3.9]	1.0 [3.8] / 0.9 [3.8]	0.7 [4.2] / 0.7 [4.2]
	Media Sector: Public versus Private					
Editorial Guide	***0.4 [1.2] / 1.5 [2.2]***	0.5 [1.3] / 0.7 [1.6]	**0.9 [2.2] / 0.8 [3.2]**	**0.9 [2.0] / 1.0 [3.1]**	***0.3 [1.2] / 0.9 [2.0]***	0.7 [4.0] / 0.6 [4.2]
Watchdog	0.4 [4.8] / 0.3 [4.8]	0.6 [4.5] / 0.6 [4.6]	0.5 [4.6] / 0.6 [4.5]	0.5 [4.6] / 0.6 [4.5]	0.1 [4.9] / 0.3 [4.8]	***0.7 [4.4] / 0.5 [4.7]***

(Continued)

Table A.5. Continued

	Sweden	Denmark	Germany	Austria	France	Spain
Mass Communicator	0.6 [4.4] / 0.6 [4.4]	0.9 [3.9] / 0.8 [3.9]	0.7 [4.3] / 0.9 [3.9]	0.7 [4.3] / 0.9 [3.8]	1.2 [3.4] / 0.8 [3.8]	0.7 [4.1] / 0.7 [4.3]
Private Media Subsector: Print versus Broadcasting						
Editorial Guide	1.6 [2.4] / 0.6 [1.4]		0.9 [3.3] / 1.1 [2.4]	1.0 [3.2] / 0.7 [2.1]	0.9 [2.1] / 0.6 [1.4]	0.6 [4.0] / 0.6 [4.4]
Watchdog	0.3 [4.8] / 0.2 [4.9]		0.6 [4.5] / 0.7 [4.0]	0.6 [4.5] / 0.6 [4.4]	0.3 [4.8] / 0.3 [4.8]	0.4 [4.7] / 0.5 [4.7]
Mass Communicator	0.6 [4.5] / 0.6 [4.2]		0.9 [3.8] / 0.8 [3.9]	0.9 [3.8] / 1.0 [4.0]	0.8 [3.9] / 1.0 [3.5]	0.7 [4.4] / 0.7 [4.1]
Political Sector: Decision Makers versus Communication Professionals						
Gladiator	0.6 [4.6] / 0.5 [4.0]	0.7 [4.4] / 0.6 [3.8]	0.6 [4.2] / 0.6 [4.1]	0.7 [4.2] / 0.5 [4.1]	0.9 [3.7] / 0.6 [4.0]	0.6 [4.3] / 0.8 [4.1]
Information Provider	0.5 [4.7] / 0.7 [3.6]	0.8 [4.3] / 0.8 [3.1]	0.6 [4.1] / 0.8 [3.6]	0.6 [4.4] / 0.9 [3.3]	0.5 [4.6] / 0.7 [3.8]	0.7 [4.2] / 0.8 [4.2]
Strategic Communicator	0.7 [4.2] / 0.7 [3.6]	0.8 [4.2] / 0.7 [3.8]	0.8 [3.6] / 0.5 [3.9]	0.7 [3.9] / 0.5 [3.9]	0.9 [3.5] / 0.6 [4.0]	0.6 [3.8] / 0.8 [4.1]
Political Sector: Executive versus Party-Political Elites						
Gladiator	0.6 [4.2] / 0.6 [4.5]	0.5 [3.8] / 0.7 [4.2]	0.8 [3.7] / 0.6 [4.3]	0.6 [3.8] / 0.6 [4.3]	0.8 [3.9] / 0.8 [3.9]	0.5 [4.1] / 0.6 [4.5]
Information Provider	0.7 [4.0] / 0.6 [4.5]	0.9 [2.9] / 0.8 [4.0]	0.8 [3.6] / 0.6 [4.0]	0.8 [3.8] / 0.8 [4.0]	0.6 [4.2] / 0.7 [4.4]	0.6 [4.3] / 0.8 [4.1]
Strategic Communicator	0.9 [3.7] / 0.7 [4.1]	0.9 [3.4] / 0.6 [4.3]	0.6 [3.5] / 0.7 [3.8]	0.3 [4.0] / 0.7 [3.9]	0.8 [3.7] / 0.9 [3.7]	0.7 [3.9] / 0.7 [4.0]
Party-Political Subsector: Left-Leaning versus Right-Leaning Elites						
Editorial guide/ Gladiator	0.6 [4.4] / 0.6 [4.5]	0.7 [4.1] / 0.6 [4.5]	0.6 [4.3] / 0.5 [4.4]	0.7 [4.3] / 0.6 [4.3]	0.7 [4.0] / 0.9 [3.5]	0.4 [4.7] / 0.5 [4.4]
Watchdog/ Info. Provider	0.6 [4.5] / 0.6 [4.5]	0.9 [4.1] / 0.9 [4.1]	0.7 [4.1] / 0.5 [4.1]	0.7 [4.4] / 0.7 [4.2]	0.4 [4.7] / 0.7 [4.4]	1.1 [3.9] / 0.8 [4.1]
Mass/Strat. Communicator	0.7 [4.1] / 0.7 [4.1]	0.7 [4.4] / 0.6 [4.4]	0.8 [3.7] / 0.7 [3.8]	0.8 [4.0] / 0.8 [3.8]	0.8 [3.5] / 0.8 [3.8]	0.8 [3.8] / 0.5 [4.0]

Note: For role specialization, italics indicate disorder, figures in bold indicate inconsistency; private print versus private broadcasting division not applicable in Denmark.

Notes

1. INTRODUCTION

1 The argument is, however, based on a historical argument rather than a normative theory as such. The necessity of consensual elites is thus based on the empirical claim that 'no democracy has ever emerged without the prior or concomitant formation of a consensually united elite, and none has persisted when such an elite has broken down' (Higley 2007, 251).

2 Survey data used in the empirical analysis have been collected within the project 'Political Communication Cultures in Europe', carried out under the auspices of the European Science Foundations' EUROCORES Programme and funded by national research councils in Sweden (VR), Denmark (DFF), Germany (DFG), Austria (FWF) and Spain (MEC). The author would like to thank the project participants for the collaborative effort in designing and conducting the project, which has laid ground for this book. See Pfetsch (2014).

2. ELITES IN MEDIATIZED POLITICS

1 The power elite tradition has been continued in the work of John Scott (1991), G. William Domhoff (2009), Ralph Miliband (2009) and Thomas R. Dye (1976), among others.

2 In large parts of his work, Bourdieu however avoids the term 'ruling class' and substitutes it by *field of power* or merely *class* (e.g. Bourdieu 1993); for a discussion of Bourdieu's terminology, see Hartmann (2005).

3 By the same token, Plasser and Plasser (2002, 7) speak of professional political consultants as a 'new power elite'.

4 Lichter et al. (1986) themselves acknowledge that this approach may be seen as problematic for the same reasons – and in fact treat the surveyed media elites as individual elites in their own right throughout their study.

5 *Agenda setting* 'refers to the idea that there is a strong correlation between the emphasis that mass media place on certain issues (e.g. based on relative place-ment or amount of coverage) and the importance attributed to these issues by mass audiences' (Scheufele and Tewksbury 2007, 9).

6 *Priming* describes a process in which 'by calling attention to some matters while ignoring others, television news influences the standards by which governments, presidents, policies, and candidates for public office are judged' (Iyengar and Kinder 1987, 63).

7 *Framing* or the use of news frames means 'to select some aspects of a perceived reality and make them more salient in a communicating text, in such a way as to promote a particular problem definition, causal interpretation, moral evaluation, and/or treatment recommendation' (Entman 1993, 52).

8 *Cultivation theory* suggests that television consumption over time 'cultivates' the audience's perception of reality (Shanahan and Morgan 1999). The political effect it describes is therefore not directed towards specific policies or political actors but rather affects broader political variables like trust.

9 Adding to such dimensions of horizontal elite integration, the term is sometimes also applied in terms of *vertical elite integration*, also denominated elite-mass congruence (Hoffmann-Lange 1992; van Beek 2010).

10 Sigal pays substantial attention to what he calls the 'journalistic creed' – a frame-work of shared values as the news makers' belief system that contains 'the con-ventions, or epistemological premises of newsmaking; the role conceptions, or newsmen's views of their jobs; and the catch-phrases, or their forensic ideology' (Sigal 1973, 65). In contrast to cultural approaches, this belief system covers only the media sector.

3. A MODEL OF ELITE COHESION IN POLITICAL COMMUNICATION

1 A similar distinction can be found in Higley and Burton's differentiation between general political and social values, attitudes towards appropriate forms of social conduct and general perceptions of the state of society (e.g. the per-ceived degree of freedom or equality). However, their focus is still on value consensus and the role of elites for the consolidation of democratic regimes (Higley and Burton 2006).

4. POLITICAL COMMUNICATION ELITES IN THE EUROPEAN CONTEXT

1 Intra-generational mobility, that is, the upward or downward mobility of the same individual or group, is in contrast more apt as a measure of societal stability as well as individual security.

2 The particular Swedish marriage of egalitarianism and class structure even extends to the aristocracy: 4 per cent of media elites in the 1990 study are aristocratic, in contrast to 2 per cent of the entire elite and 3 promille of the entire Swedish population (SOU 1990, 319).

3 In the past years, Sweden has however seen the establishment of an influential right-populist party (Sverigedemokraterna). At the time of data collection, they were still emerging as a political force and were not yet represented in parliament. Being represented in parliament, they now remain largely isolated from the other parties.

4 As has been the case in Sweden, Germany has meanwhile seen the establishment of a right-wing populist party, Alternative für Deutschland.

5 A particular situation arises however in the case of *cohabitation*, that is, when the president and the parliamentary majority/prime minister are from different parties. As presidential and legislative elections are meanwhile held within the same month, cohabitation has become very unlikely.

6 In Denmark and Germany, permanent correspondents are formally accredited to associations granting journalists privileged access to parliament, as well as governmental press conferences (*Folketingets presseloge, Bundespressekonferenz*).

7 Regional newspapers are an integral part of the French media landscape and widely read, but their outlook on national politics is very limited (Blum 2014).

8 In fact, the ominous 'spin doctor' – if at all still referred to as such – is found behind different positions (Tenscher 2003, 119). Most clearly, the Danish system has introduced the specialized formal position of 'special advisor', which comes closest to the conventional notion of a spin doctor. More general, the Nordic countries refer to 'spin doctors' in regard to formalized political positions within the otherwise-strictly apolitical administration. All other countries are far more reserved in their use of the notion and use it only colloquially to refer to individual examples: the German countries mostly assign this term to externally hired campaign experts. In France and Spain, the term usually refers to certain members of the president's and prime minister's personal staff (cabinet/gabinete) (Aira 2009, 2011).

5. INTER-SECTORAL COHESION IN POLITICAL COMMUNICATION

1 The composite indicator for pragmatism can be seen only as a rough indication for attitudinal consonance, as internal consistency is very weak. Similar cross-national levels and patterns of cohesion appear, however, when the analysis is based on average dispersion and discriminance of the individual items, rather than the composite indicator.

2 This may partly also be the result of the fact that spokespeople were asked to state the importance of this role from the viewpoint of political actors rather than from

their own, potentially lowering the intensity of their role acceptance. The case of Spain shows on the other hand that such an 'intensity gap' is not a given. This is corroborated by the fact that such 'intensity gap' neither appears for the role perceptions on the other two principles.

3   The four other reasons for conflict were measured as follows: How often do conflicts between journalists and politicians arise (1 = not frequent at all and 5 = very frequently) due to *Incorrectness*: passing on (M)/rendition (P) of incorrect information/ *Unfairness*: unfair treatment/ *Disrespect*: lack of respect for the other side/ *Compliance:* non-compliance with met agreements?

6. INTRA-SECTORAL COHESION OF MEDIA AND POLITICAL ELITES

1   Only in two cases are communication professionals' attitudes towards procedural and epistemological conditions of political communication closer to the stance of the media sector elites than to the political decision makers, namely in the case of ideology in Germany and France.

7. ELITE COHESION AS AN EXPLANATORY FACTOR

1   Exact wording: in political matters, people talk of 'left' and 'right'. Generally speaking, how would you place your views on this scale, when 1 is the left end and 7 the right end of the scale?

2   The median value corresponds to the theoretical middle of the scale (4) in five of the countries, but diverges to the left in Spain (3), which means that Spanish media elites are coded as right-leaning for scale values 4 and upwards, and as left-leaning for scale values 1 and 2. In the ensuing analysis, separability scores for Spain have additionally been calculated based on the theoretical middle of the scale (4); in all cases, discrepancies between the two measures are marginal and below graphical visibility.

3   Regression coefficients for individual countries represent the effect in relation to the perceived state of elite interaction in Sweden. As can be seen from the coefficients, Swedish elites rate at the lower end in terms of frequency of personal contact and self-reported number of friends, while they are at the higher end in terms of perceived harmony.

References

Aberbach, Joel D., Robert D. Putnam and Bert A. Rockman. 1981. *Bureaucrats and Politicians in Western Democracies*. Cambridge, MA: Harvard University Press.

Aira, Toni. 2009. *Los spin doctors: Cómo mueven los hilos los asesores de los líderes políticos*. Barcelona: Editorial UOC.

Aira, Toni. 2011. *Los guardianes del mensaje: Asesores políticos: Un modelo alternativo a los spin doctors anglosajones*. Barcelona: Editorial UOC.

Alba, Carlos R. 2001. 'Bureaucratic Politics in Spain: A Long-Lasting Tradition'. In *Politicians, Bureaucrats and Administrative Reform*, edited by Guy B. Peters and Jon Pierre, 89–100. London: Routledge.

Almond, Gabriel A. 1983. 'Corporatism, Pluralism and Professional Memory'. *World Politics* 35:245–260.

Almond, Gabriel A. and Sidney Verba. 1963. *The Civic Culture: Political Attitudes and Democracy in Five Nations*. Princeton, NJ: Princeton University Press.

Alsius, Salvador, Marcel Mauri and Ruth Rodríguez Martínez. 2011. 'Spain: A Diverse and Asymmetric Landscape'. In *Mapping Media Accountability – In Europe and Beyond*, edited by Tobias Eberwein, Susanne Fengler, Epp Lauk and Tanja Leppik-Bork, 155–167. Köln: Halem.

Altheide, David L. and Robert P. Snow. 1979. *Media Logic*. Beverly Hills, CA: SAGE.

Arriaza Ibarra, Karen and Lars Nord. 2014. 'Public Service Media under Pressure: Comparing Government Policies in Spain and Sweden 2006–2012'. *Javnost – The Public* 21 (1):71–84.

Bachrach, Peter. 1967. *The Theory of Democratic Elitism – A Critique*. London: University of London Press.

Baisnée, Olivier and Ludivine Balland. 2011. 'France: Much Ado about (Almost) Nothing?'. In *Mapping Media Accountability – In Europe and Beyond*, edited by Tobias Eberwein, Susanne Fengler, Epp Lauk and Tanja Leppik-Bork, 63–76. Köln: Halem.

Balmas, Meital and Tamir Sheafer. 2010. 'Candidate Images in Election Campaigns: Attribute Agenda Setting, Affective Priming and Voting Intentions'. *International Journal of Public Opinion Research* 22 (2):204–229.

Baugut, Philip and Carsten Reinemann. 2013. 'Informal Political Communication Cultures: Characteristics, Causes, Effects'. *German Policy Studies/Politikfeldanalyse* 9 (1):23–68.

Baum, Matthew A. and Angela S. Jamieson. 2006. 'The Oprah Effect: How Soft News Helps Inattentive Citizens Vote Consistently'. *Journal of Politics* 68 (4):946–959.

Bennett, W. Lance. 1990. 'Toward a Theory of Press-State Relations in the United States'. *Journal of Communication* 40 (2):103–127. doi: 10.1111/j.1460-2466.1990.tb02265.x.

Bennett, W. Lance and Robert M. Entman. 2001. *Mediated Politics: Communication in the Future of Democracy*. Cambridge: Cambridge University Press.

Bennett, W. Lance, Regina G. Lawrence and Steven Livingston. 2007. *When the Press Fails: Political Power and the News Media from Iraq to Katrina*. Chicago, IL: University of Chicago Press.

Bennett, W. Lance and David Paletz, eds. 1994. *Taken by Storm: The Media, Public Opinion, and U.S. Foreign Policy in the Gulf War*. Chicago, IL: University of Chicago Press.

Benson, Rodney. 2006. 'News Media as a "Journalistic Field": What Bourdieu Adds to New Institutionalism, and Vice Versa'. *Political Communication* 23 (2):187–202. doi: 10.1080/10584600600629802.

Benson, Rodney and Erik Neveu. 2005. 'Introduction: Field Theory as a Work in Progress'. In *Bourdieu and the Journalistic Field*, edited by Rodney Benson and Erik Neveu, 1–27. Cambridge: Polity Press.

Berry, Jeffrey M. and Sarah Sobieraj. 2014. *The Outrage Industry: Political Opinion Media and the New Incivility*. Oxford: Oxford University Press.

Best, Heinrich. 2008. 'New Challenges, New Elites? Changes in the Recruitment and Career Patterns of European Representative Elites'. In *Elites: New Comparative Perspectives*, edited by Masamichi Sasaki, 77–102. Leiden/Boston, MA: Brill.

Best, Heinrich and Maurizio Cotta, eds. 2000. *Parliamentary Representatives in Europe 1848–2000: Legislative Recruitment and Careers in Eleven European Countries*. Oxford: Oxford University Press.

Best, Heinrich and John Higley, eds. 2018. *The Palgrave Handbook of Political Elites*. London: Palgrave Macmillan.

Blach-Ørsten, Mark. 2014. 'The Emergence of an Increasingly Competitive News Regime in Denmark'. In *Political Journalism in Transition: Western Europe in a Comparative Perspective*, edited by Raymond Kuhn, 93–110. London: Tauris.

Blondel, Jean and Ferdinand Müller-Rommel. 2007. 'Political Elites'. In *The Oxford Handbook of Political Behavior*, edited by Hans-Dieter Klingemann and Russell J. Dalton, 818–832. Oxford: Oxford University Press.

Blum, Roger. 2014. *Lautsprecher und Widersprecher. Ein Ansatz zum Vergleich der Mediensysteme*. Köln: Herbert von Halem Verlag.

Blumler, Jay G. and Michael Gurevitch. 1995. *The Crisis of Public Communication*. London/New York, NY: Routledge.

Blumler, Jay G. and Dennis Kavanagh. 1999. 'The Third Age of Political Communi-cation: Influences and Features'. *Political Communication* 16:209–230.

Bottomore, Tom. 1993. *Élites and Society*. 2nd ed. London/New York, NY: Routledge.

Bourdieu, Pierre. 1984. *Distinction. A Social Critique of the Judgement of Taste*. Cambridge, MA: Harvard University Press.

Bourdieu, Pierre. 1993. *The Field of Cultural Production*. Cambridge: Polity Press.

Bourdieu, Pierre. 1996. *The State Nobility: Elite Schools in the Field of Power*. Cam-bridge: Polity Press.

Bourdieu, Pierre. 2005. 'The Political Field, the Social Science Field, and the Journal-istic Field'. In *Bourdieu and the Journalistic Field*, edited by Rodney Benson and Erik Neveu, 29–47. Cambridge: Polity Press.

Breen, Richard. 2007. 'Intergenerational Mobility: Core Model of Social Fluidity'. In *Blackwell Encyclopedia of Sociology*, edited by George Ritzer. Blackwell Refer-ence Online. doi:10.1111/b.9781405124331.2007.x

Breen, Richard. 2010. 'Educational Expansion and Social Mobility in the 20th Cen-tury'. *Social Forces* 89 (2):365–388. doi: 10.2307/40984537.

Bryant, Jennings and Mary Beth Oliver. 2009. *Media Effects: Advances in Theory and Research*. 3rd ed. New York, NY: Routledge.

Burgert, Denise. 2010. *Politisch-mediale Beziehungsgeflechte*. Berlin: Lit.

Bürklin, Wilhelm. 1997. 'Die Potsdamer Elitestudie von 1995: Problemstellungen und wissenschaftliches Programm'. In *Eliten in Deutschland. Rekrutierung und Integration*, edited by Wilhelm Bürklin and Hilke Rebenstorf, 11–34. Opladen: Leske + Budrich.

Burton, Michael, Richard Gunther and John Higley. 1992. 'Introduction: Elite Trans-formations and Democratic Regimes'. In *Elites and Democratic Consolidation in Latin America and Southern Europe*, edited by John Higley and Richard Gunther, 1–37. Cambridge: Cambridge University Press.

Canel, María José. 2013. 'Government Communication in Spain: Leaving behind the Legacies of the Past'. In *Government Communication: Cases and Challenges*, edited by Karen Sanders and María José Canel, 133–152. New York, NY: Blooms-bury Academic.

Choi, Yong-Joo. 1995. *Interpenetration von Politik und Massenmedien: Eine theo-retische Arbeit zur politischen Kommunikation*. Münster: Lit.

Christiansen, Peter Munk and Lise Togeby. 2007. 'Elite Transformation in Denmark 1932–1999'. In *Comparative Studies of Social and Political Elites*, edited by Fredrik Engelstad and Trygve Gulbrandsen. Amsterdam: Elsevier.

Christiansen, Peter Munk, Lise Togeby and Birgit Møller. 2001. *Den danske elite*. Copenhagen: Hans Reitzel.

Ciaglia, Antonio and Marco Mazzoni. 2014. 'Pop-Politics in Times of Crisis: The Italian Tabloid Press During Mario Monti's Government'. *European Journal of Communication* 29 (4):449–464.

Clayman, Steven E., Marc N. Elliott, John Heritage and Megan K. Beckett. 2012. 'The President's Questioners: Consequential Attributes of the White House Press Corps'. *The International Journal of Press/Politics* 17 (1):100–121. doi: 10.1177/1940161211420867.

Cohen, Jonathan, Yariv Tsfati and Tamir Sheafer. 2008. 'The Influence of Presumed Media Influence in Politics: Do Politicians' Perceptions of Media Power Matter?'. *Public Opinion Quarterly* 72 (2):331–344.

Converse, Philip E. 1964. 'The Nature of Belief Systems in Mass Publics'. In *Ideology and Discontent*, edited by David E. Apter, 206–261. New York, NY: The Free Press of Glencoe.

Cook, Timothy E. 1998. *Governing with the News: The News Media as a Political Institution*. Chicago, IL: University of Chicago Press.

Dahl, Robert A. 1961. *Who Governs?* New Haven, CT: Yale University Press.

Dahl, Robert A. 1967. *Pluralist Democracy in the United States*. Chicago, IL: Rand McNally.

Dahl, Robert A. 1971. *Polyarchy: Participation and Opposition*. New Haven, CT: Yale University Press.

Dahl, Robert A. 1989. *Democracy and Its Critics*. New Haven, CT: Yale University Press.

Dahrendorf, Ralf. 1965. *Gesellschaft und Demokratie in Deutschland*. München: R. Piper & Co. Verlag.

Dalton, Russel J. 1985. 'Political Parties and Political Representation: Party Supporters and Party Elites in Nine Nations'. *Comparative Political Studies* 18:267–298.

Davis, Aeron. 2003. 'Whither Mass Media and Power? Evidence for a Critical Elite Theory Alternative'. *Media, Culture & Society* 25 (5):669–690. doi: 10.1177/01634437030255006.

Davis, Aeron. 2007. 'Investigating Journalist Influences on Political Issue Agendas at Westminister'. *Political Communication* 24:181–199.

Davis, Aeron. 2009. 'Journalist-Source Relations, Mediated Reflexivity and the Politics of Politics'. *Journalism Studies* 10 (2):204–219. doi: 10.1080/14616700802580540.

Davison, W. Phillips. 1983. 'The Third-Person Effect in Communication'. *Public Opinion Quarterly* 47 (1):1–15. doi: 10.1086/268763.

Delli Carpini, Michael and Scott Keeter. 1996. *What Americans Know about Politics and Why It Matters*. New Haven, CT: Yale University Press.

Deuze, Mark. 2005. 'What is Journalism?: Professional Identity and Ideology of Journalists Reconsidered'. *Journalism* 6 (4):442–464. doi: 10.1177/1464884905056815.

Diezhandino, Maria Pilar, Ofa Bezunartea and Cesar Coca. 1994. *La Elite de los Periodistas*. Bilbao: Universidad del País Vasco/Euskal Herriko Unibertsitatea.

Dimock, Michael and Samuel Popkin. 1997. 'Political Knowledge in Comparative Perspective'. In *Do the Media Govern?*, edited by Shanto Iyengar and Richard Reeves, 217–224. Thousand Oaks, CA: SAGE.

Dinas, Elias, Erin Hartman and Joost van Spanje. 2016. 'Dead Man Walking: The Affective Roots of Issue Proximity between Voters and Parties'. *Journal of Political Behaviour* 38 (3):659–687.

Dindler, Camilla. 2011. 'Christiansborg uden for citat'. Dissertation University of Copenhagen.

DiPalma, Giuseppe. 1973. *The Study of Conflict in Western Society: A Critique of the End of Ideology*. Morristown, NJ: General Learning Press.

Dogan, Mattei. 2003. *Elite Configurations at the Apex of Power*. Leiden/ Boston, MA: Brill.

Domhoff, G. William. 2009. *Who Rules America? Challenges to Corporate and Class Dominance*. 6th ed. New York, NY: McGraw-Hill.

Domke, David. 2004. *God Willing? Political Fundamentalism in the White House, the 'War on Terror' and the Echoing Press*. London: Pluto Press.

Donges, Patrick. 2008. *Medialisierung politischer Organisationen*. Wiesbaden: VS Verlag für Sozialwissenschaften.

Donohue, George A., Phillip J. Tichenor, and Clarice N. Olien. 1995. 'A Guard Dog Perspective on the Role of Media'. *Journal of Communication* 45 (2):115–132. doi: 10.1111/j.1460–2466.1995.tb00732.x.

Dörner, Andreas. 2004. 'Power Talks. Zur Transformation der politischen Elite in der medialen Erlebnisgesellschaft'. In *Elitenmacht*, edited by Ronald Hitzler, Stefan Hornbostel and Cornelia Mohr. Wiesbaden: VS Verlag für Sozialwissenschaften.

Dreier, Peter. 1982. 'The Position of the Press in the U.S. Power Structure'. *Social Problems* 29 (3):298–310.

Durkheim, Émile. 1984. *The Division of Labor in Society*. London: Macmillan.

Dye, Thomas R. 1976. *Who's Running America? Institutional Leadership in the United States*. Englewood Cliffs, NJ: Prentice-Hall.

Easton, David. 1965. *A Systems Analysis of Political Life*. New York, NY: Wiley.

Eberwein, Tobias. 2011. 'Germany: Model without Value?' In *Mapping Media Accountability – In Europe and Beyond*, edited by Tobias Eberwein, Susanne Fengler, Epp Lauk and Tanja Leppik-Bork, 77–89. Köln: Halem.

Eberwein, Tobias, Susanne Fengler, Epp Lauk and Tanja Leppik-Bork, eds. 2011. *Mapping Media Accountability – In Europe and Beyond*. Köln: Halem.

Eldersveld, Samuel J. 1964. *Political Parties: A Behavioral Analysis*. Chicago, IL: Rand McNally.

Elmelund-Præstekær, Christian, David Nicolas Hopmann and Asbjørn Sonne Nørgaard. 2011. 'Does Mediatization Change MP-Media Interaction and MP Attitudes toward the Media? Evidence from a Longitudinal Study of Danish MPs'. *International Journal of Press/Politics* 16 (3):382–403. doi: 10.1177/1940161211400735.

Engelstad, Fredrik. 2007. 'Introduction: Social and Political Elites in Modern Democracies'. *Comparative Social Research* 23:1–9.

Engelstad, Fredrik. 2009. 'Democratic Elitism – Conflict and Consensus'. *Comparative Sociology* 8:383–401.

Engelstad, Fredrik and Trygve Gulbrandsen, eds. 2007. *Comparative Studies of Social and Political Elites*. Vol. 23, *Comparative Social Research*. Amsterdam: Elsevier.

Entman, Robert M. 1993. 'Framing: toward Clarification of a Fractured Paradigm'. *Journal of Communication* 43 (4):51–58.

Entman, Robert M. 2003. *Projections of Power: Framing News, Public Opinion, and U.S. Foreign Policy*. Chicago, IL: University of Chicago Press.

Entman, Robert M. 2011. 'Incivility and Asymmetric Partisan Warfare'. Louisiana State University Conference 'In the Name of Democracy: Political Communication Research & Practice in a Polarized Media Environment', 28–29 March 2011.

Esmark, Anders. 2014. 'Politicized Media? Partisanship and Collusion in the European Context'. In *Political Communication Cultures in Europe: Attitudes of Political Actors and Journalists in Nine Countries*, edited by Barbara Pfetsch, 148–170. Basingstoke: Palgrave Macmillan.

Esmark, Anders. 2017. 'Maybe It Is Time to Rediscover Technocracy? An Old Framework for a New Analysis of Administrative Reforms in the Governance Era'. *Journal of Public Administration Research and Theory* 27 (3):501–516. doi: 10.1093/jopart/muw059.

Etzioni-Halevy, Eva. 1993. *The Elite Connection: Problems and Potential of Western Democracy*. Cambridge: Polity Press.

European Journalism Centre. 2014. 'Media Landscapes'. Accessed 21/11/2014. ejc. net/media_landscapes.

Fabris, Hans Heinz. 1995. 'Der österreichische Weg in die Mediengesellschaft'. In *Österreich 1945–1995: Gesellschaft, Politik, Kultur*, edited by Reinhard Sieder, Heinz Steiner and Emmerich Tálos, 641–654. Wien: Verlag für Gesellschaftskritik.

Falasca, Kajsa and Lars Nord. 2013. 'Structures, Strategies and Spin: Government Communication in Sweden'. In *Government Communication: Cases and Challenges*, edited by Karen Sanders and María José Canel, 27–44. New York, NY: Bloomsbury Academic.

Ferree, Myra Marx, William A. Gamson, Jürgen Gerhards and Dieter Rucht. 2002. 'Four Models of the Public Sphere in Modern Democracies'. *Theory and Society* 31:289–324.

Fico, Frederick. 1984. 'How Lawmakers Use Reporters: Differences in Specialization and Goals'. *Journalism Quarterly* 61 (4):793–800.

Field, G. Lowell and John Higley. 1980. *Elitism*. London/Boston, MA/Henley: Routledge & Kegan Paul.

Fuchs, Dieter. 2007. 'The Political Culture Paradigm'. In *The Oxford Handbook of Political Behavior*, edited by Russell J. Dalton and Hans-Dieter Klingemann. Oxford: Oxford University Press.

Gäbler, Bernd. 2011. '. . . und unseren täglichen Talk gib uns heute!' Inszenierungsstrategien, redaktionelle Dramaturgien und Rolle der TV-Polit-Talkshows*. Frankfurt am Main: Otto Brenner Stiftung.

Gans, Herbert J. 1979. *Deciding What's News: A Study of CBS Evening News, NBC Nightly News, Newsweek, and Time*. New York, NY: Pantheon Books.

Genieys, William. 2010. *The New Custodians of the State: Programmatic Elites in French Society*. New Brunswick, NJ: Transaction Publishers.

Gerbner, George and Larry Gross. 1976. 'Living with Television: The Violence Profile'. *Journal of Communication* 26 (2):172–194.

Gerhards, Jürgen and Friedhelm Neidhardt. 1991. 'Strukturen und Funktionen moderner Öffentlichkeit: Fragestellungen und Ansätze'. In *Öffentlichkeit, Kultur, Massenkommunikation. Beiträge zur Medien- und Kommunikationssoziologie*, edited by Stefan Müller-Doohm and Klaus Neumann-Braun, 31–90. Oldenburg: BIS-Verlag.

Gibson, Rachel K. and Andrea Römmele. 2001. 'Changing Campaign Communications: A Party-Centered Theory of Professionalized Campaigning'. *Harvard International Journal of Press/Politics* 6 (4):31–43.

Giddens, Anthony. 1972. 'Elites in the British Class Structure'. *Sociological Review* 20 (3):345–372.

Gitlin, Todd. 2003. *The Whole World Is Watching: Mass Media in the Making & Unmaking of the New Left*. Berkeley, CA: University of California Press.

Grande, Edgar. 2000. 'Charisma und Komplexität. Verhandlungsdemokratie und der Funktionswandel politischer Eliten'. *Leviathan* 28 (1):122–141.

Green-Pedersen, Christoffer. 2002. 'New Public Management Reforms of the Danish and Swedish Welfare States: The Role of Different Social Democratic Responses'. *Governance* 15 (2):271–294.

Gulbrandsen, Trygve. 2008. 'Elite Integration and Institutional Trust in Norway'. In *Elites: New Comparative Perspectives*, edited by Masamichi Sasaki, 171–192. Leiden/Boston, MA: Brill.

Gulbrandsen, Trygve. 2012. 'Elite Integration – An Empirical Study'. *Historical Social Research/Historische Sozialforschung* 37 (1):148–166.

Gunther, Albert C. and J. Douglas Storey. 2003. 'The Influence of Presumed Influence'. *Journal of Communication* 53 (2):199–215. doi: 10.1111/j.1460–2466.2003. tb02586.x.

Gunther, Richard. 1992. 'Spain: The Very Model of the Modern Elite Settlement'. In *Elites and Democratic Consolidation in Latin America and Southern Europe*, edited by John Higley and Richard Gunther, 38–80. Cambridge: Cambridge University Press.

Guttsman, W. L. 1960. 'Social Stratification and the Political Élite'. *British Journal of Sociology* 11 (2):137–150.

Hachmeister, Lutz. 2002. 'Einleitung: Das Problem des Elite-Journalismus'. In *Die Herren Journalisten: Die Elite der deutschen Presse nach 1945*, edited by Lutz Hachmeister and Friedemann Siering, 7–34. München: Verlag C. H. Beck.

Haensch, Peter and Everhard Holtmann. 2008. 'Die öffentiche Verwaltung der EU-Staaten'. In *Die EU-Staaten im Vergleich*, edited by OscarW Gabriel and Sabine Kropp, 606–630. Wiesbaden: VS Verlag für Sozialwissenschaften.

Håkansson, Nicklas and Eva Mayerhöffer. 2014. 'Democratic Demands on the Media'. In *Political Communication Cultures in Europe: Attitudes of Political Actors and Journalists in Nine Countries*, edited by Barbara Pfetsch, 126–147. Basingstoke: Palgrave Macmillan.

Halimi, Serge. 1997. *Les nouveaux chiens de garde*. Paris: Liber-Raisons d'agir.

Hallin, Daniel C. 1986. *The Uncensored War: The Media and Vietnam*. New York, NY: Oxford University Press.

Hallin, Daniel C. and Paolo Mancini. 2004. *Comparing Media Systems. Three Models of Media and Politics*. Cambridge: Cambridge University Press.

Hallin, Daniel C. and Stylianos Papathanassopoulos. 2002. 'Political Clientelism and the Media: Southern Europe and Latin America in Comparative Perspective'. *Media, Culture & Society* 24 (2):175–195.

Hanitzsch, Thomas, Folker Hanusch, Claudia Mellado, Maria Anikina, Rosa Berganza, Incilay Cangoz, Mihai Coman, Basyouni Hamada, María Elena Hernández, Christopher D. Karadjov, Sonia Virginia Moreira, Peter G. Mwesige, Patrick Lee Plaisance, Zvi Reich, Josef Seethaler, Elizabeth A. Skewes, Dani Vardiansyah Noor, and Edgar Kee Wang Yuen. 2011. 'Mapping Journalism Cultures across Nations'. *Journalism Studies* 12 (3):273–293. doi: 10.1080/1461670X.2010.512502.

Harmgarth, Friederike. 1997. *Wirtschaft und Soziales in der politischen Kommunikation. Eine Studie zur Interaktion von Abgeordneten und Journalisten.* Opladen: Westdeutscher Verlag.

Hartmann, Michael. 2005. 'Eliten und das Feld der Macht'. In *Pierre Bourdieu: deutsch-französische Perspektiven,* edited by Catherine Colliot-Thélène, Etienne Francois and Gunter Gebauer. Frankfurt am Main: Suhrkamp.

Hartmann, Michael. 2007a. *Eliten und Macht in Europa: Ein internationaler Vergleich.* Frankfurt am Main/New York, NY: Campus.

Hartmann, Michael. 2007b. *The Sociology of Elites.* London/New York: Routledge.

Herbst, Susan. 2010. *Rude Democracy. Civility and Incivility in American Politics.* Philadelphia, PA: Temple University Press.

Herman, Edward S. and Norman Chomsky. 2002. *Manufacturing Consent: The Political Economy of the Mass Media.* 2nd ed. New York, NY: Pantheon Books.

Hess, Stephen. 1981. *The Washington Reporters.* Washington, DC: Brookings.

Hess, Stephen. 1984. *The Government/Press Connection: Press officers and their offices.* Washington, DC: The Brookings Institution.

Hess, Stephen. 1991. *Live from Capitol Hill: Studies of Congress and the Media.* Washington, DC: The Brookings Institution.

Hewitt, Christopher J. 1974. 'Elites and the Distribution of Power in British Society'. In *Elites and Power in British Society,* edited by Philip Stanworth and Anthony Giddens, 45–64. London: Cambridge University Press.

Higley, John. 2007. 'Democracy and Elites'. In *Comparative Study of Social and Political Elites,* edited by Fredrik Engelstad and Trygve Gulbrandsen, 249–263. Amsterdam: Elsevier.

Higley, John. 2009. 'Democratic Elitism and Western Political Thought'. *Comparative Sociology* 8:440–458.

Higley, John and Michael Burton. 1989. 'The Elite Variable in Democratic Transitions and Breakdowns'. *American Sociological Review* 54:17–32.

Higley, John and Michael Burton. 2006. *Elite Foundations of Liberal Democracy.* Lanham, MD: Rowman & Littlefield.

Higley, John, Desley Deacon and Don Smart. 1979. *Elites in Australia.* London/Boston, MA/Henley: Routledge & Kegan Paul.

Higley, John, Ursula Hoffmann-Lange, Charles Kadushin and Gwen Moore. 1991. 'Elite Integration in Stable Democracies: A Reconsideration'. *European Sociological Review* 7 (1):35–53.

Hofer, Thomas. 2005. *Spin-Doktoren in Österreich: Die Praxis amerikanischer Wettkampfberater. Was sie können, wen sie beraten, wie sie arbeiten.* 2nd ed. Münster: LIT.

Hoffmann, Jochen. 2003. *Inszenierung und Interpenetration: Das Zusammenspiel von Eliten aus Politik und Journalismus.* Wiesbaden: Westdeutscher Verlag.

Hoffmann-Lange, Ursula. 1979. 'Geschlossene Gesellschaft: Berufliche Mobilität und politisches Bewußtsein der Medienelite'. In *Was Journalisten denken und wie sie arbeiten,* edited by Hans Mathias Kepplinger, 49–75. Freiburg/München: Alber.

Hoffmann-Lange, Ursula. 1992. *Eliten, Macht und Konflikt in der Bundesrepublik.* Opladen: Leske+Budrich.

Hoffmann-Lange, Ursula. 2004. 'Die Elitenstruktur moderner demokratischer Gesellschaften'. In *Konjunktur der Köpfe? Eliten in der modernen Wissensgesellschaft,* edited by Oscar W. Gabriel, Beate Neuss and Günther Rüther. Düsseldorf: Droste Verlag.

Hoffmann-Lange, Ursula. 2007. 'Methods of Elite Research'. In *The Oxford Handbook of Political Behavior*, edited by Hans-Dieter Klingemann and Russell J. Dalton, 910–927. Oxford: Oxford University Press.

Holzner, Burkart. 1967. 'The Concept "Integration" in Sociological Theory'. *The Sociological Quarterly* 8 (1):51–62.

Hood, Christopher. 1991. 'A Public Management for All Seasons?'. *Public Administration* 69 (1):3–19. doi: 10.1111/j.1467–9299.1991.tb00779.x.

Huber, Claudia Kristine. 2012. *Zwischen Routine, Ratspräsidentschaft und Gipfel: Interaktionen von Medien und Politik in der Europäischen Union*. Wiesbaden: Springer VS.

Humphreys, Peter. 1996. *Mass Media and Media Policy in Western Europe*. Manchester: Manchester University Press.

Humphreys, Peter. 2012. 'A Political Scientist's Contribution to the Comparative Study of Media Systems in Europe: A Response to Hallin and Mancini'. In *Trends in Communication Policy Research*, edited by Natascha Just and Manuel Puppis, 157–179. Bristol: Intellect.

Hunter, John E., Jeffrey E. Danes and Stanley H. Cohen. 1984. *Mathematical Models of Attitude Change: Change in Single Attitudes and Cognitive Structure*. Orlando, FL: Academic Press.

Ishida, Hiroshi, Walter Müller and John M. Ridge. 1995. 'Class Origin, Class Destination and Education: A Cross-National Study of Ten Industrial Nations'. *American Journal of Sociology* 101 (1):145–193.

Iyengar, Shanto and Kyu S. Hahn. 2009. 'Red Media, Blue Media: Evidence of Ideological Selectivity in Media Use'. *Journal of Communication* 59 (1):19–39.

Iyengar, Shanto and Daniel R. Kinder. 1987. *News That Matters: Television and American Opinion*. Chicago, IL: University of Chicago Press.

Jackson, Richard. 2005. *Writing the War on Terrorism: Language, Politics and Counter-Terrorism*. Manchester: Manchester University Press.

Jebril, Nael, Erik Albæk and Claes H. de Vreese. 2013. 'Infotainment, Cynicism and Democracy: The Effects of Privatization vs Personalization in the News'. *European Journal of Communication* 28 (2):105–121.

Johnson, Allan G. 1995. *The Blackwell Dictionary of Sociology: A User's Guide to Sociological Language*. Cambridge, MA: Blackwell.

Kaltenbrunner, Andy, Matthias Karmasin and Daniela Kraus. 2010. *Der Journalisten-Report III: Politikjournalismus in Österreich*. Wien: Facultas.

Kantner, Cathleen. 2004. *Kein modernes Babel: Kommunikative Voraussetzungen europäischer Öffentlichkeit*. Wiesbaden: VS Verlag für Sozialwissenschaften.

Karmasin, Matthias, Daniela Kraus, Andy Kaltenbrunner and Klaus Bichler. 2011. 'Austria: A Border-Crosser'. In *Mapping Media Accountability – In Europe and Beyond*, edited by Tobias Eberwein, Susanne Fengler, Epp Lauk and Tanja Leppik-Bork, 22–35. Köln: Halem.

Katsirea, Irini. 2008. *Public Broadcasting and European Law: A Comparative Examination of Public Service Obligations in Six Member States*. Alphen aan den Rijn: Kluwer Law International.

Katz, Daniel and Robert L. Kahn. 1966. *The Social Psychology of Organizations*. New York, NY: Wiley.

Keller, Suzanne. 1963. *Beyond the Ruling Class: Strategic Elites in Modern Society*. New York, NY: Random House.

Kelly, Mary. 1983. 'Influences on Broadcasting Policies for Election Coverage'. In *Communicating to Voters: Television in the First European Parliamentary Elections*, edited by Jay G. Blumler, 65–82. London: SAGE.

Kepplinger, Hans Mathias. 2007. 'Reciprocal Effects: Toward a Theory of Mass Media Effects on Decision Makers'. *Press/Politics* 12 (2):3–23.

Kepplinger, Hans Mathias. 2009. 'Politiker als Protagonisten der Macht'. In *Politikvermittlung*, edited by Hans Mathias Kepplinger, 51–66. Wiesbaden: VS Verlag für Sozialwissenschaften.

Kiefer, Marie Luise. 2005. *Medienökonomik: Einführung in eine ökonomische Theorie der Medien*. München: Oldenbourg.

Kielhorn, Achim. 2001. *Rollenorientierung von Abgeordneten in Europa: Eine empirische Analyse von Bestimmungsgründen und Konsequenzen der Repräsentationsrolle von Parlamentariern in elf EU-Ländern*. Dissertation Freie Universität Berlin. Accessed 24/07/2018. https://refubium.fu-berlin.de/handle/fub188/5996.

Kitschelt, Herbert. 2007. 'The Demise of Clientelism in Affluent Capitalist Democracies'. In *Patrons, Clients and Policies: Patterns of Democratic Accountability and Political Competition*, edited by Herbert Kitschelt and Steven I. Wilkinson. Cambridge: Cambridge University Press.

Klapper, Joseph. 1960. *The Effects of Mass Communication*. New York, NY: Free Press.

Kramp, Leif and Stephan Weichert. 2008. *Journalismus in der Berliner Republik: Wer prägt die politische Agenda in der Bundeshauptstadt?* Berlin: Netzwerk Recherche.

Krüger, Uwe. 2011. 'Die Nähe zur Macht: Eliten-Netzwerke deutscher Journalisten in der Außenpolitik'. *Medien Journal* (2):33–49.

Krüger, Uwe. 2013. *Meinungsmacht: der Einfluss von Eliten auf Leitmedien und Alpha-Journalisten – Eine kritische Netzwerkanalyse*. Köln: Halem.

Kuklinski, James H. and Buddy Peyton. 2007. 'Belief Systems and Political Decision Making'. In *The Oxford Handbook of Political Behavior*, edited by Russel J. Dalton and Hans-Dieter Klingemann, 45–64. Oxford: Oxford University Press.

Lane, Jan-Erik and Svante O. Ersson. 1999. *Politics and Society in Western Europe*. London: SAGE.

Larsson, Larsåke 2002. 'Journalists and Politicians: A Relationship Requiring Manoeuvring Space'. *Journalism Studies* 3 (1):21–33.

Lasswell, Harold Dwight and Daniel Lerner. 1952. *The Comparative Study of Elites: An Introduction and Bibliography*. Stanford, CA: Stanford University Press.

Lesmeister, Christiane. 2008. *Informelle politische Kommunikationskultur. Hinter den Kulissen politisch-medialer Kommunikation*. Wiesbaden: VS Verlag für Sozialwissenschaften.

Lichter, S. Robert, Stanley Rothman and Linda S. Lichter. 1986. *The Media Elite*. Bethesda, MD: Adler & Adler.

Liebes, Tamar. 1997. *Reporting the Arab-Israeli Conflict: How Hegemony Works.* London: Routledge.

Lijphart, Arend. 1999. *Patterns of Democracy.* New Haven, CT/London: Yale University Press.

Luhmann, Niklas. 1977. 'Differentiation of Society'. *Canadian Journal of Sociology* 2 (1):29–53.

Luhmann, Niklas. 1984. *Soziale Systeme: Grundriss einer allgemeinen Theorie.* Frankfurt am Main: Suhrkamp.

Luhmann, Niklas. 2006. 'System as Difference'. *Organization* 13 (1):37–57.

Luhmann, Niklas. 2009. *Die Realität der Massenmedien.* 4th ed. Wiesbaden: VS Verlag für Sozialwissenschaften.

Maarek, Philippe. 2007. 'The Evolution of French Political Communication: Reaching the Limits of Professionalisation?' In *The Professionalisation of Political Communication*, edited by Ralph Negrine, Christina Holtz-Bacha, Paolo Mancini and Stylianos Papathanassopoulos. Bristol: Intellect.

Maarek, Philippe. 2013. 'The Wavering Implementation of Government Communication in France'. In *Government Communication: Cases and Challenges*, edited by Karen Sanders and María José Canel, 115–132. New York, NY: Bloomsbury Academic.

Mair, Peter. 2007. 'Left-Right Orientations'. In *The Oxford Handbook of Political Behavior*, edited by Russel J. Dalton and Hans-Dieter Klingemann, 206–222. Oxford: Oxford University Press.

Maurer, Peter and Eva Mayerhöffer. 2009. 'Themenmanagement von politischen Sprechern und Kommunikationsberatern unter den Bedingungen der Bonner und der Berliner Republik. Ein Zeitvergleich 1994–2008'. *Zeitschrift für Politikberatung* 2:447–466.

Maurer, Peter and Miika Vähämaa. 2014. 'Methods and Challenges of Comparative Surveys of Political Communication Elites'. In *Political Communication Cultures in Europe: Attitudes of Political Actors and Journalists in Nine Countries*, edited by Barbara Pfetsch, 57–75. Basingstoke: Palgrave Macmillan.

Mayerhöffer, Eva. 2015. 'Elite Cohesion in Political Communication: Attitudinal Consonance of Media and Political Elites in Six European Countries'. Dissertation Freie Universität Berlin.

Mayerhöffer, Eva and Barbara Pfetsch. 2018. 'Media Elites'. In *The Palgrave Handbook of Political Elites*, edited by Heinrich Best and John Higley, 417–437. London: Palgrave Macmillan.

Mayntz, Renate and Hans-Ulrich Derlien. 1989. 'Party Patronage and Politicization of the West German Administrative Elite 1970–1987 – Toward Hybridization?'. *Governance* 2 (4):384–404.

Mazzoleni, Gianpietro. 1987. 'Media Logic and Party Logic in Campaign Coverage: The Italian General Election 1983'. *European Journal of Communication* 2:81–103.

Mazzoleni, Gianpietro and Winfried Schulz. 1999. ' "Mediatization" of Politics: A Challenge for Democracy?' *Political Communication* 16:247–261.

Mazzoleni, Gianpietro and Anna Sfardini. 2009. *Politica Pop: Da 'Porta a Porta' a 'L'isola dei famosi*. Bologna: Il Mulino.

McCombs, Maxwell E. and Donald L. Shaw. 1972. 'The Agenda-Setting Function of Mass Media'. *Public Opinion Quarterly* 36 (2):176–187.

Meisel, James H. 1958. *The Myth of the Ruling Class. Gaetano Mosca and the 'Elite'*. Ann Arbor, MI: The University of Michigan Press.

Meyen, Michael and Claudia Riesmeyer. 2011. 'Service Providers, Sentinels, and Traders'. *Journalism Studies* 13 (3):386–401. doi: 10.1080/1461670X.2011.602909.

Meyer, Thomas. 2002. *Media Democracy: How the Media Colonize Politics*. Cambridge: Polity.

Miliband, Ralph. 2009. *The State in Capitalist Society*. London: Merlin Press. Original edition, 1969.

Miller, Susan Heilmann. 1978. *Reporters and Congressmen: Living in Symbiosis*, Journalism Monographs, no. 53. Lexington/Minneapolis: Association for Education in Journalism.

Mills, C. Wright. 1956. *The Power Elite*. New York, NY: Oxford University Press.

Molina, Oscar and Martin Rhodes. 2002. 'Corporatism: The Past, Present, and Future of a Concept'. *Annual Review of Political Science* 5:305–331.

Moore, Gwen. 1979. 'The Structure of a National Elite Network'. *American Sociological Review* 44 (5):673–692.

Mosca, Gaetano. 1939. *The Ruling Class*. New York, NY: McGraw-Hill.

Mueller, John E. 1973. *War, Presidents and Public Opinion*. New York, NY: Wiley.

Müller, Wolfgang C. 2006. 'Party Patronage and Party Colonization of the State'. In *Handbook of Party Politics*, edited by Richard S. Katz and William J. Crotty, 189–195. London: SAGE.

Münch, Richard. 1991. *Dialektik der Kommunikationsgesellschaft*. Frankfurt am Main: Suhrkamp.

Murschetz, Paul and Matthias Karmasin. 2014. 'Austria: Press Subsidies in Search of a New Design'. In *State Aid for Newspapers: Theories, Cases, Actions*, edited by Paul Murschetz, 133–149. Berlin/Heidelberg: Springer.

Mutz, Diana C. and Byron Reeves. 2005. 'The New Videomalaise: Effects of Televised Incivility on Political Trust'. *American Political Science Review* 99 (1):1–15. doi: 10.1017.S0003055405051452.

Mützel, Sophie. 2002. *Making Meaning of the Move of the German Capital – Networks, Logics and the Emergence of Capital City Journalism*. New York, NY: Columbia University.

Nabi, Robin L. and Mary Beth Oliver, eds. 2009. *The SAGE Handbook of Media Processes and Effects*. Thousand Oaks, CA/London/New Delhi/Singapore: SAGE.

Negrine, Ralph M. 2008. *The Transformation of Political Communication: Continuities and Changes in Media and Politics*. Basingstoke: Palgrave Macmillan.

Negrine, Ralph M., Paolo Mancini, Christina Holtz-Bacha and Stylianos Papathanassopoulos, eds. 2007. *The Professionalisation of Political Communication, Changing Media, Changing Europe*. Bristol: Intellect.

Neidhardt, Friedhelm. 1994. 'Öffentlichkeit, öffentliche Meinung, soziale Bewegungen'. In *Sonderheft 42/2002 der Kölner Zeitschrift für Soziologie und Sozialpsychologie*, 7–41. Opladen: Westdeutscher Verlag.

Neveu, Erik. 1999. 'Politics on French Television: Towards a Renewal of Political Journalism and Debate Frames?'. *European Journal of Communication* 14 (3):379–409. doi: 10.1177/0267323199014003004.

Nielsen, Poul Erik. 2010. 'Danish Public Service Broadcasting in Transition: From Monopoly to a Digital Media Environment – A Shift in Paradigms'. *Central European Journal of Communication* 3 (1):115–129.

Nord, Lars. 2007. 'The Swedish Model Becomes Less Swedish'. In *The Professionalisation of Political Communication*, edited by Ralph Negrine, Christina Holtz-Bacha, Paolo Mancini and Stylianos Papathanassopoulos, 81–96. Bristol: Intellect.

Nord, Lars. 2009. 'Political Communication in Sweden: Change, But Not Too Much'. *Central European Journal of Communication* 2:233–249.

Norris, Pippa. 2000. *A Virtuous Circle: Political Communications in Postindustrial Societies*. New York, NY: Cambridge University Press.

OECD. 2012. *Education at a Glance 2012: OECD Indicators*. Paris: OECD Publishing.

Pakulski, Jan, Heinrich Best, Verona Christmas-Best and Ursula Hoffmann-Lange, eds. 2012. 'Special Issue: Elite Foundations of Social Theory and Politics'. *Historical Social Research/Historische Sozialforschung* 37 (1).

Papatheodorou, Fotini and David Machin. 2003. 'The Umbilical Cord That Was Never Cut: The Post-Dictatorial Intimacy between the Political Elite and the Mass Media in Greece and Spain'. *European Journal of Communication* 18 (1):31–54. doi: 10.1177/0267323103018001225.

Pareto, Vilfredo. 1935. *The Mind and Society*. New York, NY: Dover.

Parry, Geraint. 1969. *Political Elites*. London: George Allen & Undwin.

Parsons, Talcott. 1951. *The Social System*. Glencoe, IL: Free Press.

Parsons, Talcott. 1971. *The System of Modern Societies*. Englewood Cliffs, NJ: Prentice Hall.

Parsons, Talcott and Gerald M. Platt. 1973. *The American University*. Cambridge, MA: Harvard University Press.

Patzelt, Werner J. 1997. 'German MPs and their Roles'. *The Journal of Legislative Studies* 3 (1):55–78. doi: 10.1080/13572339708420499.

Peffley, Mark and Robert Rohrschneider. 2007. 'Elite Beliefs and the Theory of Democractic Elitism'. In *The Oxford Handbook of Political Behavior*, edited by Hans-Dieter Klingemann and Russell J. Dalton, 65–79. Oxford: Oxford University Press.

Pettersson, Thorleif. 2010. 'Pro-Democratic Orientations, Political Shortcuts and Policy Issues: Comparative Analyses of Elite-Mass Congruence in Old and New Democracies'. In *Democracy under Scrutiny: Elites, Citizens, Cultures*, edited by Ursula van Beek. Opladen/Farmington Hills: Barbara Budrich Publishers.

Pfetsch, Barbara. 2001. 'Political Communication Culture in the United States and Germany'. *Press/Politics* 6 (1):46–67.

Pfetsch, Barbara. 2003. *Politische Kommunikationskultur: Politische Sprecher und Journalisten in der Bundesrepublik und den USA im Vergleich*. Wiesbaden: Westdeutscher Verlag.

Pfetsch, Barbara. 2004. 'From Political Culture to Political Communication Culture'. In *Comparing Political Communication: Theories, Cases, and Challenges*, edited by Frank Esser and Barbara Pfetsch, 344–366. New York, NY/Cambridge: Cambridge University Press.

Pfetsch, Barbara. 2008. 'Political Communication Culture'. In *International Encyclopedia of Communications*, edited by Wolfgang Donsbach, 3683–3686. Oxford: Blackwell.

Pfetsch, Barbara, ed. 2014. *Political Communication Cultures in Europe: Attitudes of Political Actors and Journalists in Nine Countries*. Basingstoke: Palgrave Macmillan.

Pfetsch, Barbara and Silke Adam. 2008. 'Die Akteursperspektive in der politischen Kommunikationsforschung – Fragestellungen, Forschungsparadigmen und Problemlagen'. In *Massenmedien als politische Akteure*, edited by Barbara Pfetsch and Silke Adam, 9–26. Wiesbaden: VS Verlag für Sozialwissenschaften.

Pfetsch, Barbara, Christiane Eilders, Friedhelm Neidhardt and Stephanie Grübl. 2004. 'Das "Kommentariat": Rolle und Status einer Öffentlichkeitselite'. In *Die Stimme der Medien. Pressekommentare und politische Öffentlichkeit in der Bundesrepublik*, edited by Christiane Eilders, Friedhelm Neidhardt and Barbara Pfetsch, 39–73. Wiesbaden: VS Verlag für Sozialwissenschaften.

Pfetsch, Barbara, Peter Maurer, Eva Mayerhöffer and Tom Moring. 2014. 'A Hedge between Keeps Friendship Green – Concurrence and Conflict between Politicans and Journalists in Nine European Democracies'. In *Comparing Political Communication across Time and Space: New Studies in an Emerging Field*, edited by María José Canel Crespo and Katrin Voltmer. Basingstoke: Palgrave Macmillan.

Plasser, Fritz. 1985. 'Elektronische Politik und politische Technostruktur reifer Industriegesellschaften: Ein Orientierungsversuch'. In *Demokratierituale. Zur politischen Kultur der Informationsgesellschaft*, edited by Fritz Plasser, Peter A. Ulram and Manfried Welan. Wien: Böhlau.

Plasser, Fritz and Günther Lengauer. 2010. 'Politik vor Redaktionsschluss: Kommunikationsorientierungen von Macht- und Medieneliten in Österreich'. In *Politik in der Medienarena: Praxis politischer Kommunikation in Österreich*, edited by Fritz Plasser, 53–100. Wien: Fakultas.

Plasser, Fritz and Gunda Plasser. 2002. *Global Political Campaigning: A Worldwide Analysis of Campaign Professionals and Their Practices*. Westport, CT: Praeger.

Pollitt, Christopher and Geert Bouckaert. 2011. *Public Management Reform: A Comparative Analysis – New Public Management, Governance, and the Neo-Weberian State*. Oxford: Oxford University Press.

Prewitt, Kenneth and Alan Stone. 1973. *The Ruling Elites: Elite Theory, Power, and American Democracy*. New York/Evanston, IL/San Francisco, CA/London: Harper & Row.

Putnam, Robert D. 1973. *The Belief of Politicians: Ideology, Conflict, and Democracy in Britain and Italy*. New Haven, CT/London: Yale University Press.

Putnam, Robert D. 1976. *The Comparative Study of Political Elites*. Englewood Cliffs, NJ: Prentice-Hall.

Reese, Stephen D. 2001. 'Understanding the Global Journalist: A Hierarchy-of-Influences Approach'. *Journalism Studies* 2 (2):173–187. doi: 10.1080/14616700120042060.

Reese, Stephen D., August Grant and Lucig H. Danielian. 1994. 'The Structure of News Sources on Television: A Network Analysis of "CBS News", "Nightline", "MacNeil/Lehrer", and "This Week with David Brinkley"'. *Journal of Communication* 44 (2):84–107.

Rieffel, Rémy. 1984. *L'élite des journalistes*. Paris: Presses Universitaire de France.

Rinke, Eike Mark, Michael Schlachter, Fabian Agel, Christina Freund, Timo Götz, Ulrike Täuber and Wächter Christian. 2006. *Netzwerk Berlin: Informelle Interpenetration von Politik und Journalismus*. München: Martin Meidenbauer Verlagsbuchhandlung.

Robinson, Piers. 2001. 'Theorizing the Influence of Media on World Politics: Models of Media Influence on Foreign Policy'. *European Journal of Communication* 16 (4):523–544. doi: 10.1177/0267323101016004005.

Robinson, Piers, Peter Goddard, Katy Parry, Craig Murray and Philip M. Taylor. 2010. *Pockets of Resistance: British News Media, War and Theory in the 2003 Invasion of Iraq*. Manchester/New York, NY: Manchester University Press.

Roose, Jochen. 2012. 'Die quantitative Bestimmung kultureller Unterschiedlichkeit in Europa. Vorschlag für einen Index kultureller Ähnlichkeit'. *Kölner Zeitschrift für Soziologie und Sozialpsychologie* 64:361–376. doi: 10.1007/s11577-012-0170-9.

Ross, Karen. 2010. 'Danse Macabre: Politicians, Journalists, and the Complicated Rumba of Relationships'. *The International Journal of Press/Politics* 15 (3):272–294. doi: 10.1177/1940161210367942.

Ruostetsaari, Ilkka. 2007. 'Nordic Elites in Comparative Perspective'. *Comparative Sociology* 6:158–189.

Ruostetsaari, Ilkka. 2015. *Elite Recruitment and Coherence of the Inner Core of Power in Finland: Changing Patterns during the Economic Crises of 1991–2011*. Lanham, MD: Lexington Books.

Sabatier, Paul A. 1998. 'The Advocacy Coalition Framework: Revisions and Relevance for Europe'. *Journal of European Public Policy* 5 (1):93–130. doi: 10.1080/13501768880000051.

Sabatier, Paul A. and Hank C. Jenkins-Smith. 1993. *Policy Change and Learning: An Advocacy Coalition Approach*. Boulder, CO: Westview Press.

Sampedro, Víctor and Francisco Seoane Pérez. 2008. 'The 2008 Spanish General Elections: "Antagonistic Bipolarization" Geared by Presidential Debates, Partisanship, and Media Interests'. *The International Journal of Press/Politics* 13 (3):336–344. doi: 10.1177/1940161208319293.

Sanders, Karen and María José Canel, eds. 2013. *Government Communication: Cases and challenges*. 1st ed. New York: Bloomsbury Academic.

Sanders, Karen, María José Canel Crespo and Christina Holtz-Bacha. 2011. 'Communicating Governments: A Three-Country Comparison of How Governments Communicate with Citizens'. *The International Journal of Press/Politics* 16 (4):523–547. doi: 10.1177/1940161211418225.

Sarcinelli, Ulrich. 1987. *Symbolische Politik: Zur Bedeutung symbolischen Handelns in der Wahlkampfkommunikation der Bundesrepublik Deutschland, Studien zur Sozialwissenschaft*. Opladen: Westdeutscher Verlag.

Sarcinelli, Ulrich. 2004. ' "Seiltänzer an der institutionellen Leine?" Zum kommunikativen Handlungsspielraum politischer Eliten in der Medienarena'. In *Elitenmacht*, edited by Ronald Hitzler, Stefan Hornbostel and Cornelia Mohr, 225–237. Wiesbaden: VS Verlag für Sozialwissenschaften.

Sartori, Giovanni. 1969. 'Politics, Ideology, and Belief Systems'. *The American Political Science Review* 63 (2):398–411.

Sartori, Giovanni. 1987. *The Theory of Democracy Revisited*. Chatham: Chatham Publishers.

Sasaki, Masamichi, ed. 2008. *Elites: New Comparative Perspectives*. Leiden: Brill.

Saxer, Ulrich. 1992. 'Bericht aus dem Bundeshaus: Eine Befragung von Bundeshausjournalisten und Parlamentariern in der Schweiz'. *Diskussionspunkt 24. Zürich: Seminar Publizistik der Universität Zürich*.

Scammell, Margaret. 1998. 'The Wisdom of the War Room: US Campaigning and Americanization'. *Media, Culture & Society* 20 (2):251–275. doi: 10.1177/016344398020002006.

Scheuch, Erwin K. 1988. 'Continuity and Change in German Social Structure'. *Historical Social Research/Historische Sozialforschung* 13 (2):31–121.

Scheufele, Dietram A. 1999. 'Framing as a Theory of Media Effects'. *Journal of Communication* 49 (1):103–122.

Scheufele, Dietram A. and David Tewksbury. 2007. 'Framing, Agenda Setting, and Priming: The Evolution of Three Media Effects Models'. *Journal of Communication* 57 (1):9–20. doi: 10.1111/j.1460–2466.2006.00326.x.

Schmitter, Philippe C. and Gerhard Lehmbruch. 1979. *Trends towards Corporatist Intermediation*. Beverly Hills, CA: SAGE.

Schnapp, Kai-Uwe. 1997. 'Soziale Zusammensetzung von Elite und Bevölkerung – Verteilung von Aufstiegschancen in die Elite im Zeitvergleich'. In *Eliten in Deutschland. Rekrutierung und Integration*, edited by Wilhelm Bürklin and Hilke Rebenstorf, 69–99. Opladen: Leske+Budrich.

Schnapp, Kai-Uwe. 2004. *Ministerialbürokratien in westlichen Demokratien: Eine vergleichende Analyse*. Opladen: Leske+Budrich.

Schudson, Michael. 2002. 'The News Media as Political Institutions'. *Annual Review of Political Science* 5:249–269. doi: 10.1146/annurev.polisci.5.111201. 115816.

Schwab Cammarano, Stephanie. 2013. *Rollen in der Politikvermittlung: die Interaktion zwischen Politik und Journalismus in der Schweiz, Schriftenreihe Politische Kommunikation und demokratische Öffentlichkeit*. Baden-Baden: Nomos.

Schwab Cammarano, Stephanie and Juan Díez Medrano. 2014. 'Distant North – Conflictive South: Patterns of Interaction and Conflict'. In *Political Communication Cultures in Europe: Attitudes of Political Actors and Journalists in Nine Countries*, edited by Barbara Pfetsch, 271–286. Basingstoke: Palgrave Macmillan.

Scott, John, ed. 1990. *The Sociology of Elites: Volume 1 – The Study of Elites*. Cheltenham: Edward Elgar Publishing.

Scott, John. 1991. *Who Rules Britain?* Cambridge: Polity Press.

Searing, Donald D. 1969. 'The Comparative Study of Elite Socialization'. *Comparative Political Studies* 4 (1):471–500.

Seggelke, Sabine. 2007. *Frankreichs Staatspräsident in der politischen Kommunikation: Öffentlichkeitsarbeit in der V. Republik* Münster: Lit.

Seymour-Ure, Colin. 1974. *The Political Impact of Mass Media*. London: Constable.

Shanahan, James and Michael Morgan. 1999. *Television and its Viewers: Cultivation Theory and Research*. Cambridge: Cambridge University Press.

Sigal, Leon V. 1973. *Reporters and Officials: The Organization and Politics of Newsmaking*. Lexington, KY: D.C. Heath and Company.

Sorokin, Pitirim. 1927. *Social Mobility*. New York, NY: Harper & Row.

SOU. 1990. *Demokratie och makt i Sverige: Maktutredningens huvudrapport*. Stockholm: Almänna Forlaget.

SOU. 2000. *En uthållig demokrati! Politik för folkstyrelse på 2000-talet. Demokratiutredningens betänkande*. Vol. 1. Stockholm: Fritzes.

Sparrow, Bartholomew. 2006. 'A Research Agenda for an Institutional Media'. *Political Communication* 23 (2):145–157. doi: 10.1080/10584600600629695.

Stammer, Otto. 1951. *Das Elitenproblem in der Demokratie*. Berlin: Duncker und Humblot.

Strachan, J. Cherie and Michael R. Wolf. 2012. 'Political Civility'. *PS: Political Science & Politics* 45 (3):401–404. doi: 10.1017/S1049096512000455.

Street, John. 2005. 'Politics Lost, Politics Transformed, Politics Colonised? Theories of the Impact of Mass Media'. *Political Studies Review* 3 (1):17–33. doi: 10.1111/j.1478–9299.2005.00017.x.

Strömbäck, Jesper. 2008. 'Four Phases of Mediatization: An Analysis of the Mediatization of Politics'. *Press/Politics* 13 (3):228–246.

Strömbäck, Jesper. 2009. 'Selective Professionalisation of Political Campaigning: A Test of the Party-Centred Theory of Professionalised Campaigning in the Context of the 2006 Swedish Election'. *Political Studies* 57 (1):95–116. doi: 10.1111/j.1467–9248.2008.00727.x.

Strömbäck, Jesper. 2015. 'Mediatization'. In *The International Encyclopedia of Political Communication*, edited by Gianpietro Mazzoleni. Hoboken, NJ: Wiley.

Strömbäck, Jesper and Lars W. Nord. 2006. 'Do Politicians Lead the Tango?: A Study of the Relationship between Swedish Journalists and their Political Sources in the Context of Election Campaigns'. *European Journal of Communication* 21 (2):147–164. doi: 10.1177/0267323105064043.

Strömbäck, Jesper, Mark Ørsten and Toril Aalberg, eds. 2008. *Communicating Politics: Political Communication in the Nordic Countries*. Göteborg: Nordicom.

Stroud, Natalie J. 2007. 'Media Use and Political Predispositions: Revisiting the Concept of Selective Exposure'. *Political Behavior* 30 (3):341–366.

Suleiman, Ezra N. 1984. *Bureaucrats and Policy Making. A Comparative Overview.* New York, NY/London: Holmes & Meier.

Suleiman, Ezra N. 2004. *Dismantling Democratic States*. Princeton, NJ: Princeton University Press.

Tenscher, Jens. 2003. *Professionalisierung der Politikvermittlung? Politikvermittlungsexperten im Spannungsfeld von Politik und Massenmedien*. Wiesbaden: Westdeutscher Verlag.

Tesser, Abraham and David R. Shaffer. 1990. 'Attitudes and Attitude Change'. *Annual Review of Psychology* 41 (1):479–523. doi: 10.1146/annurev.ps.41.020190.002403.

Thye, Shane R. and Edward J. Lawler, eds. 2002. *Group Cohesion, Trust and Solidarity*. Oxford: Elsevier Science.

Tunstall, Jeremy. 1970. *The Westminster Lobby Correspondents*. London: Routledge.

Turner, Frederick C. 1992. *Social Mobility and Political Attitudes: Comparative Perspectives*. New Brunswick, NJ: Transaction Publishers.

Van Aelst, Peter and Rens Vliegenthart. 2013. 'Studying the Tango'. *Journalism Studies* 15 (4):392–410. doi: 10.1080/1461670X.2013.831228.

van Beek, Ursula J. (ed.). 2010. *Democracy under Scrutiny. Elites, Citizens, Cultures*. Opladen: Barbara Budrich Publishers.

van Kempen, Hetty. 2007. 'Media-Party Parallelism and Its Effects: A Cross-National Comparative Study'. *Political Communication* 24 (3):303–320. doi: 10.1080/10584600701471674.

Vatter, Adrian. 2009. 'Lijphart Expanded: Three Dimensions of Democracy in Advanced OECD Countries?'. *European Political Science Review* 1 (1):125–154. doi: 10.1017/S1755773909000071.

Vatter, Adrian. 2014. *Das politische System der Schweiz*. Baden-Baden: Nomos.

Walgrave, Stefaan. 2008. 'Again, the Almighty Mass Media? The Media's Political Agenda-Setting Power According to Politicians and Journalists in Belgium'. *Political Communication* 25:445–459.

Walgrave, Stefaan and Peter Van Aelst. 2006. 'The Contingency of the Mass Media's Political Agenda Setting Power: Toward a Preliminary Theory'. *Journal of Communication* 56:88–109.

Wasner, Barbara. 2004. *Eliten in Europa*. Wiesbaden: VS Verlag für Sozialwissenschaften.

Weber, Max. 1948. *From Max Weber: Essays in Sociology* (Translated, Edited and with an Introduction by H. H. Gerth and C. Wright Mills). Milton Park/ New York, NY: Routledge.

Weichert, Stephan and Christian Zabel. 2007. 'Die Seele des Alpha-Journalisten. Zum Selbstverständnis der journalistischen Funktions- und Leistungselite'. In *Die Alpha-Journalisten. Deutschlands Wortführer im Porträt*, 14–54. Köln: Halem.

Weischenberg, Siegfied, Maja Malik and Armin Scholl. 2006. *Die Souffleure der Mediengesellschaft. Report über die Journalisten in Deutschland*. Konstanz: UVK.

Wenzler, Michel. 2009. *Journalisten und Eliten: Das Entstehen journalistischer Nachrichten über Energie- und Kulturpolitik*. Konstanz: UVK.

Wolfsfeld, Gadi. 1997. *Media and Political Conflict: News from the Middle East*. Cambridge: Cambridge University Press.

Wolfsfeld, Gadi. 2011. *Making Sense of Media and Politics: Five Principles in Political Communication*. New York, NY: Routledge.

Wörgetter, Sylvia. 2007. 'Der politische Kommentar in Österreich'. In *Mediendemokratie Österreich*, edited by Peter Filzmaier, Peter Plaikner and Karl A. Duffek, 251–258. Wien: Böhlau.

Xenos, Michael and Patricia Moy. 2007. 'Direct and Differential Effects of the Internet on Political and Civic Engagement'. *Journal of Communication* 57 (4):704–718.

York, Chance. 2013. 'Cultivating Political Incivility: Cable News, Network News, and Public Perceptions'. *Electronic News* 7 (3):107–125. doi: 10.1177/1931243113507926.

Zaller, John. 1992. *The Nature and Origins of Mass Opinion.* Cambridge: Cambridge University Press.

Zandberg, Eyal and Motti Neiger. 2005. 'Between the Nation and the Profession: Journalists as Members of Contradicting Communities'. *Media, Culture & Society* 27 (1):131–141. doi: 10.1177/0163443705049073.

Index

Note: Page references for figures are italicized and tables are bold.

About the Author

Eva Mayerhöffer is assistant professor of journalism at the Department of Communication and Arts, University of Roskilde. She holds a PhD in political communication from Freie Universität Berlin. Her research focuses on elites in modern democracies, political communication, comparative media studies, journalism cultures and populism.